MW00353568

NARRATIVE APPROACHES
TO BRAIN INJURY

BRAIN INJURIES SERIES

Other titles in the series:

Anxiety and Mood Disorders following Traumatic Brain Injury:
Clinical Assessment and Psychotherapy
    Rudi Coetzer
A Relational Approach to Rehabilitation: Thinking About Relationships
after Brain Injury
    Ceri Bowen, Giles Yeates, & Siobhan Palmer
Practical Neuropsychological Rehabilitation in Acquired Brain Injury:
A Guide for Working Clinicians
    edited by Gavin Newby, Rudi Coetzer, Audrey Daisley, and
    Stephen Weatherhead

NARRATIVE APPROACHES TO BRAIN INJURY

Edited by

*Stephen Weatherhead
and David Todd*

KARNAC

First published in 2014 by
Karnac Books Ltd
118 Finchley Road, London NW3 5HT

Copyright © 2014 to Stephen Weatherhead and David Todd for the edited collection, and to the individual authors for their contributions.

The rights of the editors and contributors to be identified as the authors of this work have been asserted in accordance with §§ 77 and 78 of the Copyright Design and Patents Act 1988.

All rights reserved. No part of this publication may be reproduced, stored in a retrieval system, or transmitted, in any form or by any means, electronic, mechanical, photocopying, recording, or otherwise, without the prior written permission of the publisher.

British Library Cataloguing in Publication Data

A C.I.P. for this book is available from the British Library

  ISBN 978 1 78049 044 1

Edited, designed and produced by The Studio Publishing Services Ltd
www.publishingservicesuk.co.uk
e-mail: studio@publishingservicesuk.co.uk

Printed in Great Britain

www.karnacbooks.com

CONTENTS

ABOUT THE EDITORS AND CONTRIBUTORS   vii

SERIES EDITORS' FOREWORD   xi

GLOSSARY   xv

INTRODUCTION   xix
    Stephen Weatherhead and David Todd

CHAPTER ONE
Understanding narratives: a beacon of hope or   1
Pandora's box?
    Ava Easton and Karl Atkin

CHAPTER TWO
Brain injury narratives: an undercurrent into the
rest of your life   27
    Katy Flynn, Anna Daiches, and Stephen Weatherhead

CHAPTER THREE
Narrative approaches to goal setting   51
   David Todd

CHAPTER FOUR
Narrative therapy and trauma   77
   Maggie Carey

CHAPTER FIVE
Exploring discourses of caring: Trish and the   101
impossible agenda
   Sarah Walther, Amanda Redstone, and Anette Holmgren

CHAPTER SIX
Narrative practice in the context of communication   117
disability: a question of accessibility
   Rozanne Barrow

CHAPTER SEVEN
Helping children create positive stories about a parent's   143
brain injury
   Audrey Daisley, Simon Prangnell, and Ruth Seed

CHAPTER EIGHT
Using narrative ideas and practices in indirect work   165
with services and professionals
   Lincoln Simmonds

CHAPTER NINE
Outcome evidence   185
   David Todd and Stephen Weatherhead

INDEX   213

Karl Atkin is a sociologist with an interest in health and illness and a background in qualitative research in multi-disciplinary and culturally diverse settings. He holds a personal research chair in the Department of Health Sciences, University of York, where he is also head of research. His work has a particular focus on understanding the social consequences of various longstanding, chronic conditions, including sickle cell and thalassaemia disorders, encephalitis, and heart failure.

Rozanne Barrow is a practising speech and language therapist and currently holds the position of Speech & Language Therapist Manager at Beaumont Hospital in Dublin, Ireland. Beaumont is a large teaching hospital and is the national centre for neurosciences in Ireland. In addition, she is a visiting lecturer to the University of Dublin, Trinity College, and is an associate trainer for Connect—the Communication Disability Network in the UK. She has worked within acute, rehabilitation, and community care contexts in the UK and New Zealand. Her main focus of research has centred on investigating the experience of living life in the context of stroke and aphasia, with particular reference to the role the "stories we live by" play in this experience.

Currently, she is exploring the potential use of qualitative method-ologies within everyday working practice.

Maggie Carey is co-director of Narrative Practices Adelaide, the centre for narrative training, supervision, and therapy that Michael White established before his death in 2008. She has practised narrative therapy since the early 1990s. Her therapeutic work has centred largely on women and children who have experienced violence or abuse, and on using narrative practices in responding to communities of shared experience, including those who live with mental health concerns, with disability, homelessness, and grief, loss, and trauma in Aboriginal communities.

Anna Daiches has been a chartered clinical psychologist for sixteen years and is currently in the role of Clinical Director of the Doctorate in Clinical Psychology at Lancaster University. Anna's research and clin-ical interests are broad, but thematically seek to promote humanity, compassion, inclusivity, and connectivity in our systems and inter-actions with each other. Narrative, whether in therapy, research, or round a campfire, is a beautiful vehicle for this.

Audrey Daisley is a consultant clinical neuropsychologist at the Oxford Centre for Enablement (a post-acute neuro-rehabilitation unit which is part of Oxford University Hospitals NHS Trust). She is the lead for the Family Support Service there and has particular interest and commitment to helping children who are affected by brain injury in the family.

Ava Easton is the Chief Executive of the Encephalitis Society. She is involved in a number of research studies looking into the processes and outcomes of encephalitis. Her PhD is in neuro-narratives. Ava has produced and published several papers on various aspects of encephalitis and its after-effects, and lectures both nationally and internationally on acquired brain injury and encephalitis and its consequences, for health, education, and social care professionals.

Katy Flynn is a clinical psychologist who currently works in eating disorder services. Her fascination with stories/narratives is rooted in her Irish background, where storytelling was a central part of family life. She has an interest in narrative therapy and draws upon this approach in her clinical work. Her research interests include using narrative analysis to explore the stories of people who have experienced traumatic health difficulties. The research described in this book was completed as part of her doctoral training.

Anette Holmgren is a Danish psychologist. She is Co-director of DISPUK, a private training institute and therapy centre north of Copenhagen. Anette has been working as a therapist, supervisor and educator more than twenty years. She has written and edited several books and articles on narrative therapy and counselling.

Simon Prangnell is a clinical psychologist currently working in the South Worcestershire CAMHS team. Prior to this, he worked in the Department of Clinical Neuropsychology at the Oxford Centre for Enablement, where he specialised in working with individuals and families affected by acquired brain injury or neurological illness.

Amanda Redstone is a co-founder and director of The Institute of Narrative Therapy in the UK. She has eighteen years' experience of being a therapist and counsellor in primary care, a trainer, and a supervisor. She has written a number of articles for journals on narrative therapy and supervision.

Ruth Seed is a trainee clinical psychologist on the Manchester Doctoral Course. She studied psychology, followed by an MSc in Rehabilitation Psychology at the University of Nottingham, graduating in 2009. She worked as an assistant psychologist at a Brain Injury Rehabilitation Trust unit, and then in the Neuropsychology Department at the Oxford Centre for Enablement. She has a particular interest in working systemically in learning disability services with adults, children, families, and staff teams.

Lincoln Simmonds is a clinical psychologist who is passionate about using ideas from narrative therapy in his work. He has presented workshops, supervised other practitioners, and written about using narrative therapy approaches. His chapter is derived directly from narrative therapy ideas that he has adapted and applied within his work. He has always been amazed by the enthusiastic responses, renewed hope, and an increasing sense of authorship in their own lives of the people with whom he has been fortunate enough to share the ideas.

David Todd is a clinical psychologist working with individuals and their families after acquired brain injury. He is involved in developing and facilitating rehabilitation programmes in post-acute, community and residential settings. He works therapeutically with people in managing relationships, emotions, and cognition as directed by the individual's personal goals. He is active in contributing practice-based evidence and producing research, and teaches on Leeds University's Doctorate in Clinical Psychology

Sarah Walther works full time as a narrative therapist in East Lancashire Hospitals NHS Trust and is also co-director of the Institute of Narrative Therapy. She has published and presents internationally, and her recent interests include responses to social inequity, the effects of trauma, and making visible the "shoulds" of life. Sarah's reading, writing, and practice development projects always emerge from, and return to, the very real, everyday practice dilemmas she experiences in her work.

Stephen Weatherhead is a clinical psychologist specialising in brain injury. He co-founded Neuro Family Matters (www.neurofamily matters.co.uk) in 2010 in order to provide flexible, individualised psychological support to individuals and families. He specialises in the Mental Capacity Act, with a particular emphasis on assessment, multi-agency working, and systemic perspectives. He is a clinical tutor and lecturer in health research on the Lancaster University Doctorate in Clinical Psychology.

A range of creation myths from mystical traditions describes the coming together of two disparate forces, creating a third, emergent, ever-expanding dimension of our universe. The stories of how the parental forces meet are varied. It seems fitting to take a couple of these accounts in turn as metaphors for the coming together of narrative practice and neuro-rehabilitation, as presented in this stimulating book.

The first story is one of a violent collision, a defining event that shakes everything up, forming something new from the shattered elements. This book proposes perhaps the most radical position in the Brain Injury Series to date, its systemic, relational cousin (Bowen, Yeates, & Palmer, 2010) laying some diplomatic, connective groundwork. Post-structural approaches and traditionally realist, positivist neuroscientific approaches have often been positioned at opposite ends of a very wide spectrum (e.g., Abrams, 2004). So, perhaps the opposite ends have finally looped around and impacted on each other, with neuroscientific decontextualised certainty reeling back from this first hit. At the same time, a narrative approach seems to have stumbled across a world where the spotlight has commonly turned away from context, power, co-production of meanings, and has been fixed inwards. These narrative pioneers must think there is much work to do, and this has been a fine start. Their message is strong, vibrant, unique, and exciting. Even the layout of words and text has been played with in this book (reminiscent of R. D. Laing), to stimulate the creation of new meaning for the reader. Characteristically for narrative authors, the relationship of the reader to the text constantly changes during the reading.

But all narrative practitioners know that there is never one story. Other accounts of the creation dialectic in the cosmos draw attention to a reciprocation between two disparate qualities, with each giving way, accommodating, perhaps waiting for the other. Has neuroscience been waiting for narrative therapy? Perhaps—neuropsychological accounts of memory describe semanticisation, a process whereby episodic memories become more narrative-like in structure over time (Meeter & Murre, 2004). No clear explanation has been provided for how this change might occur, and while some look to the neuronal level, others wonder if the way in which memories are remembered, including the interpersonal dimension and involvement of others, might be responsible (Gingell, 2005)—the co-remembering of a collective. In neuropsychological research on awareness of disability following brain injury and dementia, a finding that service users who identify no meaning in problem accounts of their own functioning can access and participate in third-person narratives describing the same essential content (Meeter & Murre, 2004), an unlikely literature to find essentially an account of externalising techniques.

In post-structural theory, too, writers have noted that the often cited exemplars of material power bases and differences such as money, roles, jobs, possessions, living environment (along with the social gatekeeping practices to these dimensions) should be widened to include dimensions of embodiment, neurobiology being no exception (Parker, 1992). Harré (2002) describes neurobiological capacity and function as a dimension of discursive resource, recruited during the co-production of shared and contested meanings. When undermined (Harré uses Alzheimers Disease as an example), the patterning of this social meaning production can be altered and constrained (while retaining space for socio-cultural determinism here). By including altered neurobiological substrate on the narrative practice map (as the contributors to this book clearly do), the resultant social enquiry and targeted empowerment can be all the more potent and far-reaching (e.g., a therapeutic deconstruction of "agency" or "sexual potency" with a survivor of ABI will need to access a socio-cultural participation point to open up an emancipatory and supportive meaning structure, while also finding perhaps a new assemblage of words to give meaning for the first time to confusing and contradictory experiences in these domains following ABI).

So, with both the excitement of a dramatic impact and the possibilities of a nuanced and novel co-accommodation of narrative and neuro-rehabilitation traditions, the future for socially orientated rehabilitation and community-based brain injury services seems tangibly rich and exciting in the midst of these ideas. We hope the reader will agree.

Giles Yeates and Ceri Bowen

References and Bibliography

Abrams, D. (2004). Chair of the BPS Research Board Report. *The Psychologist*, May, p. 260.

Bowen, C., Yeates, G. N., & Palmer, S. (2010). *A Relational Approach to Rehabilitation*. London: Karnac.

Gingell, S. (2005). On the role of the hippocampus in the acquisition, long-term retention and semanticisation of memory. University of Edinburgh: Unpublished Doctoral Thesis.

Harré, R. (2002). *Cognitive Science: A Philosophical Introduction*. London: Sage.

McGlynn, S. M., & Kaszniak, A. W. (1991). Unawareness of deficits in dementia and schizophrenia. In: G. P. Prigatano & D. L. Schacter (Eds.), *Awareness of Deficit after Brain Injury: Clinical and Theoretical Issues* (pp. 84–110). New York: Oxford University Press.

Meeter, M., & Murre, J. M. J. (2004). Consolidation of long-term memory: evidence and alternatives. *Psychological Bulletin, 130*: 843–857.

Parker, I. (1992). *Discourse Dynamics: Critical Analysis for Social and Individual Psychology*. London: Routledge.

Reisberg, B., Gordon, B., McCarthy, M., & Ferris, S. H. (1985). Clinical symptoms accompanying progressive cognitive decline and Alzheimer's disease. In: V. L. Melnick & N. N. Duber (Eds.), *Alzheimer's Dementia* (pp. 295–308). Clifton: Humana Press.

For my wonderful little family—Claire, Euan and Emily,
my brave sisters Coleen and Nicky,
and my amazing dad—you will always be with us.

SJW

To Mum, Joe, Dan, and Hannah for all your support.

DJT

GLOSSARY

Absent but implicit: The difference between the narratives that have already been given meaning and those that have not or have been neglected (i.e., the stories of self that lie beyond the problem story).

Aphasia/dysphasia: An impairment that affects a person's ability to process language following an acquired brain injury. People with aphasia know what they want to say but find it difficult to translate their thoughts into spoken and/or written words. Similarly, they may experience difficulty in understanding and interpreting spoken and written language.

Cognitive linguistic impairment: Specific difficulties in communication which have arisen in connection with other cognitive functions (i.e., attention, memory, executive functioning, visual–spatial skills) that can in some way affect the individual's ability to use language and communicate effectively.

Constructivist epistemology (see "Social constructionism"): The view that reality is constructed according to individual belief systems, rather than an objective "truth".

De-centred position: Privileging the life expertise and preferences of the person who is consulting the therapist, rather than those of the therapist/theoretical model.

Discourses: Particular ways of talking about a subject containing meanings that are understood by groups of people or by a particular culture.

Dominant discourses: The unquestioned acceptance of an understanding of the subject or problem, situated in a powerfully compelling socio-cultural context.

Double listening: Paying attention to what something is not, as well as to what it is (e.g., an expression of sadness also speaks of someone's hopes for happiness).

Dysarthria: An impairment of speech due to muscle weakness and/or unco-ordination, making their speech difficult to understand. Speech can sound slurred, effortful and/or unco-ordinated. If very severe, the person may not be able to speak at all.

Encephalitis: Severe inflammation of the brain.

Epistemology: The branch of philosophy which studies knowledge and its adequacy/strength.

Executive functions: Cognitive processes, principally associated with the prefrontal areas of the frontal lobe, which control and manage other cognitive processes.

Externalising conversations: Therapeutic interactions and techniques providing space to work towards the understanding that "the person is not the problem, the problem is the problem".

Knowledges: Reflects the "postmodernist" view that there is no one objective "truth" and that there are many multiple possible interpretations of any event.

Modernism: Positivistic emphasis on rationality, materialism, and reductionism.

Naturalistic descriptions (or fallacy): Attempting to give factual definitions of value-laden terms.

Non-structuralist perspectives: Emphasising intention and agency in understanding identity; inviting us to consider the actions, hopes, dreams, and wishes of people in relation to "what it is they give value to".

Outsider witness: Narrative practice in which listeners are invited to a consultation in order for the individual to acquire new images and knowledge about the problem and their preferred future.

Palsy: Paralysis, often localised to one side/one area of the body. Accompanied by loss of feeling in that area.

Positivism: The view that all true knowledge is scientific and that all things are ultimately measurable, with a definitive "truth" to be found.

Postmodernism: The position that reality is not mirrored in human understanding of it, but is, rather, constructed as the mind tries to understand its own personal reality.

Preferred stories: The stories/accounts that are most useful and helpful to ourselves or the person whom we seek to help.

Privileged meaning: As distinct from "correct" meaning; reflecting that what is presented as dominant discourse is one of multiple possible perspectives.

Problem-saturated stories: Narratives people may have for themselves and their own lives that are dominated by problems that work to oppress them.

Relativism: The view that there are no absolute truths: that is, that truth is always relative to some particular frame of reference, such as a language or a culture.

Re-membering conversations: These provide a context for people to revise or reorganise the "membership" or how they experience themselves and others in order to develop new knowledge.

Right hemisphere language impairment: This affects a person's ability to process the more pragmatic/holistic aspects of language. For example, the person may have difficulty in making inferences, understanding metaphor, and managing topics. In addition, their ability to deal with the "choreography" of conversation is affected (i.e., turn-taking skills, sensitivity to conversation partner's needs).

Scaffolding: Using questions to help people move from what is already familiar to them, to developing new possibilities.

Social constructionism (see "constructivist epistemology"): The view that individuals and groups participate in the construction of their perceived social reality through an ongoing dynamic process.

Structuralist perspectives: Describes the problems people experience as a surface manifestation of an underlying structural disorder, requiring expert assessment, identification, and remedy. In this context, an understanding of identity is a core and fixed entity.

Subjugated meaning (see "Absent but implicit"): What is "left out" from the dominant discourses presented, because it has been oppressed/marginalised by other dominant views/accounts.

Thicken: To further develop a narrative.

Unique outcomes: Exceptions to the problem that wouldn't be predicted by the problem's narrative, such as exploring times when the brain injury 'is not present'.

Zone of proximal development: The distance between the actual developmental level as determined by independent problem solving and the level of potential development as determined through problem solving under guidance.

Introduction

Stephen Weatherhead and David Todd

Our hopes for this book

Editing a book is a challenge for novice and expert alike. Some of those challenges are logistical ones, such as getting it done on time; others are more intellectually engaging, such as how does one balance the multiple perspectives that are presented across the chapters? How can the chapter authors be given freedom to write in a way that lights their flame, while the editors hold on to a shared philosophy and vision for the book as a whole? We have been privileged to work with some great authors who have made addressing these challenges relatively painless.

We set out to create a book that brings together narrative approaches and brain injury rehabilitation in a manner that fosters an understanding of the natural fit between the two. We live our lives by narratives/stories, whether they are stories of our personal or professional life, or our lived, wished for, or yet-to-be-experienced stories. Brain injury can affect those narratives at many levels, and the impact can be far-reaching. Creating a space for those stories to emerge and change is as important as understanding the functional neuroanatomy and cognitive profile of the injury.

We have tried to produce a book that balances theory with the practical application of that theory. There is a range of stances within the content of the book. Some of the authors are narrative therapists, others have accessed some narrative therapy training; some work in a way that is informed by narrative ideas in a more broad sense, and there are some who have simply recognised that therapy can be a space to hear and work with the stories people live through. As editors, we value all of those positions equally. We have asked each author to position themselves explicitly within their writing. We hope this will enable you as a reader to feel a greater interaction with the book and its contributors. You will be able to see how the authors view the work they do, what they personally value, and how their values are enacted within their professional roles.

We would encourage you to spend some time reflecting on some of these issues yourself. To get you started, perhaps have a think about the following. What does narrative mean to you? What personal and professional stories stick out in your own mind? What values do you hold on to in your life? How do those values interact with the values of the people you work with? What do you value about those interactions, and what do others value about the way in which you work? We hope that this book helps you along your own journey, and aids the interactions you have on a daily basis.

You will see that each author/group of authors has written their chapter in their own style. Some have created a lot of space for the actual words used by people who have experienced a brain injury, and others give some specific examples of how we can structure inter- actions to create space for the inherent narratives. Inevitably, some of these styles will sit better with you than others. If this book is to make a difference to you (as it has to us), then you will need to enjoy it. Therefore, do not feel obliged to read it in the same order in which the chapters are presented.

We have tried to create a thread to the internal narrative of the book as a whole. You will see that it begins with an exploration of narratives within brain injury broadly, then moves to considering professional interactions with those narratives. Once the context has been set, we move to look at focusing our work through goal setting, and thinking about the issues clinicians or therapists might meet, such as trauma, communication difficulties, working with carers, families, and other forms of indirect work. We conclude with a chapter looking at the journey of our work through the process of gathering outcome evidence.

Despite having created this path, we would encourage you to explore it in your own way. Perhaps start with the chapter where the title captured your attention, or is focused on an issue you are exploring yourself, or flick through the pages to see if any of the content captures your eye in how it is structured. We hope each chapter sits well on its own, as well as forming part of the book as a whole. We shall leave that judgement to you.

"Building-site brain"

Narrative Approaches to Brain Injury was developed to reflect and encourage multiple different perspectives and sources of knowledge in supporting recovery and adjustment following acquired brain injury. The cover image for the book provides an opportunity to introduce some of the themes explored within its pages—what does the image suggest to you about life after brain injury? Here are some thoughts from us.

The "building-site brain" cover image of *Narrative Approaches to Brain Injury* was intended to illustrate a number of concepts. First, we wanted to draw a focus to the Vygotskian concept of "scaffolding", a technique of bridging a person's zone of proximal development, or the distance between what the person can achieve on his/her own and what the person can achieve with calibrated assistance. Scaffolding is an important concept in narrative approaches and reflects the importance of the therapist entering the person's "phenomenological field"; our ability to understand the lived-in experience of the person after brain injury (Prigatano, 1999). Second, the image depicts an ongoing process, suggesting that both a person's narrative and the brain itself are dynamic, respectively reflecting the availability of alternative possibilities and perspectives in people's lives and the neuroscience of brain plasticity.

To us, the cover image suggests the activity of building, and is intended to reflect the process of recovery and adjustment after brain injury. Just as there are a number of construction workers on a building project, there are a number of people involved in working together to support a survivor of brain injury to achieve their goals, including the members of the person's family and perhaps a multi-disciplinary rehabilitation team. Also, just as work on a building site is a process devised by an architect and co-ordinated by the project manager, recovery and rehabilitation following brain injury should as much as possible also be directed and controlled by a designated individual: the person who has suffered the injury.

Conversely, another, more abstract, perspective of the image could be seen as representing the dismantling of the brain structure. Such an interpretation could be taken to reflect the deconstructionist philosophy of narrative therapy, perhaps in offering an alternative view to the dominant biomedical narrative of treatment following brain injury. This perspective would reflect one aim of the book in endorsing the consideration of non-structuralist orientations, which includes opening up the possibility of unique outcomes and multiplicity in selfhood, both before and after brain injury.

The cover picture represents a connection of the brain to its environment, reflecting the narrative view that the person (and his brain) is embedded in the world he is in. This contextualisation reflects the application of narrative approaches to facilitate alternative possibilities; widening the focus outwards from neuropathology to the contextual factors enables consideration of the resources available to the person, and the cultural and social influences on their lives.

Finally, despite representing the themes described above, the image is also intended to be humorous, which reflects the authors' experiences that there exists a genuine prospect of hope and joy, even after the often devastating trauma of an acquired brain injury. For us, also, humour reflects the need for therapists and clinicians to remain personable and genuine in their approach, while maintaining sensitivity and empathy.

The ambiguity of the "building-site brain" image itself illustrates a key strength of narrative approaches to brain injury, that is, diverse points of view are possible. Did you, the reader, take a different meaning from cover image of this book? Just as art is open to interpretation and there are many possible narratives about the meaning of an image, *Narrative Approaches to Brain Injury* discerns multiple perspectives about a person's life, identity, and that person's future possibilities after brain injury, and we welcome your views.

Applying narrative therapeutic principles to working with people who have experienced a brain injury

The aim of this book is to explore and critically appraise the benefit of applying approaches informed by narrative therapy and narrative practice to supporting a person's recovery and adjustment following an acquired brain injury. This aim may seem antithetical to some practitioners in the worlds of both neuro-rehabilitation and narrative therapy because of the central conflict between empiricists and post-modernists on the nature, possession, expression, and application of knowledge. On the surface, clinical neuropsychology and narrative therapy are two fields that appear to be diametrically opposed in terms of their epistemological approach.

Narrative therapy looks at the interaction of knowledge, language, and power in relation to a person's understanding of her experience/story/narrative. It combines social and psychological understandings of these discourses in relation to problems that have become so pervasive that the person sees herself as defined by that problem. There are few settings in which this is more pertinent than in life after a brain injury.

A brain injury can affect every aspect of a person's identity and accompanying narratives. Those narratives are influenced by a range of societal, family, social, and individual levels.

Social narratives of brain injury are often loaded with worst-case scenarios that fuel stereotypes. Legal and medical discourses within which many neuropsychological or brain injury services are provided have led to those services being (perhaps rightly) accused of a paternalistic approach to rehabilitation. I (SW) remember hearing a moving presentation by a father whose adult son had experienced a brain injury, my paraphrasing of which is "Brain injury services are like the extended family coming for Christmas: you don't see them for ages, and then they don't know when it's time to leave". Hearing this has certainly made me regularly check when the right time to become involved is, and when is the right time to leave. For families where there has been a brain injury, rehabilitation is influenced by narratives relating to illness, personal and social resources, and family roles. The consequence for many people is that a diagnosis of brain injury brings with it a pervasion of confusion, fear, and uncertainty, or a belief that it can all be "fixed" and they will "get back to normal" soon.

All of this interacts with the individual's lived experience of his brain injury and its effect on him personally. Knowledge of his own past can be affected by memory problems, lost relationships, and trauma. His present sense of self can also be influenced by cognitive problems, as well as the social, emotional, and behavioural problems that can occur after an acquired brain injury. A person's perspectives on his future self can be especially affected by long-term effects on work, relationships, abilities, and personal resources.

Narrative therapy techniques and the underpinning philosophy are closely linked, and are intended to reduce the impact of any given problem by helping the person to develop a perspective on her experience of life, which is not wholly consumed by the problem. It cannot make the brain injury go away, but then, no psychological therapy can. However, it can stop a person feeling wholly defined by it.

Addressing areas of incongruence between approaches

As described, our hopes as editors are that this book explores the benefits of applying narrative approaches to working with brain injury, which, we believe, necessitates drawing from a continuum of approaches. As the reader will recognise, the book's authors respectively approach the different chapters from a range of stances, and for each chapter an explicit attempt has been made to position the author's stance in terms of where it sits on the philosophical and epistemological continuums. In valuing all of those positions equally, our shared philosophy is to promote mutual enrichment, while allowing each perspective to retain its core values or identity. Being comfortable with diversity, therefore, is of importance to our shared philosophy. This can be a challenge when that diversity is one of diverse theoretical/philosophical perspectives and practice. This has been a big part of our thinking throughout, and will continue to be in the future.

Reinforcing the shared philosophy of multiple perspectives in this book has been important from the perspective of the contributors whose practice is diligently informed by an underlying postmodernist and non-structuralist philosophy. We feel lucky to have received contributions from a range of professionals, both narrative therapists and therapists working with narratives. We hope that all of them feel reassured that the integrity of their approach is both respected and protected. We also hope this book creates a space both for individual and collective ideas. In addition, we hope that the cross-pollination of ideas and knowledge in this book will, in fact, promote the clarity of narrative approaches and contribute to a reduction of the marginalisation of non-dominant therapeutic approaches. By considering narrative perspectives and describing the practical application of narrative approaches within brain injury services, we seek to create a space for philosophical and theoretical debate, but, more importantly, we want to provide evidence of how narrative approaches can directly contribute to improving services for survivors of brain injury.

Narrative approaches within the historical context of brain injury research and practice

The rise to prominence of the fields of clinical neuropsychology and neuro-rehabilitation over the past few decades has been predicated by a growing desire by those within these professions to create a more traditionally scientific empirical base, with standardised tests for validation, cross-validation, and replication (Stuss & Levine, 2002). In turn, rehabilitation programmes for individuals with acquired brain injuries have historically focused primarily on cognitive deficits and behavioural challenges. However, evidence of the effectiveness of interventions seeking to improve emotional and psychosocial outcome after brain injury has been more limited (e.g., Kneebone & Lincoln, 2012).

From a biopsychosocial perspective, Puente and McCaffrey (1992) argued that an understanding of brain injury that fails to place the person in the context of his life situation "has spawned a body of knowledge replete with questionable data and unfounded conclusions" (p. ix). The importance of developing new approaches to address this gap between brain and person is clear; reduced social, community, and occupational functioning not only hampers the quality of life for brain injury survivors but also presents broader socioeconomic consequences. The increasing crisis in healthcare funding has meant that a need for alternative ways of responding to long-term conditions has been recognised (e.g., Edmondson, 2003).

The need for a holistic approach to supporting post-injury recovery and adjustment is perhaps most clearly exemplified by the

complex constellation of physical, cognitive, and emotional difficulties following mild traumatic brain injury (MTBI). Around 80% of all
traumatic brain injuries are mild; however, of these, up to 15% may
present with ongoing problems, including clinical levels of anxiety
and/or depression (Kraus & Chu, 2005). These data highlight controversy about the causes and management of persisting problems after
MTBI, including the tension between viewing persisting problems as
related to a brain injury that need to be compensated for, or maintained by psychological mechanisms that may be managed (Williams,
Potter, & Ryland, 2010). However, many clinicians and researchers
take the view that the mechanism involves an intricate interplay of
biological, psychological, and social factors (e.g., Carroll, Cassidy,
Holm, Kraus, & Coronado, 2004). Unfortunately, perhaps the only
area that clinicians do agree on in considering this major public health
issue is that there is a lack of effective strategies to support improvement with these problems (Al Sayegh, Sandford, & Carson, 2010).

In recent years, more holistic approaches to working with people
after brain injury have been developed in brain injury rehabilitation
settings (e.g., Ben-Yishay, 1996; Wilson, 2000). In addition to addressing cognitive impairment and behavioural difficulties, psychotherapeutic work with individuals with acquired brain injury has
increasingly focused on common emotional difficulties (e.g., Coetzer,
2010), relational approaches (e.g., Bowen, Yeates, & Palmer, 2010), and
on the individual's own relationship to their psychological and
contextual experiences (e.g., Kangas & McDonald, 2011). Such initiatives have focused on adapting services to meet the needs of the individual and espouse an approach considering neurological, cognitive,
emotional, behavioural, and existential issues following a brain injury,
in a systemic context. However, it is noted that these are not new
ideas, and in many respects these initiatives reflect the approaches of
the early pioneers in understanding the sequelae of brain injury.
Indeed research into the impact of a brain injury has traditionally been
based on "the method of converging operations" requiring information from diverse subject populations and multiple investigatory techniques, which Banich (1997) describes as "a strategy akin to changing
your eyeglasses often" (p. 50).

Considering ideas informed by postmodernist and non-structuralist philosophy when working with people following brain injury is
not a "paradigm shift" or controversial within the historical context,

but, instead, part of a natural continued development consistent with the tradition of clinical neuropsychology and neuro-rehabilitation. However, despite the emphasis of this book on the compatibility of narrative approaches to supporting people following brain injury, we seek to illustrate the potential for contributing to significant change in the current narratives of brain injury. Further anticipated developments in "neuro-narratives" include increasing recognition of the limitations of bio-medicine following hospital discharge, and increased awareness of brain injury survivors not as passive tragic victims, but as actively engaged with their recovery (e.g., Bury, 2001). Researchers and clinicians are increasingly offering feasible alternatives to the dominant bio-medical narrative of brain injury in the process of recovery and adjustment.

Prigatano (2000) suggested that therapeutic interventions need to be more than science, they need to utilise other sources of knowledge, including art, literature, history, and philosophy. Narrative approaches emphasise that what works for one person might not work for someone else; however, this book seeks to provide practitioners with tools to see "the unique in the familiar and the familiar in the unique" (Easton & Atkin, 2011, p. 39).

References

Al Sayegh, A., Sandford, D., & Carson, A. J. (2010). Psychological approaches to treatment of postconcussion syndrome: a systematic review. *Journal of Neurology, Neurosurgery & Psychiatry, 81*: 1128–1134.

Banich, M. T. (1997). *Neuropsychology: The Neural Bases for Mental Function.* Boston, MA: Houghton Mifflin.

Ben-Yishay, Y. (1996). Reflections on the evolution of the therapeutic milieu concept. *Neuropsychological Rehabilitation, 6*: 327–343.

Bowen, C., Yeates, G., & Palmer, S. (2010). *A Relational Approach to Rehabilitation: Thinking about Relationships after Brain Injury.* London: Karnac.

Bury, M. (2001). Illness narratives: fact or fiction. *Sociology of Health and Illness, 23*: 263–285.

Carroll, L. J., Cassidy, J. D., Holm, L., Kraus, J., Coronado, V. G., & WHO Collaborating Centre Task Force on Mild Traumatic Brain Injury (2004). Methodological issues and research recommendations for mild traumatic brain injury. *Journal of Rehabilitation Medicine, 43*: 113–125.

Coetzer, R. (2010). *Anxiety and Mood Disorders Following Traumatic Brain Injury: Clinical Assessment and Psychotherapy.* London: Karnac.

Easton, A., & Atkin, K. (2011). Medicine and patient narratives. *Social Care and Neurodisability,* 2: 33–41.

Edmondson, R. (2003). Social capital: a strategy for enhancing health? *Social Sciences & Medicine,* 57: 1723–1733.

Kangas, M., & McDonald, S. (2011). Is it time to act? The potential of acceptance and commitment therapy for psychological problems following acquired brain injury. *Neuropsychological Rehabilitation,* 21: 250–276.

Kneebone, I. I., & Lincoln, N. B. (2012). Psychological problems after stroke and their management: state of knowledge. *Neuroscience & Medicine,* 3: 83–89.

Kraus, F., & Chu, L. D. (2005). Epidemiology. In: J. M. Silver, T. W. McAllister, & S. C. Yudofsky (Eds.), *Textbook of Traumatic Brain Injury* (pp. 3–26). Washington, DC: American Psychiatric Publishing.

Prigatano, G. P. (1999). *Principles of Neuropsychological Rehabilitation.* New York: Oxford University Press.

Prigatano, G. P. (2000). Neuropsychology, the patient's experience, and the political forces within our field. *Archives of Clinical Neuropsychology,* 15: 71–82.

Puente, A. E., & McCaffrey, R. J. (1992). *Handbook of Neuropsychological Assessment: A Biopsychosocial Perspective.* New York: Plenum Press.

Stuss, D. T., & Levine, B. (2002). Adult clinical neurosychology: lessons from studies of the frontal lobes. *Annual Review of Psychology,* 53: 401–433.

Williams, W. H., Potter, S., & Ryland, H. (2010). Mild traumatic brain injury and postconcussion syndrome: a neuropsychological perspective. *Journal of Neurology, Neurosurgery & Psychiatry,* 81: 1116–1122.

Wilson, B. A. (2000). Brain injury: recovery and rehabilitation. *WIREs Cognitive Science,* 1: 108–118.

CHAPTER ONE

Understanding narratives: a beacon of hope or Pandora's box?

Ava Easton and Karl Atkin

This chapter considers the use of narratives by people who have been affected by neurological illness and disability and, in particular, their naturally occurring, organic generation of narratives rather than those created as part of a therapeutic intervention. Much research has examined the content of people's narratives, but little explores why people turn to narratives following brain injury and what impact such narratives might have for both readers and authors. Consider the following extract, for example, from Ruthann Knechel Johansen (2002), writing about her son, Erik, who survived a traumatic brain injury:

The Navajo say:	Those who tell the stories rule the world.
But a story that is told	is not the story enacted.
A cold wind played	outside our house one
February night in 1995	as the family sat inside
again around	the kitchen table
When I finished reading	the draft of chapter one,
a tale familiar	from frequent telling, Erik said,
"You must go on, for until	you finish writing, I will not be finished."
You and I, he said.	I and he? I thought.

Neither will be finished	till the story be told out,
till *he* becomes	a *you* again.
I pondered puzzled:	how writing his story
could complete him.	Perhaps he meant
he could not be	himself unless I wrote
him into the present.	Was it an ending
or release	he called for?
Did I need to	write him across *his* gaps-
Or were the gaps	now more *mine* than his,
A teller and the tale	seeking communion with the told.

We begin our reflection on works such as the one above, by looking at the literature on writing narratives, before discussing the challenges generated by working with the existing literature. The chapter then goes on to consider the use and impact of reading narratives among a brain injury population, using primary empirical research. In presenting this research, we reflect on how narratives can support adjustment and recovery following acquired brain injury, while acknowledging that, for some, narratives might not be such a positive experience. Finally, the chapter considers the value of narratives for professionals and organisations that work with people affected by acquired brain injury. Much of this chapter is based upon the doctoral work of Ava Easton (Chief Executive of the Encephalitis Society) who co-authored the chapter with Karl Atkin (who holds a personal research chair at University of York).

> When thinking about your own practice, can you identify positive instances of people telling the story of their illness experience. When have people struggled to tell their story? How would you explain the difference?

What does the literature tell us?

The concept of self and identity is one that endures through time. There are, however, certain conditions under which it might be disrupted and altered, brain injury being one such instance (Chamberlain, 2006; Fraas & Calvert, 2009; Lawton, 2003; Muenchberger, Kendall, & Neal, 2008; Nochi, 2000; Segal, 2010). Writing narratives following traumatic circumstances is not uncommon and might help people come to terms with what has happened to them, contributing in some way towards acceptance of living a life under what the German physician, Rudolf Virchow calls "altered circumstances" (Bell, 2000; Gerhardt, 1989; Hydén, 1997; Teske, 2006; Whitehead, 2006). Our self-identity is created partly through our on-going narration (Bruner, 2002; Harrison, 2008; Murray, 1999; Teske, 2006). Narratives enable us to present our view or experience of the world, in a way that we have some control over, although often with the hope that our accounts will find validation through our interactions with others (see Bourdieu, 1990). Narratives, therefore, express how we see ourselves and how we present ourselves to others. They are personal creations that exist and assume meaning within a social context.

Given this, one might expect a substantive literature on the impact or influence writing narratives has on those who read and write them. There is, however, a specific dearth of literature considering their impact among those affected by neuro-illness or disability, other than those generated in rehabilitation or therapeutic settings. Further, and historically, researchers have also tended to focus on the content of narratives rather than their social meaning and use (Riessmann, 2004). Consequently we know little about the motivations and outcomes for readers and authors (Alcauskas & Charon, 2008) and Medved (2007) states "What is missing from the literature is research on narratives from individuals who have been abruptly left with cognitive impairments" (p. 605). The lack of specific literature around acute and critical illness is also described by Rier (2000) and Lawton (2003).

> What do you think are the reasons for the lack of literature on the motivations for, and impact of, narratives upon authors and readers?

Unlike their instrumental narrative use in rehabilitation settings, often with therapeutic goals in mind, many narratives are, for the most part, written for less obvious purposes. Understanding the value of narratives from the point of view of those who produce them provides an important addition to more traditional psychosocial research and helps to facilitate a more rounded and nuanced insight into people's experiences. Bio-medicine has sometimes struggled with such approaches (Kreiswirth, 2000; Smith & Squire, 2007). Lorenz

(2010, p. 163) recounts a conversation with a director of research at a renowned rehabilitation hospital in the USA. Lorenz asked if he had room on his staff for a qualitative researcher. The director responded by saying qualitative research with brain injury survivors was pointless because ". . . you just keep hearing the same story over again . . .". Some authors also suggest that the contributions of people with neuro-disabilities are often not considered reliable, valuable, or important (Cloute, Mitchell, & Yates, 2008; Lorenz, 2010; Segal, 2010). Research suggests those affected worry that their narratives are not taken as seriously as they should be by others. Their authenticity (and value) is, in effect, questioned. Patients certainly feel this, and various accounts suggest their experience is not afforded due respect and, in turn, they are left feeling "fraudulent" (Easton, 2012). A sense of not being believed may have a particular impact on a population whose "broken brains" and cognitive difficulties are already invisible (Atkin, Stapley, & Easton, 2010). In addition, there is evidence of reluctance among researchers to interview and engage with people who have complex disabilities, such as cognitive problems or speech impairments (Lawton, 2003; Paterson & Scott-Findlay, 2002; Thorne et al., 2002). Such barriers go some way in explaining the lack of literature in both brain injury and in exploring the impact of narratives among those who read and write them.

Writing narratives: motivations, intentions, and impact

The prospect of why and when people *write* narratives as opposed to why they *read* them seems to offer a more tangible subject for evaluation. The use of narratives as a primary resource for creating meaning and purpose, along with their capacity to bring structure to complex and unexpected events, is discussed at length in the literature (Bruner, 2002; Jones & Turkstra, 2011; Riessman, 2004; Skultans, 2000; Teske, 2006). The role of narratives in framing ". . . the exceptional and the unusual into a comprehensible form" is also reinforced by Bruner (1990, p. 47), and that our motivation to write stories comes from a desire to understand the world around us, particularly when that world takes an unpleasant or unexpected turn (Riessman, 1990; Aronson, 2000; Bruner, 2002; Teske, 2006). Therefore, it is easy to appreciate how narratives enable people to document how their illness has had an impact upon their lives and often the lives of those closest to them, facilitating opportunities to reconcile and come to terms with what they have experienced (Harrington, 2005; O'Brien & Clark, 2006). Autobiographical accounts following neurological disease or injury (neuro-narratives) provide a particularly rich source of material.

In the same way that adjustment following neuro-disability is constantly changing, so, too, are people's narratives (Segal, 2010). Narratives, although created at a single point in time, like time itself do not remain fixed, but can represent a reference point around which to make sense of experience (Harrison, 2008; Hovey & Paul, 2007). Our stories and how we choose to present them can be complex. They might not always be chronologically sequential; we reflect and revise our stories, particularly in response to those of others, and one person's experience and interpretation of an event might differ greatly from another. People also choose what aspects of their "selves" and their experiences they choose to share, and those they wish to conceal (Harrison, 2008). It is the process of reinterpretation that occurs within these constantly changing circumstances that help us make sense of our experiences, and come to terms with what might be a very different sense of self, following neuro-illness or disability. Narratives are not only personal creations, either, but are simultaneously constructed from our social experiences, realised in our social environments, through interaction with others. Consequently, they attract social meanings, which can differ according to the perspectives of both the story-giver and the receiver (Bruner, 1994; Jenkins, 2006). Reconciling the personal and the social are at the heart of understanding their meaning, as an individual exercises and realises active agency, which is defined and reached through the processes of social negotiation (see Bourdieu, 1990).

Consider an event in your life which had a significant impact on how you saw yourself. What was your story of this event? How important was it to you to tell your story? Did others' responses change the way you told the story? Did you tell the story differently according to who you were talking to? Did your story change over time?

Making sense of individual experience

Dealing with, or making sense of, one's experience is a recurring theme in the literature, with many authors identifying this as having a significant role in why people write their narratives (Aronson, 2000; Bruner, 2002; Charon, 2001; Jones & Turkstra, 2011; Lillrank, 2003; Medved, 2007; O'Brien & Clark, 2006; Pinhasi-Vittorio, 2008; Whitehead, 2006). This suggests that people's stories are less about solving their problems or finding solutions but more about their process: the journey as opposed to the destination (Bruner, 2002). According to Arthur Frank (1995), these are known more as quest narratives. In some cases, writing was an attempt to reconcile their current feelings of alienation and estrangement when people compared themselves to the way they were before their brain injury. Nowhere is this more clearly illustrated than by Luria (1987). *The Man with a Shattered World* is one of the most famous neuro-narratives of the twentieth century and provides an excellent example of a documentary narrative being used to create structure and coherence for experiences which are seen as outside the control of the individual. In a more recent account, Pinhasi-Vittorio (2008) introduced Ned, whose poetry enabled him to express himself and restore his self image; writing his poetry enabled him to organise his thoughts, reflect on them, and, through this process, a "new" Ned began to emerge.

The process of telling one's story can be a cathartic experience (Aronson, 2000; Robinson, 2000). The process of writing and publishing provides validation and, in some instances, can be a request for understanding and support from others (Frank, 1997; Hydén, 1997; Murray, 2000; Skultans, 2000). We are, by nature, collective beings and the groups we belong to shape our identity. Groups can also provide us with stability, meaning, and direction (Haslam, Jetten, Postmes, & Haslam, 2009; Jones & Turkstra, 2011). Following a serious traumatic brain injury, Linge (1997) recalls that during his journey of recovery, his story appeared in several different publications during the 1980s, resulting in many letters and calls which he felt reduced his sense of isolation and fostered a new found sense of hope. With hope there comes the possibility of a future, and so the process of looking forward and not back is an important stage in people's recovery (see Smith & Sparkes, 2005; Whitehead, 2006).

In making sense of one's experience, there comes an opportunity to turn the "negative" into a "positive" (Fraas & Calvert, 2009; Kemp,

2000; Noble, 2005); this is what Arthur Frank (1995) calls a "restitution narrative". The desire to positively reframe is evident in the online diary of Ivan Noble, which reached international audiences through the BBC News website (http://news.bbc.co.uk/2/hi/health/4211475. stm, accessed 23 April 2010). Ivan, suffering from a malignant brain tumour, describes "an urge to keep going and to try to make something good come out of something bad" (Noble, 2005). Similarly, following his operation to remove a brain tumour, Martin Kemp (2000) described writing his book as a way of remembering and replacing the bad with the good times. It is, perhaps, the process of writing which creates an opportunity to reframe one's experience. It appears to be a strategy and an outcome that, although used therapeutically, also occurs naturally and indirectly as a direct result of writing and reflection.

The collective use of narratives: writing for an audience

Writing narratives could imply a desire to achieve more collective, public, or community outcomes, and might be written with a specific audience in mind (see Frank, 1995), thereby connecting the private with the public. Communication skills can be impaired following neurological illness/injury and can pose a major problem when attempting to re-engage with one's family and community (Hydén, 2008). Effective communication is about being listened to, and being taken seriously by other people. Writing one's narrative could provide an uninterrupted opportunity that more fully illustrates the person's experience as they see it and over which they have more control. These narratives can then be shared with those interested in hearing their story. This is demonstrated by Kate Bainbridge (2005), who, although left with severe communication problems following acute disseminated encephalomyelitis (ADEM), wrote and published a book about her experiences. Another example illustrates a patient reciting a poem during a primary care consultation in order to express her difficulties. The Practice was so taken by this approach that they developed and ran poetry workshops for their patients (Opher & Wills, 2004), resulting in improvements in patient–practitioner communication, along with reduced levels of patient-reported isolation and loneliness. Consequently, for those whose ability to communicate in conventional senses has been impaired, then it would seem that narratives offer an alternative solution or medium.

Despite what appears to be a genuine desire, both politically and medically, to move away from paternalistic practices, where emotional concerns are ignored, open communication is often difficult to achieve and power imbalances continue to occur between patients and practitioners (Bell, 2000; Bury, 1991; Carbaugh, 2007; Frank, 1997; Lillrank, 2003; Mattingly, 1994). The literature suggests that health services, as well as those who are responsible for providing them, risk ignoring the patient's own understanding of their illness and disease (see Atkin, Stapley, & Easton, 2010). Consequently, the patient may attempt to find other ways to ensure his experiences are heard. Johansen (2002, p. 56) illustrates this when documenting the story of her son's brain injury:

> although this medical institution existed for the welfare of its patients, all of whom relied on it for their healing, they were often reduced to objects submissive to the will and convenience of the attending experts. Patient's voices and personal agency were disregarded as largely invisible decision makers manipulated their body parts and organs. The vocabulary and tone of voice with which many staff communicated to patients was frequently condescending or patronizing.

How do you listen to patient or client stories? What do you get from them? How well do you feel you understand them? Are some patients or clients easier to understand than others? Why do you think that is?

She goes on to describe the chasms between the medical case notes constructed by the doctors, which she describes as based firmly in the present, disregarding the past, and the "biographical narrative we had lived with our son", therefore ". . . contributions we as parents might have made . . . were not sought by the medical professionals, social workers or chaplains" (Johansen, 2002, p. 45).

What changes could you make in your own practice that might improve your capacity to hear your patients/clients? How would these changes benefit them? To what extent would they improve your ability to care?

Adams (1995) provides a further illustration of the desire to be seen as a person first and patient second. He was asked by Tom, an inpatient survivor hospitalised in 1931 following the pandemic of encephalitis lethargica (occurring approximately 1915 to 1926), to record his experiences. Tom wanted his and his fellow-survivors' social and emotional experiences acknowledged, rather than them be seen as "patients with a rare and strange pathology" (p. 79). In documenting her brother's brain death, Crow (2006) and her family reconstructed medical communications into narratives that were more meaningful for them. For example, the news from the doctor that the brain injury was "the worst injury he'd ever seen" (p. 178) was translated by the family as evidence of his tenacity, that he was a "fighter", and, perhaps more importantly, a potential survivor. Crow's narrative also describes her anger with the medical profession, about both their treatment of her brother and their inaccessibility to them as a family.

These accounts raise a potential gap between the practice of health professionals and the expectations and experiences of patients and their families. Often, recipients of health care want their opinions sought and listened to. In the case of brain injury, information is often felt to be insensitive, overtly medical in its use of language, and, at times, delivered with little regard to the impact it might have upon the recipients, who, in turn, are struggling to come to terms with the unexpected trauma unfolding before them (Easton, 2012). Encounters such as those described above demonstrate the need to document experiences, but also speak of the need to influence and change understanding, behaviour and practice (see Atkin, Stapley, & Easton, 2010). For example, a good medical outcome following neurological illness or injury can be considered being able to walk and talk at discharge, but often pays no regard to the cognitive, emotional, behavioural, and social problems experienced by people (Easton, 2012).

Patient narratives can also be useful in educating other patients and families about the recovery process (Fraas & Calvert, 2009) and, as such, there is evidence of authors writing to provide guidance for people directly affected, or family members experiencing the trauma associated with neuro-illness/disability (Hogan, 1999; Lillrank, 2003). One example is the book *Stepped Off* (Pape, 2005), which describes the author's recovery from having sustained life-threatening head injuries following a motorcycle accident in the Scottish Highlands. In particular, his primary intention in writing the book was to give direction to others, because "[his wife] often said she would have benefited from reading a book like this whilst I was so ill in hospital, to give her an idea of what to expect, if and when I recovered" (p. 2). Understandably, traumatic experiences foster a desire in some to provide direction and guidance for others, particularly since it might be one of few positive things they feel they can do when, from their point of view, their lives are out of control.

Reading narratives: an empirical case study

Following our review of the literature, we now offer a more detailed empirical case study, using qualitative material from the doctoral work of one of the authors (Easton, 2012). Our intention is to offer a more detailed, descriptive account, reflecting the complexity and subtlety of people's experience, following encephalitis. Specifically, our analyses focus on why people read neuro-narratives, since this is, as we have seen, often missing from the literature. This work, conducted in accordance with iterative and interpretive traditions of qualitative research (see Hammersley & Atkinson, 1995), presents material from twenty-one semi-structured interviews with people directly affected by the encephalitis (n=12) and their family members (n=9). A qualitative methodology is particularly effective in exploring complex, sensitive, and potentially contested themes, while in-depth interviews enable us to understand how people interpret what is happening to them (Denzin & Lincoln, 1998).

Time and ambivalence

Those interviewed tended to find encephalitis-related narratives through the Encephalitis Society newsletters and website (www.encephalitis.info), but were not restricted to these sources, with many respondents finding narratives elsewhere, such as in newspapers and magazines. Most people's experiences of encephalitis-related narratives were generally positive, although there is a minority for whom it was negative and a few whose feelings fluctuate. Most of the respondents described having read encephalitis-related stories for a number of years, describing them as uplifting, grateful, lucky, interesting, comforting, reassuring, invaluable, and fascinating. Those who have more negative feelings described stories as "depressing", "sad", "bad", "horrifying", "unfair", "harrowing", "painful", "not uplifting", and "upsetting". Those who expressed more ambivalent feelings said much depended on what they felt like when they read the narrative. If they felt down, for example, they would avoid stories. This is why some only wanted to read more positive accounts. Others felt compelled to read the stories, whatever their content, with one person describing them as like looking "inside Pandora's box":

> ". . . there's that pull, once you've seen them, there's that pull of 'ooooh, its awful', it's like Pandora's Box, the temptation to open the lid and have another look even though it's really painful, um, and the horror of some of the stories." (Ginny, parent, aged forty-seven)

Reading stories is not necessarily a case of liking or disliking them. Readers' views change over time and people's response to them is complicated by a variety of different factors. There are also those, like Ginny, above, who are compelled to read narratives in spite of knowing they are likely to experience distress. Another respondent, Pauline, the wife of a man affected by encephalitis, expressed a similar view. As with Ginny's child, Pauline's husband was moderately to severely affected by the after-effects of encephalitis and both women seemed to be using the stories to find answers to what the future might hold. In Pauline's case, her husband's diagnosis was unclear and he had been diagnosed with varying conditions over the years, none of which the doctors were able to confirm. It was her response to this uncertainty that led her to continue reading stories, in the hope that she might recognise her husband in one of them and finally find a diagnosis. Ginny was searching the stories for a doppelganger of her child, which might then be a prediction of what the future might hold. Pauline, however, seemed better able to rationalise the negative stories, by relating them to the more positive ones. Ginny, on the other hand, said she could lose sight of the positive and tended to identify with worst-case scenarios. Comparing one's experience with that of others is a key finding in the research.

Do you have any patients or clients like Ginny and Pauline? How might you help them?

Those we spoke to read stories for multiple and varied reasons, and, like other interests, they are subject to changes over time. Many people said they continued to read stories, the same now as they always had done, although some respondents said they read encephalitis-related narratives more in the early days of their illness experience, while others described reading more now than in the early days. No common approach emerged. Interpretation could change over time, too. Some people found negative stories more helpful after the acute or critical phase was over. For these readers, concerns about reading stories early on in their encephalitis journey centred on fears of what they might learn:

> ". . . it was a bit scary at the beginning when you're sort of reading, you know, how other people are and then thinking 'oh god, is that what I've got to come?' or you know, so . . . it's all a bit of an unknown when I first had it . . ." (Claire, person affected, aged thirty-four)

Reading stories and locating experience

One of the reasons people said they read stories was an attempt to locate their experience of a condition, about which little collective understanding exists. Making sense of one's own, or one's family member's, experiences following encephalitis was common:

> "Well you don't know anything about the illness, this is your first, um, contact, the experiences of others, so completely in the dark, and reading, that enlightens you . . ." (Vince, parent, aged forty-five)

A person directly affected by the condition agreed:

> ". . . I'd never ever heard of it before and it was for me, it was such a life-changing thing, for a minute I was on a school trip in Stratford and then the next minute I was in hospital for five months. For me it was such a big, life-changing thing but I did want to read, when I could, I wanted to read them just to try and make sense of it all, and try and understand what was going on and that I wasn't some weird person and it was the only one that'd ever happened." (Rachel, person affected, aged twenty-six)

Stories were also providing alternative ways of viewing and approaching the difficulties that life after encephalitis presented people with:

"I think other people with encephalitis is a great source to you because no matter what type of encephalitis or how you feel about it or what you do yourself, whether you are upbeat or down or whatever, if you read about somebody else there's always something in that story you pick out that can make you think 'oh, they did that, maybe I could do that, maybe that's a good way to cope'." (Belinda, person affected, aged fifty-three)

The usefulness of reading other people's stories much depended on whether the reader "connected" with the author or the story. One family member described preferring stories written by the person affected; a sibling preferred stories written by other brothers and sisters; a person affected (who did not have children) said they could not relate to stories about children. Some people struggled to connect, or chose not to connect, because they found the story too distressing, especially where children were affected or where people died. In one case, a respondent expressed distress when people had seemed to have made a better recovery than him.

While those directly affected by encephalitis used stories to help them understand what was happening to them, family members could use them to understand the affected person:

"He has, he's very, very limited communication . . . so I'm actively trying to find ways, you know, maybe to understand J more and to be able to move deeper into his world, if you know what I mean, so that I can bring him into ours." (Susan, parent, aged forty)

Some family members used stories to accept and cope with challenging behaviours, reminding themselves that the person affected could not help the way they were. They were, in effect, using the stories to embrace and legitimise behaviour as a result of the injury to the brain, which in other circumstances might be unacceptable or considered deviant.

"If there is anything I read and think oh wow this is just like T or this is just more to do with his behavioural issues . . . I'll say you need to read this to my husband or even to his brothers or read it out and say 'look this is why T acts as he does, we need to be a bit more understanding because of this, that, and the other'." (Brenda, parent, age 46)

Many respondents used stories in order to compare their own experience. This was a common theme and one of particular significance because, as we have seen, encephalitis is a rare condition and one which people have little or no collective understanding of.

"I think there's always hopes and intentions when you're reading, certainly a story, and I'm, I just can't really explain myself with this, I know certainly I often read and you're often looking to find a mirror image of what you've been through, somebody else who's been through exactly the same and I don't know why that is, you just hope to find somebody . . ." (Susan, parent, aged forty)

Some people, but usually family members, used the experiences of others to make very specific comparisons: for example, looking out for new symptoms, comparing their treatment with that of others.

"Well in the back of your mind, you're only really looking out for yourself and, um, and you want to look at, read other people's stories about their level of problems and their level of recovery and you're trying to compare it with your own and really you're just trying to get something for yourself out of it. It's quite a selfish thing really." (Vince, parent, aged forty-five)

It would seem that some relatives specifically adopt a role of "overseer" early on in their experience of encephalitis, hunting for information about symptoms, treatments, and outcomes. However, for some—both those affected by the condition and family members— reading and comparing prompted a good deal of worry, with a minority concerned that the stories might be indicative or predictive of their future. This caused anxieties.

"I think that was probably a fear, in the earlier days. I think it's not such a rational fear now but it might have been about, oooh, perhaps I don't want to read too much about it in case something or other depressing about, how I might be in the future or whether it could come back. I think I had a rational, irrational fear about it coming back, um, which hopefully I don't have now." (Margaret, person affected, aged fifty-eight)

Ginny, who we have already met, described in quite a graphic sense how reading stories actually influenced the way she viewed and felt about her child, who was affected.

> "I was prepared, but I don't know if that's a good thing or a bad thing, in how it makes you feel towards your child. Perhaps that's it, you suddenly look at your child, you know each child and you accept whatever, but you're suddenly looking at your child as like a description of something awful that could happen, not as your child and I think if you haven't understood everything about the illness and what it is you wouldn't view them as that. It's, it's the suddenly it's not a child, it's all this, you know, it's going to be awful, you know she's going to be dreadful, and of course, you don't know and actually even when the behaviour is dreadful you love them to bits." (Ginny, parent, aged forty-seven)

Knowing others have come out the other side can be especially reassuring. In some instances, stories inspired people to continue their recovery journey. More generally, respondents were using stories to compare their experiences and gain a sense of perspective. However, again, not all people reported positive effects from making such comparisons. Some respondents for whom reading was a negative experience described feelings of anger and resentment that other people were faring better, at least, at the time of their reading:

> "... at the beginning you feel slightly angry because why should they be OK from it when I'm not, kind of thing. I dunno, just confused and thinking you know, what, ... why have I done this, why am I more ill than others, why? You know, why have I got these side-effects and they haven't ... there's definitely more wrong with me." (Rachel, person affected, aged twenty-six)

Most respondents stated that reading other people's stories made them positively feel part of something: a collective, a group:

> "... it's brought me into a fold. I know that somebody else is out there suffering the same as me, even if it, nobody else knows it, but I know it. I know there is somebody else out there the same as me ..." (Harold, person affected, aged seventy-four)

This sense of belonging to a group seemed important to many of those we spoke to and some spoke of how this identification elevated their mood, making them feel uplifted, encouraged, inspired, and motivated.

> Had you realised the variety of ways in which people were using neuro-narratives, and the very positive role they play for many? Had you also considered the potential negative consequences?

Connecting with others

The literature suggests one use of narratives was to promote understanding or to make changes in others' behaviour. Those directly affected by encephalitis and family members could associate with this and nearly all described a lack of understanding or respect for their post-encephalitic difficulties. Some directly affected by encephalitis felt this lack of understanding could equally apply to close family members. Being believed, therefore, became a major difficulty:

> "Probably because it felt like you'd found keys that were opening doors, for awareness, confirmation, to validate and I just needed others to know what I was reading, what G was reading, and I think it's because it stems from not being believed. So that's what we were actually using it for, and helping them to come to terms that you know, you're not on your own either going through this. Other, others have experienced it very similar but again its quite a recurring thought that all the time it was validating, proving, we are telling the truth!" (Pauline, wife, aged forty-nine)

Using stories as a communication tool to change behaviour did, therefore, occur, but those we spoke to also used them to broker greater insights and to initiate discussion with others about issues, in some cases prompting the person affected to disclose or discuss things that might otherwise have remained hidden:

> "They, they helped me to understand them and in turn its helped me to help G because there would have been things he wouldn't have told me that he was experiencing but other people have and then I've been able to go to G . . ." (Pauline, wife, aged forty-nine)

None the less, while most people were comfortable in using stories to improve communication, some seemed reluctant. One grandparent, Anne, said that she felt her own daughter's (the mother of the child affected) refusal to engage with stories resulted in a significant lack of understanding toward her granddaughter, who had been affected severely by encephalitis:

> "... with reading them and finding out that other people were experiencing the same things she was, you know, the sort of naughtiness, the forgetfulness and things like that, you are able to turn round and say well it is part of the problem and therefore you need to accept it, you know. I think because my daughter doesn't read them so much that's maybe why she's not so accepting of C's condition and what happens with her." (Anne, grandparent, aged fifty-nine)

Professional and organisational use of narratives

The final part of this chapter returns to the literature and considers professional use of narratives. Theoretically, there is evidence that professionals are becoming increasingly sympathetic to patients' narrative (Fraas & Calvert, 2009; Prigatano, 2000). People's narratives can provide important understanding and insights for practitioners (Alcauskas & Charon, 2008; Bennett, 2007; Fraas & Calvert, 2009; Lorenz, 2010; O'Brien & Clark, 2006; Pinhasi-Vittorio, 2008). Some authors go further, suggesting that by reading narratives they engender a greater capacity to empathise and, thus, achieve an increased sense of self-satisfaction in their work (Alcauskas & Charon, 2008; Charon, 2001; Johansen, 2002). This is illustrated by returning to a study mentioned earlier in the chapter, in which a GP practice worked to improve patients' outcomes (Opher & Wills, 2004). The study details the case of a young woman with a brain injury who frequently attended her GP surgery with innumerable medically unexplained symptoms. A writing course facilitated by the surgery saw her consultation rates drop drastically, as she began to document her feelings and experiences by way of poetry. Her doctor states how he had to review *his* view of her and acknowledged that, through their long relationship, he had "lost sight of her humanity and had become incapable of giving her the respect I owed her" (p. 157).

Have you ever lost sight of the person? Why do you think that is? How can policy and practice best facilitate patient or client stories?

As well as acting as a reminder of our humanity, and refocusing professionals on the individual, people's stories are also rich in evidence and information that might help professionals in diagnosing and managing a person's illness (e.g., Ragan, Mindt, & Wittenberg-Lyles, 2005, p. 261). For these reasons, narratives are, and should remain, an important aspect of any medical consultation. Understanding the subjective experience of illness, however, has not always been a traditional part of the physician or scientist's work (Feinberg, 2005) particularly in modern society. Indeed, one author–patient suggests that "[narratives] can lend perspective and vitality to issues that are . . . written about in a quantitative and analytic fashion" (Mullan, 1999, p. 124). Our human experiences, therefore, are more complex and kaleidoscopic than can be captured in scientific language and concepts alone (Harrington, 2005; Hydén, 1997). Returning to one of the few encephalitis narrative papers (Adams, 1995), the stated reason for working with Tom (an encephalitis lethargica patient) in order to capture his story was because the author felt that the voice of the patient was drowned out by "the intimidating clamour of professional discourse" (p. 78) and that accounts such as Tom's provided a "valuable counterbalance to a discourse dominated by professional imperatives" (p. 81).

Patients can use narratives to distance themselves from the sometimes more negative medical language that is used to describe their injury (Pinhasi-Vittorio, 2008). A meta-study of chronic illness experience studies explicitly states that people with conditions affecting the brain are rarely included (Thorne et al., 2002). Much of the literature that exists on acquired brain injury, other neurological conditions, and, in particular, encephalitis, are concerned with acute clinical and pharmacological management, life-saving procedures, and psychological findings and debates. Prigatano (2000) suggests professionals working with brain injury survivors need to understand their patient's experiences. Hearing a patient's story is undoubtedly one way of achieving this, especially when this can be contextualised and triangulated with other material and information.

That narratives have the potential to successfully inform therapeutic and nursing interventions is well documented (Bennett, 2007;

Chamberlain, 2006; Fraas & Calvert, 2009; Nochi, 2000; Pennebaker, 1997; Robinson, 2000). This is perhaps not surprising, as it has been suggested that a narrative approach is an extension of what we do naturally, and that since our realities are socially constructed and maintained via the stories we tell, then a narrative approach can enable a person to retell their story following illness/trauma, reframing themselves and their situation. Hogan (1999) makes the compelling argument that a narrative approach empowers patients, enabling them to be the authors of their own interventions as opposed to being someone about whom reports are written. Hogan (1999) concludes that people's stories can help provide professionals with a deeper understanding of those they treat, a view shared by others such as Carroll (1998), who recommends that the patient's perspective and knowledge of their condition should be welcomed by the professionals involved in their care, helping to broaden a scientific approach and embracing personal, social, and cultural perspectives. Moving from theory to practice, some authors have demonstrated significant changes in perspectives of practitioners after listening to patient narratives (Fraas & Calvert, 2009), a finding which could result in improved outcomes for the patient.

Conclusion and discussion

Despite growing interest in the use of patient narratives, much of the previous research has focused on their content, rather than the meaning for those who write and read them. The literature also tends to focus on the experience of longstanding chronic conditions, rather than those who have an acquired brain injury. None the less, this related literature does provide insights into the potential value of narratives, both in making sense of what is happening to a person and in improving the relationship between patient and healthcare professional.

Our empirical case study further explored the potential value and use of narratives written by people affected by encephalitis or their family members. These narratives assisted in helping many understand and make sense of their experiences, creating a sense of belonging and reduced feelings of isolation, while encouraging people not to give up. The value of this should not be underestimated, especially when engaging with a condition that often has no personal or collective meaning (Easton, 2012). To encounter others speaking the same language as you and describing similar experiences can be incredibly powerful. For most of those we spoke to, reading stories is a positive experience, suggesting the potential of narratives for general wellbeing and recovery. The narratives of others, however, are not for everyone; some find them distressing, while others might find them less helpful, at certain times, than at other times. This reflects the complexity of the use and meaning of narratives and also reminds us of the difficulties of over-generalisation when establishing good practice.

None the less, there is a positive role for writing one's story when it is used as a vehicle to support health professionals in better understanding their clients and seeing beyond the disease. There is, however, an important distinction between stories being written for therapeutic use (a conscious and explicit aim) and stories written which result (unconsciously) in therapeutic outcome (Robinson, 2000). There is a necessary tension here, since the use of stories as a therapy, or even their use in less explicit ways, for example, keeping a diary with a view to encouraging people to cope better with their condition, means that the person's narrative is no longer completely their own. One alternative, if one wants to assess or illustrate the progress of a brain injury survivor, is to simply listen to their story at varying points in time, noting the subtle changes rather than to try to influence, direct, or become heavily involved in the production of *their* story (see Frank, 1998; Lorenz, 2010). Professionals, be they doctors, nurses, or therapists, should consider carefully, as should researchers, why, how and when they become involved in a person's narrative. Witnessing a person's narrative can of course be a positive and life affirming event. However this may not always be so, and there is always a risk of trauma and distress when "playing with another person's life" (Harrison, quoting Plummer, 2008, p. 41; Cloute, Mitchell, & Yates, 2008); A "duty of care" must exist. A good illustration of this is provided by Gelech and Desjardins (2011) who considered the "lost self" interpretation of brain injury survivors' experiences. They found survivors who resisted this view of themselves post-injury, and suggest that attempts to encourage them to pursue narrative as a therapeutic tool had the potential to result in suffering and distress (see also Segal, 2010). They go on to warn that inappropriate therapeutic discourses might compromise the patient–practitioner relationship and say it is necessary to consider to what extent therapists' moral evaluations of a person's pre-injury self plays a role in the way they direct their narrative interventions.

We are not suggesting that a narrative approach should be discouraged, simply that an awareness is required that particular types of narrative are not useful for all people at all times. In such instances practitioners could assist people in exploring alternative, or more multi-faceted, ways of coping. Organisations that publish people's narratives also have a duty of care and should consider a number of things, including presenting a good balance of narratives, ensuring that most people will connect in a positive way at some level. We must also be mindful of to whom, and when, we give narratives. As this chapter has shown, they remain a tool of enormous importance to many, but for a few they can be a source of distress, and they might struggle to avoid them, particularly in these days of the Internet and social media. Their value in offering insight to health and social care professionals should not be understated, either, and can help practitioners see the person and not the condition.

Acknowledgements

The authors would like to thank, and dedicate this chapter to, the members of The Encephalitis Society, without whom this piece of work would not exist.

References

Adams, J. (1995). 'I am still here': a life with encephalitis lethargica. *Oral History*, 78–81.

Alcauskas, M., & Charon, R. (2008). Right brain: reading, writing, and reflecting: making a case for narrative medicine in neurology. *Neurology, 70*: 89–94.

Aronson, J. K. (2000). Autopathography: the patient's tale. *British Medical Journal, 321*: 1599–1602.

Atkin, K., Stapley, S., & Easton, A. (2010). "No-one listens to me, no one believes me": self-management and the experience of living with encephalitis. *Social Science and Medicine, 71*: 386–393.

Bainbridge, K. (2005). *Kate's Story*. London: Headway.

Bell, S. (2000). Experiencing illness in / and narrative. In: C. Bird, P. Conrad, A. Fremont, & S. Levine (Eds.), *Handbook of Medical Sociology* (pp. 184–199). Upper Saddle River, NJ: Prentice-Hall.

Bennett, B. (2007). Gaining understanding from patients' stories to inform neuroscience nursing practice. *British Journal of Neuroscience Nursing, 3*: 308–312.

Bourdieu, P. (1990). *In Other Words: Essays Towards a Reflexive Sociology.* Stanford, CA: Stanford University Press.

Bruner, J. (1990). *Acts of Meaning.* Cambridge, MA: Harvard University Press.

Bruner, J. (1994). The "remembered" self. In: U. Neisser & R. Fivush (Eds.), *The Remembering Self: Construction and Accuracy in the Self-narrative* (pp. 41–54). Cambridge: Cambridge University Press.

Bruner, J. (2002). *Making Stories: Law, Literature, Life.* Cambridge, MA: Harvard University Press.

Bury, M. (1991). The sociology of chronic illness: a review of research and prospects. *Sociology of Health and Illness, 13*: 451–468.

Carbaugh, D. (2007). Ethnography of communication. In: W. Donsbach (Ed.), *The Blackwell International Encyclopedia of Communication.* Available at: http://works.bepress.com/donal_carbaugh/12.

Carroll, L. W. (1998). Understanding chronic illness from the patient's perspective. *Radiologic Technology, 70*: 37–41.

Chamberlain, D. J. (2006). The experience of surviving traumatic brain injury. *Journal of Advanced Nursing, 54*: 407–417.

Charon, R. (2001). Narrative medicine: a model for empathy, reflection, profession, and trust. *Journal of the American Medical Association, 286*: 1897–1902.

Cloute, K., Mitchell, A., & Yates, P. (2008). Traumatic brain injury and the construction of identity: a discursive approach. *Neuropsychological Rehabilitation, 18*: 651–670.

Crow, L. (2006). Extreme measures: a personal story of letting go. *Death Studies, 30*: 177–186.

Denzin, N. K., & Lincoln, Y. S. (1998). *The Landscape of Qualitative Research.* London: Sage.

Easton, A. (2012). The role of narratives in recovery following encephalitis. Unpublished doctorate dissertation. University of York.

Feinberg, T. E. (2005). Four fictional odysseys through life with a disordered brain. *Cerebrum*, 51–64.

Fraas, M. R., & Calvert, M. (2009). The use of narratives to identify characteristics leading to a productive life following acquired brain injury. *American Journal of Speech–Language Pathology, 18*: 315–328.

Frank, A. (1995). *The Wounded Storyteller*. Chicago, IL: Chicago University Press.

Frank, A. (1997). Illness as moral occasion: restoring agency to ill people. *Health*, 1: 131–148.

Frank, A. (1998). Just listening: narrative and deep illness. *Families, Systems and Health*, 16: 197.

Gelech, J. M., & Desjardins, M. (2011). I am many: the reconstruction of self following acquired brain injury. *Qualitative Health Research*, 21: 62–74.

Gerhardt, U. (1989). *Ideas about Illness – An Intellectual and Political History of Medical Sociology. New Studies in Sociology*. Basingstoke: Macmillan.

Hammersley, M., & Atkinson, P. (1995). *Ethnography: Principles in Practice*. London: Routledge.

Harrington, A. (2005). The inner lives of disordered brains. *Cerebrum*, 7: 23–36.

Harrison, B. (2008). Editor's introduction: researching lives and the lived experience. In: *Life Story Research* (pp. 23–48). London: Sage.

Haslam, A., Jetten, J., Postmes, T., & Haslam, C. (2009). Social identity, health and well-being: an emerging agenda for applied psychology. *Applied Psychology*, 58: 1–23.

Hogan, B. A. (1999). Narrative therapy in rehabilitation after brain injury: a case study. *NeuroRehabilitation*, 13: 21–25.

Hovey, R., & Paul, J. (2007). Healing, the patient narrative-story and the medical practitioner: a relationship to enhance care for the chronically ill patient. *International Journal of Qualitative Methods*, 6: 53–66.

Hydén, L.-C. (1997). Illness and narrative. *Sociology of Health and Illness*, 19: 48–69.

Hydén, L.-C. (2008). Broken and vicarious voices in narratives. In: L.-C. Hydén & J. Brockmeier (Eds.), *Health, Illness and Culture: Broken Narratives* (pp. 36–53). Abingdon: Routledge.

Jenkins, R. (2006). *Social Identity*. Abingdon: Routledge.

Johansen, R. K. (2002). *Listening in the Silence, Seeing in the Dark: Reconstructing Life after Brain Injury*. London: University of California Press.

Jones, C. A., & Turkstra, L. S. (2011). Selling the story: narratives and charisma in adults with TBI. *Brain Injury*, 25: 844–857.

Kemp, M. (2000). *True: The Autobiography of Martin Kemp*. London, Orion Books.

Kreiswirth, M. (2000). Merely telling stories? Narrative knowledge in the human sciences. *Poetics Today*, 21: 293–318.

Lawton, J. (2003). Lay experiences of health and illness: past research and future agendas. *Sociology of Health and Illness*, 25: 23–40.

Lillrank, A. (2003). Back pain and the resolution of diagnostic uncertainty in illness narratives. *Social Science & Medicine*, 57: 1045–1054.

Linge, F. R. (1997). What does it feel like to brain damaged? And: faith, hope and love: non-traditional therapy in recovery from serious head injury, a personal account. In: N. Kapur (Ed.), *Injured Brains of Medical Minds. Views from Within* (pp. 317–340). Oxford: Oxford University Press.

Lorenz, L. S. (2010). *Brain Injury Survivors: Narratives of Rehabilitation and Healing*. London: Lynne Rienner.

Luria, A. R. (1987). *The Man with a Shattered World: The History of a Brain Wound*. Cambridge, MA: Harvard University Press.

Mattingly, C. (1994). The concept of therapeutic 'emplotment'. *Social Science & Medicine*, 38: 811–822.

Medved, M. I. (2007). Remembering without a past: individuals with anterograde memory impairment talk about their lives. *Psychology Health & Medicine*, 12: 603–616.

Muenchberger, H., Kendall, E., & Neal, R. (2008). Identity transition following traumatic brain injury: a dynamic process of contraction, expansion and tentative balance. *Brain Injury*, 22: 979–992.

Mullan, F. (1999). Me and the system: the personal essay and health policy. *Health Affairs*, 18: 118–124.

Murray, M. (1999). The storied nature of health and illness. In: M. Murray & K. Chamberlain (Eds.), *Qualitative Health Psychology: Theories and Methods* (pp. 47–63). London: Sage.

Murray, M. (2000). Levels of narrative analysis in health psychology. *Journal of Health Psychology*, 3: 337–347.

Noble, I. (2005). *Like a Hole in the Head*. London: Hodder and Stoughton.

Nochi, M. (2000). Reconstructing self-narratives in coping with traumatic brain injury. *Social Science and Medicine*, 51: 1795–1804.

O'Brien, M., & Clark, D. (2006). Online illness narratives about living with motor neurone disease: a quantitative analysis. *British Journal of Neuroscience Nursing*, 2: 410–414.

Opher, S., & Wills, E. (2004). Workout with words – a poetry project in a GP surgery. *British Journal of General Practice*, 54: 156–157.

Pape, S. (2005). *Stepped Off*. Frederick, MD: PublishAmerica.

Paterson, B., & Scott-Findlay, S. (2002). Critical issues in interviewing people with traumatic brain injury. *Qualitative Health Research*, 12: 399–409.

Pennebaker, J. W. (1997). Writing about emotional experiences as a therapeutic process. *Psychological Science, 8*: 162–166.

Pinhasi-Vittorio, L. (2008). Poetry and prose in the self-perception of one man who lives with brain injury and aphasia. *Topics in Stroke Rehabilitation, 15*: 288–294.

Prigatano, G. (2000). A brief overview of four principles of neuropsychological rehabilitation. In: A.-L. Christensen & B. P. Uzzell (Eds.), *International Handbook of Neuropsychological Rehabilitation* (pp. 115–125). New York: Kluwer Academic/Plenum.

Ragan, S. L., Mindt, T., & Wittenberg-Lyles, E. (2005). Narrative medicine and education in palliative care. In: L. M. Harter, L. M. Japp, & C. S. Beck (Eds.), *Narratives, Health, and Healing: Communication Theory, Research, and Practice* (pp. 259–276). Hillsdale, NJ: Lawrence Erlbaum.

Rier, D. A. (2000). The missing voice of the critically ill: a medical sociologist's first-person account. *Sociology of Health and Illness, 22*: 68–93.

Riessman, C. K. (1990). Strategic uses of narrative in the presentation of self and illness: a research note. *Social Science and Medicine, 30*: 1195–2000.

Riessman, C. K. (2004). A thrice-told tale: new readings of an old story. In: B. Hurwitz, T. Greenhalgh, & V. Skultans (Eds.), *Narrative Research in Health and Illness* (pp. 309–324). Oxford: Blackwell.

Robinson, M. (2000). Writing well: health and the power to make images. *Journals of Medical Ethics, 26*: 79–84.

Segal, D. (2010). Exploring the importance of identity following acquired brain injury: a review of the literature. *International Journal of Child, Youth and Family Studies, 1*: 293–314.

Skultans, V. (2000). Editorial. Narrative illness and the body. *Anthropology and Medicine, 7*: 5–13.

Smith, B., & Sparkes, A. (2005). Men, sport, spinal cord injury, and narratives of hope. *Social Science & Medicine, 61*: 1095–1105.

Smith, C., & Squire, F. (2007). Narrative perspectives: two reflections from a continuum of experience. *Reflective Practice, 8*: 375–386.

Teske, J. A. (2006). Neuromythology: brains and stories. *Zygon, 41*: 169–196.

Thorne, S., Paterson, B., Acorn, S., Canam, C., Joachim, G., & Jillings, C. (2002). Chronic illness experience: insights from a metastudy. *Qualitative Health Research, 12*: 437–452.

Whitehead, L. C. (2006). Quest, chaos and restitution: living with chronic fatigue syndrome/myalgic encephalomyelitis. *Social Science & Medicine, 62*: 2236–2245.

CHAPTER TWO

Brain injury narratives: an undercurrent into the rest of your life

Katy Flynn, Anna Daiches, and Stephen Weatherhead

Individuals who have experienced a brain injury are experts in their own experiences. Listening to their stories, as told in their own words, permits us to gain valuable insights into dominant narratives surrounding brain injury. To enable this, six people who had experienced a traumatic brain injury (TBI) and undergone neurosurgery were interviewed. Their stories powerfully portray the experience of living with a brain injury.

Sustaining a brain injury is a traumatic experience, the repercussions of which can (and often do) last a lifetime. Brain injuries usually lead to numerous hospital appointments, and sometimes multiple surgical interventions. During those repeat medical visits, the person can often feel as though their life is on hold until all the appointments have been completed. In effect, they are in a temporal void. Employment, social, and even rehabilitation interventions may all be put on hold at different stages. This is often reflected in personal narratives, which express a feeling of being unable to move on practically, and psychologically.

In preparing this chapter, six people were interviewed in order to gain an insight into their individual and shared narratives. We present their stories, as explored using narrative analysis. All six of the interviewees have experienced a brain injury and have undergone at least two neurosurgical interventions. The specific neurosurgical intervention that connects them, and which led us to ask them to participate in the interviews, is cranioplasty.

As many readers may not be familiar with cranioplasty, we thought it might be useful to give a brief outline. Sometimes, after a person has sustained a brain injury, it may be necessary to remove a section of the skull (e.g., due to brain swelling, infection, need to access large portions of the brain). This procedure is a called a craniotomy (or craniectomy). The replacement of the skull piece is referred to as a cranioplasty. It is not always possible to replace the piece of skull at the time, particularly if it is infected or damaged due to the initial injury, so there can often be a wait for a few weeks or months, before the cranioplasty is performed.

The narrative of cranioplasty as a procedure is itself an interesting one. It has been carried out for centuries, perhaps as far back as prehistoric times, and there is definitive evidence of it being used by the Incans (Sanan & Rengachary, 1999). The surgery was first documented as part of Western surgical practice in the seventeenth century, and became relatively popular during the Second World War in order to repair skull damage incurred by military personnel (particularly in the air force).

> We would encourage you to consider one or two interventions, either medical or psychological. Consider their historical development, their political underpinnings, and the processes of the decisions made around them.

Over recent decades, there have been numerous explorations of the most appropriate form of material for the cranioplasty. Ideally, the original piece of skull bone will be put back in, but infection or fragmented bone segments often mean that an alternative material is needed. A further complication is how to store the bone piece in the interim. The most suitable storage place was widely accepted for some time to be in the patient's own abdomen. This comes with obvious medical and psychological implications. Other materials that have been used include canine bone, and human ribs. The former was off-putting to many, and the latter option resulted in an aesthetically displeasing "washboard effect" in the shape of the skull. Polymers, or, more commonly, metals have been the material of choice for almost as long as the procedure has been conducted. Indeed, there is evidence of gold plates being used in ancient Peru (Sanan & Rengachary, 1999). Probably the most common material used today is a titanium mesh mould.

Currently, there is no definitive perspective on logistical aspects of the surgery, such as timing and materials. In fact, the procedure itself is somewhat controversial, with some clinicians questioning its merit. We are still in the early stages of understanding cranioplasty's impact from a cognitive and neurophysiological perspective. There are some indications that it can lead to improvements (Agner, Dujovny, & Gavriria, 2002; Fodstad, Love, Ekstedt, & Lilisquist, 1984; Grant & Norcross, 1939; Suzuki, Suzuki, & Inabuchi, 1993), and the risks of further brain injury are certainly reduced by replacing the missing piece of bone. Furthermore, there is obvious value in terms of the cosmetic benefits of having one's skull reformed to its original shape, and there may well be significant therapeutic value (Dujovny, Aviles, Agner, Fernandez, & Charbel, 1997).

However, there are also downsides to consider. Undergoing further neurosurgical intervention inevitably comes with risks; risks associated with the surgery itself, as well as secondary long-term risks such as seizures and cognitive decline. The impact of these issues is felt severely by the individual, her family, and close friends, but they are often not acknowledged by wider social networks and society, mainly due to the complex (often subtle) presentation of difficulties once a person is beyond the acute phase. Consequently, the situation of living with a "hidden disability" is compounded further.

Professional narratives and our still limited understanding of the brain does not help this experience. In brain injury research, there is a paucity of large-scale robust research from which to draw evidence and understanding. Thankfully, this is because populations from which researchers can draw are relatively low in number. However, this does mean that the impact of some conditions can be underestimated. Again, if we look specifically at cranioplasty as our working example, there is a widespread assumption that once a person has undergone the procedure, they can fairly quickly return to "normal" life. This is rarely the case; the residual neuropsychological impact can have many long-term implications.

> What do you think the wider dominant narratives/social discourses about brain injury are, and how do you interact with those narratives?

In cranioplasty, we do not even have an agreed understanding of the underlying neurological mechanisms of deficits. The closest we have is that it overcomes the "Syndrome of the trephined" (ST). ST was first described by Grant and Norcross (1939), and has also been labelled post-concussion syndrome, or post-trauma syndrome. ST leads to a range of clinical symptoms, including dizziness, headaches, psychological distress, and cognitive deficits (Dujovny, Aviles, Agner, Fernandez, & Charbel, 1997). Possible causes of ST have been linked to atmospheric pressure, cerebral blood flow, cerebrospinal fluid, and the sunken skin flap (sinking into the gap left by the missing bone) causing cortical irritation, but the exact relationship is unclear. Performing a cranioplasty overcomes the issue of a sunken skin flap, thus providing a theoretical rationale for the improvement.

When it comes to exploring the effect a brain injury has on a person's sense of self, research, to date, is still in its infancy. Obviously, even less is known about how the additional experience of a cranioplasty affects people who have already experienced the trauma of a brain injury. From a clinical and research perspective, my (SW) interest in the area was sparked through discussions with my then supervisor (Dr Gavin Newby), and a consultant in rehabilitation medicine (Dr Colin Pinder). This spark turned into a flame through interactions with a client. This client (Warren) is discussed in more detail below. I (SW) had been working with Warren for about five months while he was awaiting his cranioplasty. His fatigue levels were very high, and he had significant cognitive deficits. For example, despite seeing him once a week, he could never remember my name, never mind the content of the therapy sessions. Warren recognised me on arrival, but if I phoned him (which I did regularly to remind him of planned visits), I had always to prompt his recall of me by referring to myself as "The brain guy", as this was how he remembered me.

The day after Warren had the cranioplasty, I called him at the hospital to see how he was, and the conversation went as follows:

SW: Hi Warren, how are you doing?
Warren: Oh, hi Steve, I'm doing great thanks.
SW: You recognise my voice?

Warren: Yes, it's Steve, the brain guy isn't it?
SW: (Stunned silence)

This is obviously an extreme example, and there are many other factors that could explain the interaction. Despite this, I am sure you can appreciate how the experience would cause me to take a greater interest in cranioplasty. An opportunity arose to develop this interest further through discussions with Anna Daiches and Katy Flynn.

I (AD) grew up within an extended family where fable and folk-lore were our primary means of communication, used to cement bonds and confirm family identity and to offer both teaching and legislation for the younger generation. How we individually and collectively story our worlds has fascinated me ever since. We are often more familiar with narrative forms in fiction rather than non-fiction. Indeed, many will find Dickens a more persuasive social historian than Engels. However, what drew me to the profession of clinical psychology was the power of the non-fiction case study in articulating not only theory and practice, but also, more importantly, capturing human experience, typically at times of struggle and transition. In terms of our work described here, it was the narratives that drew me, despite the subject matter. Being what I could only describe as "comically squeamish", reading through transcripts which described traumatic brain injury in minute detail was difficult. However, I am glad to have persevered and been able to bear witness to these powerful stories.

I (KF) have always had an interest in narratives/stories. From an early age I was an avid reader of "stories" in the form of fiction and non-fiction books, and my interest in how the lives of characters and people are portrayed through both poetry and prose led me to study English Literature at A-Level and in some undergraduate modules. My undergraduate degree was in psychology, and, after a few months, I requested that this be combined with cognitive neuroscience, as I was intrigued by the study of brain function and dysfunction and how it can enhance our understanding of people. My first experience of brain injury narratives was as an assistant psychologist. I met the parents of a boy who had a traumatic brain injury and listened to them describe their "story" of him before and after the accident. Their highly emotive story of loss and resilience had a profound effect on me, and a year later, as a trainee clinical psychologist, this experience influenced my decision to look in more depth at the narratives of people who had experienced a brain injury.

I (KF) conducted and analysed the interviews, with SW and AD acting as supervisors. It is important to note here that we, as clinicians/researchers, chose to focus specifically on cranioplasty. However, as you will see very clearly, the people who were interviewed (Sean, Warren, Nicola, Princess, Dorothy, Mary)[1] presented stories that are pertinent not just to cranioplasty, but also to the experience of living with a brain injury. We find the narratives to be powerful, and appreciate being given the opportunity to hear them. We hope that you will, too.

We have tried to present the narratives in a way that we hope to be meaningful to the individuals that were interviewed. In order to do so, we analysed the interviews using a narrative analysis. Narrative analysis should not be confused with narrative therapy. The latter is a therapeutic intervention, whereas narrative analysis is a qualitative methodology for interpreting interview data.

Narrative analysis involves exploring how people make sense of their world through telling stories of their experiences. The approach can be distinguished from other forms of qualitative analysis by its focus on self-presentation at an overall level (Burck, 2005), which allows interpretations to be informed by the context and temporal organisation of stories. There is a wide variability in how narrative analysis is conceptualised and conducted, and the present analysis was guided by several established texts in narrative analysis (Crossley, 2000; Lieblich, Tuval-Mashiach, & Zilber, 1998; Riessman, 1993). Focused readings of interview transcripts and the creation of summary stories which included reflections on both content and structure revealed that, although there were noteworthy differences between individual's narratives, there were also many similarities.

The individuals' narratives are presented as a shared story with four "acts", which convey their sense of identity and "self" through regressive and progressive phases: (1) the loss of my self; (2) mourning my old self; (3) searching for my self; (4) trying to accept a different self.

Progressive narratives are when interviewees' stories are moving forward and show signs of individual improvement, while regressive narratives are when things are getting worse (Gergen & Gergen, 1988). As you will see, the different narratives convey the multi-dimensional impact a brain injury can have on a person's sense of self and identity.

To begin, we present a brief introduction to the aetiology of the injury of each of the individuals whose narratives are represented.

Sean is a twenty-year-old male who had his accident when he was eighteen. He was on holiday with friends and had a quad bike accident. He had the cranioplasty eleven months after his accident. Despite his relatively young age, since the injury Sean has become keen on helping others to learn from his experiences. He has spoken to pupils at his old school about wearing a helmet, and is now a co-investigator on a large research project.

Warren is a forty-year-old male who had his accident when he was thirty-eight. He was assaulted outside a pub. He had the cranioplasty eight months after the assault. The fatigue and cognitive deficits he acquired did not prevent him fully engaging in the interview, or from showing how he has a great sense of humour!

Nicola is a forty-four-year-old female who had her accident when she was forty-three. She slipped and fell down her stairs. She had the cranioplasty ten days after the accident. Nicola talked about her "steely determination", and how central her husband and the rest of her family have been in helping her to get through.

Princess is a twenty-one-year-old female who had her accident when she was twenty. She was on holiday with her boyfriend and had a motorcycle accident. She had the cranioplasty six months after the accident. Princess was overjoyed that the cranioplasty was done in time for her twenty-first birthday, which her family and friends celebrated by planning a Las Vegas themed surprise party for her!

Dorothy is a seventy-five-year-old female who had her accident when she was seventy-two. She was involved in a car accident. She had her first cranioplasty five months after the accident, and it stayed in for 3–4 weeks before being removed due to infection. She had her second cranioplasty one year after the accident, and it stayed in for four months before being removed due to infection. Dorothy's daughter and husband were involved in the interview, and their support and love for Dorothy shone through, despite all the difficulties they have had to face together.

Mary is a sixty-four-year-old female who had her accident when she was sixty-two. She slipped on ice and fell over. She had the cranioplasty seven months after the accident. My (KF) last contact with Mary was a happy one, as she informed me of her joy at her engagement to her partner, who was an important person in her journey to recovery.

A shared story

Act 1: The loss of my self: the accident. "Wham . . . and everything changed"

Act 1 of the shared narrative explores the accident which caused the brain injury, which could be described as the epicentre of the narratives. The effects of the traumatic brain injury (TBI) on the individual can be viewed in a non-linear way; the accident acted as an epicentre, which sent out several "waves" that had an impact on individuals' sense of self.

For the individuals interviewed here, the shared story begins with the accident that caused the individuals' brain injuries. Each person had their own memory of this pivotal moment in their lives, but, for all of them, it was the point at which their lives changed.

All the interviewees began talking about their accident in the first three minutes of their interview. Warren, Nicola, and Princess briefly skimmed over their previous life before focusing on the accident. Sean and Mary began a year before the accident, and then went straight into describing what happened. Dorothy began her story with "I was nursing there before the accident, and, erm, it's changed my life completely."

Sean described being on an idyllic holiday, and then, after a long pause, he dramatically stated "and then tragedy struck". The word "struck" conveyed forcefulness and shock. Nicola brought up the accident on four separate occasions, and each time she emphasised her astonishment, disbelief, and "incredulousness" that something like this could have happened to her. The trauma was so acute that she continued to experience it throughout the narrative. Dorothy used the onomatopoeic word "wham" to describe how everything changed as a result of the accident, and this vividly emphasised the speed and suddenness of the accident, and just how out of her control it was.

Several of the interviewees' descriptions of their accident sounded quite rehearsed. For example, when Nicola first discussed how her injury happened, it was almost as if she was reciting a monologue. Her language in this section of her narrative contained less pauses and filler words, and had a clear ending: "that's it really, that's all I can tell you." Sadly, each of the interviewees has probably had to tell a lot of people about the accident, so their accounts may well have become rehearsed over time. These rehearsed stories may also have functioned as a way for the individuals to create some distance for themselves from unbearable emotions.

Van Der Kolk (1998) discusses how "autobiographical memory gaps and continued reliance on dissociation makes it very hard for these patients [people with amnesia following trauma] to reconstruct a precise account of both their past and current reality" (p. 98). All of the interviewees mentioned not being able to remember at least some details;[2] however, all the interviewees apart from Warren were still able to produce a cohesive narrative of the accident. This is in line with Nochi (1998), who also found that the interviewees had consistent self-narratives despite memory blanks: "they made a story about the accidents using 'objective' information, hearsay and guesses" (p. 871). If the event is not personally remembered, then information may be collated and an account scripted. Mary's account was literally scripted, as someone who had witnessed her fall had written down what they had seen on a piece of paper. She brought this to the interview, and asked me to read it out loud. By asking me to do this, she distanced herself from the event, which again may have functioned as a way to keep safe from difficult emotions.

The language used by the interviewees conveyed their lack of control at the time of the accident, and afterwards with the hospital admissions, travel, and emergency operations. For example, Sean described how a massive lorry "sent" him down a gully and how he was "catapulted" off the bike. However, the control that individuals felt that they had over the cause of their accident differed. Sean described how before the accident he "loved, loved doing anything, erm, that was a bit of risk involved, that got the adrenaline going". He took the risk of going on a quad bike without wearing a helmet, and when he reflected on the accident he questioned his choices: "Why did I do that, why didn't I have a helmet on?" This contrasted with Nicola, who slipped when she was going upstairs to bed, and felt that she had no control over the accident. She also felt as if she had little control over things like that happening again: "I just think, God I could be taken away from them [her niece and nephew] at any time, 'cause honestly Katy it was such a brief moment." Nicola's direct address to me and her use of my name increased my own empathy; I felt her shock and horror.

When Princess talked about the accident she used the word "scared" several times. Again, the theme of having no control over her life featured in her narrative, and this had made her and her parents fearful. Princess switched between blaming herself for the accident because she was not able to "hold on" to the motorbike, and feeling as if the accident was beyond her control: "We were doing everything right."

Warren's narrative differs from the others because he did not explicitly describe the details of his accident. This could have been because he assumed that the listener already knew about the accident, or perhaps talking about it might have brought up too many difficult emotions, or it might have been evidence of his memory difficulties. Cloute, Mitchell, and Yates (2008) describe how not being able to recall events means that people are less able to "own their experience, constructing a position of disempowerment" (p. 664).

Many of the interviewees also reported not being able to remember much about their time in hospital. Nicola described her memories as "like snapshots", which expressed how distant she felt from herself at this time. These feelings of dissociation were developed further when she described how her sister wrote a diary of Nicola's time in hospital. Nicola's narrative of this time is informed by her sister's descriptions. Nicola, like all of the interviewees, mentioned details about the days or dates of when things happened. This might have been an attempt to pin these "snapshot" memories together, to provide a chronological narrative of this time. Warren also conveyed a sense of being very distant from himself in hospital; he stated how he literally lost himself in the operating theatre: "As far as I'm aware I died and came back to life."

Both Princess and Warren used striking, horrific imagery to describe how they looked before they had the cranioplasty: "me head like gone [crying] . . . half head" (Princess); "the living dead because I had half my head" (Warren). Warren's use of the oxymoron "living dead" created a sharp emphasis and enhanced the monstrous imagery. On listening to this experience, I (KF) felt shock and some fear at the image, but also empathy, as he felt as if he was only half in the "real world". Hellawell and Brewin (2004) describe how trauma memories and flashbacks are associated with a greater use of perceptual detail, characterised by more mention of death, and by the primary emotions of fear, horror, and helplessness. Many of the narratives in Act 1 are certainly indicative of trauma.

Act 2: Mourning my old self: the past. "If only I could turn back time"

Act 2 highlights the first "wave" of the journey that interviewees described trying to negotiate. Individuals appeared to begin "mourning for their old selves; the past", and many of them expressed how they longed to be able to "turn back time".

The narratives of all the interviewees were framed within progressive descriptions of their previous "self", before the traumatic accident. The language that Sean and Princess used vividly conveyed a sense of independence and freedom. Sean described how he was a "typical teenage boy" on holiday after finishing Sixth Form College, who could do "whatever I wanted, whenever I wanted." The fast, staccato rhythm and the alliteration used in these phrases reflected enthusiasm; however, the tempo and rhythm also suggested that his life was running out of control. Princess described going to live in another country for the summer before starting her police training, and she stated, "I've never been so happy in my life." Sean and Princess painted idealised pictures of their previous lives, which emphasised the discrepancy between their lives before and after the accident. This is consistent with Lange, Iverson, and Rose (2010) who report a "good-old-days" (p. 442) bias in people who have experienced a brain injury.

Sean's and Princess's narratives in this act contrast with the more "up and down" stories of the others. Like Sean, Dorothy talked about the independence she had before the accident: "I was able to get around and do everything I wanted to do." However, when Dorothy "had" to give up nursing after having children, it was "as though I'd lost a limb." The imagery created by this simile highlighted just how much giving up her career affected her identity. Similarly, Mary and Nicola did not idealise their past, but talked about happy and difficult times. For example, they describe the death of their husband and father, respectively, as great losses. Warren talked about how he "used to be able to do anything" before the accident. However, he also talked about coming from a "broken home" and how he had "always felt like a loner". Despite this, like the others, he longed to return to the life he had before that accident: "If only I could turn back time" (Warren).

The tense that the interviewees used to describe their lives before the accident disclosed much about how they viewed this time of their lives. Princess's description of life before the injury was firmly in the past tense: "I'd be one of those girls, coz I was only young, I'd go out every day." Her language implied that she was looking back into a distant past. She repeated "I was only young" several times throughout her story, which highlighted how naïve she felt that she was then, and how the accident had made her "grow up". Sean switched between the past and present tense. He used the present tense when describing his life just before the accident, when he was on holiday for the first time with his friends. This put him back in the moment, and, as the listener, I (KF) felt that the past was still within his reach and that he had not given up hope: "I'm here on my own, I've got so much independence now." However, he stated this just before he talked about the accident, and the use of mixed tense can be indicative of ongoing trauma (Hellawell & Brewin, 2004).

A central theme to come from Nochi's (1998) research, which was reflected for these individuals, is a "loss of self by comparison". Descriptions of the interviewees' selves before the accident were often framed as a comparison, as they compared their current selves to the images they had maintained of themselves in the past. However, progressive narratives of the past also functioned as a way for the interviewees to demonstrate how they felt that they had control and agency over their lives, to some extent, before the accident: "I felt I was getting somewhere. I had missions—challenges to complete" (Warren).

Act 3: Searching for my self: cranioplasty. "They've not put the jigsaw back properly"

Act 3 represents a second wave, "searching for my self: cranioplasty". The cranioplasty literally makes the skull whole again, but individuals were still scrambling to fit the "jigsaw" pieces of their identity together.

There were several important differences between the interviewees within this act. However, the main themes are captured by Nicola's comment, "They've not put the jigsaw back properly." Literally, this sentence represents how the plate or the replaced skull bone felt in their heads: "It's deeper on that side" (Warren); "I've still got the screw ... err ... protruding" (Sean). However this phrase was also a metaphor about identity. The word "they've" coveys how most of the interviewees felt that other people, not themselves, had control during this act. The metaphor "jigsaw" can be interpreted as representing the life of each interviewee, and how their accident has left them with a view of it being fragile and easily pulled apart into pieces. "Back" communicates how most individuals strive to return to how they were before the injury. Most of the interviewees did not feel as if their self was "whole", and memory loss meant that most of the interviewees had gaps (or missing jigsaw pieces) in their complete picture of themselves: "One minute I've got an average everyday normal life and the next I've got nothing. And there's a big gap in that, in between that, where I lost my memory. I don't know what happened" (Warren).

The accident, not the cranioplasty, was the central event in interviewees' narratives. However, all of the interviewees mentioned the cranioplasty, and this affected the progressive or regressive terrain of the interviewees' narratives in different ways.

The amount of control that the interviewees felt that they had over the cranioplasty operation varied. Sean had a choice about having a cranioplasty, but struggled with the lack of control that he had over the outcome of the operation. Before the cranioplasty operation, he desperately tried to maximise the control he had by assertively questioning professionals about the outcome: "I don't want to come out of that operation theatre with a perfect head, but have epilepsy then for the rest of my life" (Sean). Like Sean, Princess was given a choice about her cranioplasty operation. Princess's narrative conveyed a real sense of having control over her life at this point. Out of all the narratives, she was the only one to emphasise how the doctors warned her about the risks of the operation: "They were saying quite bad things about it. Trying to push me off getting it!" Despite this, she chose to have it, and she described how well it went in an almost idealised way: "I was like in and out of hospital basically." Princess also described how she fought to have an operation to improve her facial palsy. Choosing to have both the cranioplasty and the palsy operation gave her the sense of feeling physically in control of her body again, after this was taken away from her by the accident.

Although Mary could not remember if she had a choice over the cranioplasty, there was a strong sense of her being in control as she said, "I felt like I wanted to go and get it done. I did." Both Warren and Nicola lacked memory about the cranioplasty. Unlike the other interviewees, Nicola's accident, craniotomy, and cranioplasty happened in quick succession and she was unconscious for most of this

time: "The whole craniotomy thing, there, there was absolutely nothing I could do about that."

Dorothy had two cranioplasty operations; however, both plates
became infected and were removed. She was waiting to see if she
would have a third cranioplasty. She was the only participant who
had experienced a "failed" cranioplasty. This affected her narrative,
which was passive and helpless: "I'll just go along with it . . . because
there's nothing else I can do." When she did try to assert herself more,
she was dismissed by the doctor:

> "I told the doctor how I was trying to remember the things and I get
> headaches. He said don't remember them. Let it go. He said there's
> nothing important now. I said it is to me. I like to remember things.
> Anyway he said let it go. It'll come back when it's ready . . . I don't
> like not remembering though." (Dorothy)

Many of the interviewees applied a medical model of understanding to their recovery. Sean described having a cranioplasty as "a bitter
pill to swallow"; Dorothy stated several times that "I still think the
doctor knows better." Princess wanted to have the palsy operation
because the surgeon said "he'd get me smiling," and because "I'll
never be like happy till it's gone [the palsy]." She literally believed an
operation would make her happy. This is consistent with the literature,
as Cloute, Mitchell, and Yates (2008) identified "medical model refer-
encing" as a central theme in their study of brain injury and identity.
The use of this language places the person in the passive "patient" role,
dependent on "experts" to help them fix their difficulties.

After the cranioplasty, some of the interviewees started to regain
control of their lives. For Mary, the cranioplasty was just one part of
an overall progressive story of recovery: "It's just got better and
better." Several times she stated how the cranioplasty helped to
increase her confidence and independence. Even things which could
be portrayed as negative, such as her tiredness, were presented in a
positive way: "I used to sleep a lot . . . It just builds you up." In previous acts, Princess described feeling "scared", but after the cranioplasty
she described how "the fear had gone". She felt "secure" and safe with
the cranioplasty, and this allowed her to start to regain control of her
life. However, she described how this was happening slowly: "It's like
being a child again."

Sean expressed how he felt a great deal of anger about his cranio-plasty for the first six months because his seizures returned: "I hated the fact that I had done it [chosen to have the cranioplasty]". He slowly regained control over his seizures as they started to reduce, but his freedom was still affected: "I know cranioplasties don't affect everyone in the same way but for me it's stopped me drinking. It's stopped me driving. It's stopped me being a normal sociable person. A confident person."

Warren also lacked control after his cranioplasty and this was conveyed by the simile "I feel like a robot." He was referring to the metal in his body and how physically he was not the same, but "robot" also suggested that he was no longer in control of his own body, and that he was very distant from who he used to be. Like Dorothy, he was "lost—I'm a different person" (Dorothy).

Act 4: Trying to accept a different self. "An undercurrent into the rest of your life"

The story represented here ends with Act 4, "trying to accept a differ-ent self". However, this is not the end of interviewees' brain injury narratives; their brain injury is, instead, experienced as an "undercur-rent" into the rest of their lives.

For most of the interviewees, this final act did not signal the end of their brain injury narratives. A brain injury is not a finite event, and the interviewees' journeys through their brain injury experiences had not ended. They still yearned for the self that they were before. However, for most, there was the dawning realisation that this expe-rience had affected them too much for them to return to their "old" self. Nicola captured this when she stated how "it does have an under-current into the rest of your life." On the surface, most of the six inter-viewees described coping and acting to some extent like they did before the accident. However, the "undercurrent" of the brain injury was still a present and powerful force.

Mary described how "It's nice to be back again. It is nice to be back again, yeah." This indicated that she felt as if she was so different after the injury that her "self" had literally "gone away". She felt that her "old" self was back, and attributed much of this to the cranioplasty. Contrastingly, the narratives of the other interviewees suggest that they found it more difficult to accept their selves at the time of the interview:

"I suppose the old Nicola was . . . she was just normal; she just got on with things and wouldn't get upset like this. So, that was the old one I suppose. Just, y'know, the old—I don't even like the term the 'old Nicola' but it was just, she didn't have this in her head all the time, thinking about it. (slower) Because I do spend every waking minute thinking about it." (Nicola)

Nicola talked about her "old" self in the third person, and this is consistent with Nochi's (1998) findings: "when an individual cannot define his or her functional change, he or she may feel alienated from the self" (p. 872). Sean kept coming back to his "quest" to become "normal". At one point in his narrative, he stated that it was "only over the past year since I've been properly normal again," and at another point he questioned if he was "ever going to have a normal life again." His perception of how close to his "quest" he was changed throughout, and was influenced by his conflicting feelings about the cranioplasty. This could be because he did not really know what being "normal" meant to him any more. He used to believe that normality was his "old" self, but the accident and cranioplasty had changed him physically and psychologically so he could not go back: "I've grown up so much with this accident."

Princess stated how "I'm a different [Princess] now. So, I've like changed completely. So, I do think like, that was the old part of me, this is the new [Princess]." Like Sean and Nicola, her narrative conveys tension between her personified "old" self and "new" self: "I was a gobby cow before . . . but now, I'll sit there quiet and if someone's making me feel bad about myself I'll just ignore it." Many of the interviewees' accounts are shaped by the notion of a "unitary self" (McAdams, Josselson, & Lieblich, 2006) which "experiences multiplicities and contradictions as tensions rather than valued complexities" (Burck, 2005, p. 253).

Dorothy and Warren struggled to accept their selves in the present and their narrative tones were particularly pessimistic. The effect of their brain injury was more than an "undercurrent" in their lives. For Warren, the brain injury had the effect of a "drain" which he felt as if his life was going down. Sections of his narrative were fast, jumpy, and frantic, which created an atmosphere of desperation as he grasped for parts of his life which were lost to him. Dorothy described her injury and the subsequent "failed" cranioplasties as "like a brick wall", a dead end that she could not get past and which prevented her life from progressing. Compared to other interviewees, their narratives lacked progression: "I'm back to square one again" (Dorothy).

Interviewees' narratives also highlighted how society had an effect in shaping their identity. At an ideological level, "investigation of narratives informs us of the cultural assumptions that permeate our society and our very identity" (Murray, 2000, p. 343). Nicola presented a striking image of society's perceptions of people with a brain injury: "They expect me to be rocking and licking glass or something y'know." Nicola's view of society was consistent with McLellen, Bishop, and McKinlay (2010), who found that people who were unfamiliar with brain injury believed that people with a brain injury were less employable, polite, flexible, intelligent, and mature. This "narrow-minded point of view or ignorance" (Nicola) can have a significant impact on rehabilitation following brain injury, as stigma can affect life chances and cause stress (Link & Phelan, 2006).

One reason why other people and society have such an influence is because "reduced independence" is a key theme that links all narratives. This led to a reliance on others: "I'm an awful burden to him [husband]" (Dorothy); "That annoys me in a way that I can't—I'm not self sufficient" (Nicola). Before the accident, Sean had just learnt to drive and he loved the independence this gave him. However, as a result of the seizures caused by his brain injury and subsequent cranioplasty, he was not allowed to drive: "That's the biggest thing I miss at the moment." He described waiting for a bus, which mirrored his life after the accident: "It is just a waiting game. Which is horrible." Dorothy had lost a great deal of independence as she was in a wheelchair: "I don't like it . . . because it's other people pushing me. And I want to do it for myself. I don't want to be pushed around. I don't want to be an invalid." Like Sean, the cranioplasty contributed to Dorothy's loss of independence, as her lengthy hospital stays reduced her mobility further.

Sean repeatedly described the accident as having "a massive strain on everything in my life." Although Sean, Princess, and Nicola described going back to college or work, and "normality", they did not have complete control over this as they felt that the "strain" of the brain injury was still there. Nicola showed some acceptance of the lack of control that she felt that she had over her life: "Anything can happen at any given time, you just have to appreciate what you've got." Princess described how the palsy on her face was a visual reminder: "It just knocks you down again doesn't it [crying], it makes you remember that you had an accident." This implied that she was trying to "get up" and carry on with her life. However, memories of the accident metaphorically knocked her down again. She continued to relive the trauma of the accident, and this prevented her from moving on.

Sean desperately believed that you could see dangers if you looked closely enough: "hazard perception". He longed to live in a world where people could predict and have some control over what happens. Sean tried to have control over the negative things that might happen to other people by going into schools and educating young people about head injuries and possible dangers on holiday. He stated, "I've got a responsibility to help people now." The word "responsibility" suggested that he did not chose to help people, but that he felt that he must help people. This might further add to the "massive strain" that he felt. Feeling the need to go into schools and tell his story of brain injury might be another indicator of trauma. A predominant theme in the trauma literature is the "urge to bear witness . . . the need for 'survivors' to testify to other people the truth of their experience" (Crossley, 2000, p. 110).

Sean's desire to help people extended further. In part of the interview, my (KF) own professional role clearly influenced Sean's narrative. He talked with some envy about people, like the researcher, who "help" people as part of their jobs:

> "It's like the way you help people get over things like this; it must be so good for you to see. Like if you see a person three or four years down the line and they're back to normal, and you know inside you that must have had something to do with me . . . Like and if you've brought someone from thinking there is no point in living any more to being normal again then there is no better thing to, to even think about." (Sean)

This extract suggests that one of the reasons why helping people is so important for Sean is because with it comes the ability to control "bad things" happening to others. The power for change belongs with the helper, not the individual being helped: "that must have had something to do with me." The theme of "helping" is also present in other narratives. Princess stated that "I want a career where I'm actually needed," and Warren said, "That's all I want to do now, help people." However, he then added, "and it's so frustrating 'cause I can't help myself," which communicated his sense of powerlessness.

Several of the interviewees described someone else with a brain injury who was worse off than them: "There was one girl who was in the bed opposite me who was a dance instructor who, who knocked her head, had a stroke, had to have her leg amputated" (Nicola). This finding is consistent with Nochi (2000), who found that interviewees' repositioned their narratives by comparing themselves to others who appeared worse off, and that this was a coping strategy.

Many of the interviewees strived to present coping narratives; however, their language at times suggested that the "undercurrent" of the brain injury was preventing them from coping as well as they would like. For example, the word "lucky" was mentioned several times: "I've been very very lucky" (Sean); "and that could have been me. I've just been so lucky" (Princess); "The whole experience has shown me how much people care, and how lucky I am" (Nicola). Although "lucky" is a positive word, it implies that fate is in control, not the interviewees themselves. It also suggests that society has imposed rules about how the interviewees should feel about a brain injury.

Contrastingly, Mary compared herself to "normal" people who had not experienced a brain injury. She described differences in herself now, but expanded on this by saying that other people were no different: "Now I have to wear glasses all the time but it doesn't bother me. I mean there's a lot of people who have to wear glasses don't they" (Mary).

For most of the interviewees, their stories end with thoughts about the future. Much of Mary's narrative is about the future, as she contemplated a life living with her partner. Both Sean and Nicola used the metaphor of a road to describe how the journey for them was not over: "There's a few bumps in the road still to come I'm sure, it's just how you get over them" (Sean); "It's not the end of the road" (Nicola). Both accounts seemed hopeful and optimistic about the "road to recovery". However, the hope felt somewhat forced when Nicola said, "You've got to have hope through all this or you'd have nothing." On the surface she appeared hopeful, but there is still an "undercurrent" of despair.

Warren used a simile to describe how he viewed his future: "It's like a walk in the dark, wandering aimlessly into—into time basically." Sean and Nicola have a "road" that leads them to where they want to be; however, he does not have this direction and is "wandering aimlessly". Time is the only thing that is moving on. "Walk in the dark" conveyed his fear and confusion. It also expresses what it feels like to go through life with the cognitive difficulties that he has acquired. Dorothy did not think about the future: "If I think about it I'll go crazy." The "brick wall" of her accident was still in place, and her narrative was unable to progress. Similarly, Warren described how "My life has come to a long standstill." The juxtaposition of "wandering aimlessly" and "long standstill" portrayed his bewilderment and disorientation, his wandering does not lead anywhere. Crossley (2000) identifies how "living in the empty present" is a form of temporal orientation that can be used by people as a way to try and cope with traumatic experiences. However "the inability to project into the future, to live with hopes, possibilities and aspirations . . . is comparable to a prison" (Crossley, 2000, pp. 150–151).

* * *

These interviews offer an insight into how a brain injury and subsequent interventions affect a person's narrative. For each of the interviewees, while the initial incident that led to the injury was the central event, the cranioplasty was a "wave" in participants' journeys towards acceptance, normality, or recovery. For some, the current of the cranioplasty "wave" pulled them back and stories were regressive, and for others it propelled them forward and they told a progressive narrative. However, others barely noticed this "wave" amid a stormy ocean of the other obstacles that a brain injury presents.

Acknowledgements

The authors would like to thank David Todd and the Cumbria Community Acquired Brain Injury Service, Gavin Newby, Beth Fisher, Bernie Walsh, and Anne Mansfield of the South Cheshire Acquired Brain Injury Service, Colin Pinder, Lancaster University DClinPsy Programme, and all of the interviewees.

* * *

There is one more thing we would like to share in concluding this chapter: a poem. This was not written as a poem: it is, in fact, an excerpt from the interview with Princess. One way of exploring the data from interviews is to change the layout on the paper. The order and content is unchanged, it is just the breaks in textual layout that are reorganised to create poetic stanzas. Princess's "poem" was particularly powerful and captures the experience in a very poignant fashion.

Princess's Poem

The battle between my old self and my new self

Like before the op, the accident, I was completely different
So I'm a different [Princess] now
So, I've like changed completely
So, I do think like, that was the old part of me, this is the new [Princess].

A lot more scared of everything.
So, don't come near me in a club,
Coz if someone's going to hit me or something
I'll put you in front of me
I'm not like over the top fragile
I can stick up for myself and things like that.
But I'd rather not argue,
I'd rather just let something go than get into confrontation.

So I'm just a lot more, not confident enough to shout back at someone
    if they're shouting at me.
I'd rather just run away.
I was a gobby cow before
If someone said like boo to me I'd be like what?
I'd shout back like, I'd give a lot back.
But now, I'll sit there quiet
And if someone's like making me feel bad about myself I'll just ignore it.

I'm going to college, and I think that's really good
Because I'm concentrating I think that's great
But, like there obviously is some new bad bits
But there obviously is some new better bits.

It's just like getting used to yourself again coz,
Like people are always pushing me

And saying things like 'you used to be like this, you used to do that'
And coz I don't do that now
They have to accept it
And not try to push me into things again
But obviously I do want to go back to being what I was like,
But, with a bit more of what I'm like now.

So like, I'm not so. Coz I wouldn't care,
I'd jump over a fence, and it'd be a quicker route round,
But now I walk all the way round,
Just silly things like that.

I used to not care.
If someone was going to overtake me on the motorway I'd let them
Instead of pulling out to overtake over someone else.
Yeah, I do think I'm better now.
But obviously like people liked me before as well.
So obviously they liked the bits before,
But because I'm like this now
Like they have to start liking me like this
I guess?

I've got old friends in Essex and my accent's changed
Coz I used to be a bit of a scally
And I'd be like 'y'alright mate,'
And it'd be very very confident, very loud

And because I've had so much done with me throat and everything
Me voice has gone a lot softer
And coz I don't speak the same
Coz I'm not as gobby or as confident I think my voice has changed.

So, people always say, like, your voice isn't the same.
And that makes you feel like crap but then you think
Well this is my new voice isn't it?
So. Get used to it.

Well yeah, coz I think, I don't know what it used to be like.
Coz everyone tells me it was a lot more stronger and louder
People just say to me now you're a lot quieter
But I don't think I used to walk in and be like [shouts] 'alright Suz'
   dead loud,
I just think like I used to be a bit more confident
So my voice was obviously a bit stronger
But like, I think it's coz I used to be a bit louder.

And coz it used to be a bit more confident and cocky,
That's why it's changed.
But that'll come back in time.

So, it's not changed completely.
It's just I'm just not the same girl.

Notes

1. The individuals who were interviewed were given the opportunity to either have their own names used, or to choose a pseudonym.
2. There might, of course, also be cognitive explanations for this.

References

Agner, C., Dujovny, M., & Gavriria, M. (2002). Case report: neurocognitive assessment before and after cranioplasty. *Acta Neurochirurgica, 144*: 1033–1040.

Burck, C. (2005). Comparing qualitative research methodologies for systemic research: the use of grounded theory, discourse analysis and narrative analysis. *Journal of Family Therapy, 27*: 237–262. doi: 10.1111/j.1467–6427.2005.00314.x.

Cloute, K., Mitchell, A., & Yates, P. (2008). Traumatic brain injury and the construction of identity: a discursive approach. *Neuropsychological Rehabilitation, 18*: 651–670. doi: 10.1080/09602010701306989.

Crossley, M. L. (2000). *Introducing Narrative Psychology: Self, Trauma and the Construction of Meaning*. Buckingham: Open University Press.

Dujovny, M., Aviles, A., Agner, C., Fernandez, P., & Charbel, F. T. (1997). Cranioplasty: cosmetic or therapeutic? *Neurology, 47*: 238–241.

Fodstad, H., Love, J. A., Ekstedt, H. F., & Lilisquist, B. (1984). Effect of cranioplasty on cerebrospinal fluid hydrodynamics in patients with the syndrome of the trephined. *Acta Neurochirurgica, 70*: 21–30.

Gergen, K. J., & Gergen, M. M. (1988). Narrative and the self as relationship. *Advances in Experimental Social Psychology, 21*, 17–56. doi: 10.1016/S0065–2601(08)60223-3

Grant, F. C., & Norcross, N. C. (1939). Repair of cranial defect by cranioplasty. *Annals of Surg, 110*: 488–512.

Hellawell, S. J., & Brewin, C. R. (2004). A comparison of flashbacks and ordinary autobiographical memories of trauma: content and language.

Behaviour Research and Therapy, 42: 1–12. doi: 10.1016/s0005-7967 (03)00088-3.

Lange, R. T., Iverson, G. L., & Rose, A. (2010). Post-concussion symptom reporting and the "good-old-days" bias following mild traumatic brain injury. *Archives of Clinical Neuropsychology, 25*: 442–450. doi: 10.1093/arclin/acq031.

Lieblich, A., Tuval-Mashiach, R., & Zilber, T. (1998). *Narrative Research: Reading, Analysis and Interpretation.* London: Sage.

Link, B. G., & Phelan, J. C. (2006). Stigma and its public health implications. *The Lancet, 367*: 528–529. doi: 10.1016/S0140-6736(06)68184-1.

McAdams, D. P., Josselson, R., & Lieblich, A. (2006). *Identity and Story: Creating Self in Narrative.* Washington, DC: American Psychological Association.

McLellan, T., Bishop, A., & McKinlay, A. (2010). Community attitudes toward individuals with traumatic brain injury. *Journal of the International Neuropsychological Society, 16*: 705–710. doi: 10.1017/S1355617710000524.

Murray, M. (2000). Levels of narrative analysis in health psychology. *Journal of Health Psychology, 5*: 337–347. doi: 10.1177/135910530000500305.

Nochi, M. (1998). "Loss of self" in the narratives of people with traumatic brain injuries: a qualitative analysis. *Social Science & Medicine, 46*: 869–878. doi: 10.1016/S0277-9536(97)00211-6.

Nochi, M. (2000). Reconstructing self-narratives in coping with traumatic brain injury. *Social Science & Medicine, 51*: 1795–1804. doi: 10.1016/S0277-9536(00)00111-8.

Riessman, C. K. (1993). *Narrative Analysis.* London: Sage.

Sanan, A., & Rengachary, S. S. (1999). History of calverial reconstruction. In: S. S. Rengachary & E. C. Benzel (Eds.), *Calvarial & Dural Reconstruction* (pp. 1–23). Rolling Meadows, IL: American Association of Neurological Surgeons.

Suzuki, N., Suzuki, S., & Inabuchi, T. (1993). Neurological improvement after cranioplasty: analysis by dynamic CT scans. *Acta Neurochirurgica, 122*: 49–53.

Van Der Kolk, B. A. (1998). Trauma and memory. *Psychiatry and Clinical Neurosciences, 52*: 97–109. doi: 10.1046/j.1440-1819.1998.0520s5S97.x.

CHAPTER THREE

Narrative approaches to goal setting

David Todd

I am a clinical psychologist working in rehabilitation programmes within both residential and community settings with people who have had an acquired brain injury. Goal setting is recognised as the crux of effective recovery, adjustment, and adaptation during the multi-disciplinary rehabilitation process. This chapter outlines the contribution narrative approaches have made to conceptualising goal setting, and describes goal-setting activities consistent with narrative practice.

Goal setting in brain injury rehabilitation

The scope of this chapter aims to describe goal setting across the pathway of rehabilitation services following brain injury; this includes working in a variety of settings with a range of clinical professionals, addressing biological, neurological, and physiological signs of injury, in addition to facilitating psychological, behavioural, and existential change. Hence, some of the culturally accepted terminology and definitions outlined in this chapter do not always sit comfortably with narrative therapy principles; however, the aim here is to describe the need and relevance of narrative approaches in the goal-setting process within the current context of rehabilitation provision.

Our own stories about our lives are dynamic and developing phenomena, formed by reflecting on our past and planning for our future as much as responding to our present situation (Collicutt McGrath, 2007). The foundations and processes of rehabilitation focus on the long-term adjustment to functional losses, which can be viewed as a structured subset of an ongoing adjustment, adaptation, and development process of self-understanding, but perhaps within the context of significant personal change and acquired impairment. After brain injury, memory difficulties can often affect a person's connection with their past, while problems with executive functioning can disrupt links to future possibilities, leading to a restriction to the "here and now". This can conflict with our innate existential need to feel as though we are on a journey, in order to retain a sense of hope and meaning, while maintaining our sense of who we are.

In recent years, goal setting has been referred to as the cornerstone of effective rehabilitation with people who have an acquired brain injury (e.g., Kuipers, Foster, Carlson, & Moy, 2003). It has been proposed that the process of goal setting is the most appropriate way to plan, direct, and measure the success of rehabilitation (Wilson, Evans, & Gracey, 2009). However, it has also been argued that current models and theories provide an incomplete explanation of how goals should be applied in clinical rehabilitation. It has been argued that for rehabilitation to advance as a scientific discipline, it needs conceptual and theoretical advances, based not solely on empiricism (e.g., Siegert & Taylor, 2004).

National guidelines, legislation, and research

Focus in national guidelines has been placed on supporting "patient choice" and employing a "service-user-centred approach" to rehabilitation following brain injury, involving individuals in decisions about their own care and rehabilitation (e.g., *National Service Framework for Long-Term Conditions*, Department of Health, 2005). In addition, in England and Wales (*Mental Capacity Act*, Department of Constitutional Affairs, 2005) and in Scotland (*Adults with Incapacity (Scotland) Act*, HMSO, 2000) it has been enshrined in law that people should be empowered to make decisions for themselves wherever possible, and those who lack mental capacity to make specific decisions should be protected to ensure they are placed at the heart of the decision-making process.

Although person-centred rehabilitation and care planning is outlined as best practice, national guidelines and legislation do not detail how to implement these key elements of service practice. In addition, there remain mixed research findings as to the additional benefit of taking a collaborative approach to goal setting, with some research indicating that a goal assigned to a service user by clinicians is as effective as one that is set by the service user, provided the purpose or rationale for the goal is given (Hart & Evans, 2006). Holliday, Cano, Freeman, and Playford (2007) found that, although increased participation of service users in goal setting did not lead to improvement in standardised functional outcome measures, goals were reported to be more relevant to individuals, and were more likely to result in the transfer of skills beyond the rehabilitation environment.

Based on meta-analytic reviews of goal setting and its application, goal commitment has been found to be a moderator of goal achievement (Locke & Latham, 2002), and it has been argued that the easiest way to ensure a person is committed to a goal is for them to have participated in setting that goal (Wilson, Evans, & Gracey, 2009). McPherson, Kayes, and Weatherall (2009) concluded that "research about goal setting in rehabilitation remains heterogeneous in terms of purpose, proposed mode of action, the approach to delivery and any expectation of outcome" (p. 297). This lack of convergence of research findings raises questions about the form and content of brain injury rehabilitation outcome measures (see Chapter Nine, "Outcome evidence"), and adds weight to the proposition that there is currently an incomplete explanation of how goal setting should be applied in brain injury rehabilitation. This proposition has led to a demand for a theoretically based framework to facilitate an effective process of person-centred goal setting (e.g., Siegert & Taylor, 2004).

Challenges and ethical dilemmas

A number of practical challenges have been identified in the application of person-centred goal setting with people who have had a brain

injury; Hart and Evans (2006) note that impairments in deficit awareness might lead people with brain injuries to aim for goals that are
more ambitious than clinicians may believe are appropriate for them.
However, a depressed or anxious individual with low self-efficacy
who lacks belief in his or her own capabilities may resist, or have
negative emotional reactions to, the goal-setting process.

Following the experience of loss after brain injury, people often
undertake a process of acceptance, adjustment, and adaptation in the
days, weeks, and years that follow; working through this process may
involve defensive denial or avoidance of impairments to protect
against narcissistic injury to the self (Klonoff, 2010). In addition, early
in the rehabilitation process, individuals are unlikely to have a
detailed understanding of the brain injury, or its implications for functional abilities and future roles. Consideration is required of how and
when clinical assessments are performed in relation to the goal-setting
process, and how information is shared with the individual and their
families. Indeed, prior to the goal-setting process, other activities
might be indicated in order to prevent unnecessary social disability
and to ensure the best use of resources. Such work could include additional support for service users and their families to develop trusting
relationships with health services, provision of early education on
symptom management, or signposting to relevant non-health services
(e.g., Cathers, Fryer, Hollingham, Hyde, & Woolridge, 2011).

The potential obstacles to person-centred goal setting with individuals following brain injury are reflected in the ethical debate on
the approach and practice of rehabilitation services. For example, in
reviewing ethics in goal planning for rehabilitation, Levack (2009)
describes the tension between the ethical principle of autonomy
(respecting a person's right to self-determination) and the principles
of beneficence and non-maleficence (doing good and avoiding harm),
while also considering the perspective of utilitarianism (maximising
benefits to the community served), including consideration of finan-
cial and organisational factors.

Narrative approaches and goal setting

Markus and Nurius (1986) proposed that people have mental representations of "possible selves", influenced by social and cultural

context, which include both what they would like to become ("hoped-for selves") and what they are afraid of becoming ("feared selves"). These possible selves enable the construction of one's own self-narra-tive, including the thoughts, behaviours, and actions associated with this discourse. In a review of goal setting, Karniol and Ross (1996) stated, "in general, people imagine various futures, consider the advantages and disadvantages of each, select their preferred end states, and then develop plans to achieve their desired goals while avoiding negative outcomes" (p. 595).

The philosophy and practices of narrative approaches can provide a theoretical foundation to goal setting in neuropsychological rehabil-itation, and can be employed to balance the important ethical dilem-mas described above. A narrative approach to goal setting can inform a framework for conceptualising the challenges identified within a person-centred approach to brain injury rehabilitation. This chapter seeks to outline how narrative approaches can be practically useful in informing and guiding the structure, process, and implementation of goal-setting interventions.

Principles of narrative approaches that I have found useful in the goal-setting process

- Facilitating people to find the power to define themselves based on their own knowledge of the details of their lives.
- Identifying meaningful narrative discourses post-brain injury in driving an individualised and effective process of rehabilitation.
- Supporting people to recognise "absent but implicit" goals, as well as explicit goals; providing opportunity to increase available directions for adjustment and adaptation, and thicken conclu-sions about self-worth after brain injury.
- Providing an opportunity to explicitly discuss power relations in the rehabilitation process and continually re-examine and nego-tiate the terms of involvement in decision making.
- Enabling the individual, family members, and rehabilitation team to collaboratively unite against the problem, agreeing language and terminology and developing shared definitions of goal setting.
- Promoting the ability of people to act over deterministic forces (including "The Brain Injury" and specific acquired impairments).

Structure

As described, recent literature has suggested that theoretical frameworks should be developed in order to support a move towards more formal and structured person-centred goal-setting approaches in brain injury settings (e.g., Siegert & Taylor, 2004). However, within the social constructionist and non-structuralist philosophy of narrative approaches, the use of a formalised structure is problematic due to the risks of failing to separate person from problem, implicitly advocating that there is a "right" way to approach this issue, and developing a positivist foundation on which this work is facilitated. A universally applied process is likely to be insufficiently flexible to adapt to the individual, risking the assumption of a homogeneous approach to working with all persons following brain injury, and so might foster the construction of narrow descriptions of rehabilitation goals over the influence of individualised narratives.

In a survey, Wilson, Rous, and Sopena (2008) found that a sample of rehabilitation clinicians was influenced by numerous models and theories, illustrating that multiple theoretical perspectives are necessary in clinical practice. In addition, a narrative approach to goal setting considers that not all cultures endorse the goal-orientated internal locus of control that is predominant in rehabilitation within the Western world (Kielhofner & Barrett, 1998). However, in this chapter, the view that a broad and flexible structure and process of brain injury rehabilitation goal setting is outlined, based on the integration of key theoretical models and practical interventions influenced by, and consistent with, narrative approaches. These narrative approaches are considered both within and alongside current taxonomies of goal setting in brain injury rehabilitation.

Goal description

Conceptual dimension

Rehabilitation goals can be classified at a conceptual level. The World Health Organization's *International Classification of Functioning, Disability and Health* (*ICF*) (WHO, 2001) developed a holistic framework for classifying health conditions at the levels of impairment (signs and symptoms), activity (functioning and observed behaviour), and participation (social positions and roles). Significantly, all of these dimensions are influenced by the contextual factors for each individual. This means that the model of functioning and disability proposed in the *ICF* classification outlines an interactional relationship among the various health factors within the context of environmental and personal factors. This includes the influence of the context within which rehabilitation takes place; for example, an acute inpatient setting is often predominantly physically focused, in contrast to community settings, where more emphasis is likely to be placed on participation in social roles and family relationships.

It is acknowledged that, as a structured framework built on a coding system, the *ICF* does not sit comfortably with narrative approaches; it can be argued that it creates space for individual context, but does not necessarily accommodate personal stories. However, this framework is consistent with narrative approaches in that it does not classify people, as many diagnostic systems do, but, instead, attempts to describe the situation of the person within an array of different domains. Threats and Worrall (2004) posited that the *ICF* is not something to be done *to* someone, but rather something to be done *with* them. Importantly, in the context of current mental health service provision in the UK, in which certain resources are being configured and commissioned based on the diagnostic categories of the World Health Organization's *International Statistical Classification of Diseases and Related Health Problems* (10th edition) (WHO, 2010) (e.g., *Payment by Results*, Department of Health, 2011), the WHO's *ICF* offers the opportunity for thicker descriptions of individual rehabilitation goals to be developed and recognised at service and organisational levels.

Temporal dimension

Rehabilitation goals are usually classified across different timescales, with short-term goals, medium-term goals, and long-term goals. Neuropsychological rehabilitation promotes linking goals together to make the connections between the person's longer-term hopes and aspirations and more immediate goals. Much guidance on setting "ideal" goals has emphasised the importance of rehabilitation goals being quantifiable and SMART (typically, Specific, Measurable, Achievable, Realistic/Relevant, Timed). However, it is not always appropriate or helpful to quantify goals through SMART criteria; for example, it was stated by the researcher who actually developed SMART goals that goals need not necessarily be SMART, and it might instead be appropriate for some goals to be ambitious or abstract (Doran, 1981).

Discharge from the rehabilitation service is not the end-point in terms of adjustment and adaptation to brain injury for the individual, and consideration needs to be given to maintaining progress after discharge. For example, there is evidence that a common problem in goal setting is the lack of continuity from inpatient to community rehabilitation and long-term goals (Playford, Siegert, Levack, & Freeman, 2009). Long-term goals can be described as components of hoped-for futures based on the individual's life priorities and values; these personally important long-term goals represent a preferred narrative that plays a vital role in marking out each individual's rehabilitation journey.

Process

Hearing the person's narrative and assessing strengths

Throughout the process of rehabilitation, a continued focus on the individual's personal narratives, experiences, and post-intervention aims and hopes is needed. This focus informs regular goal setting and can mitigate the possible negative effects of invisible assumptions or beliefs held by rehabilitation clinicians. Speculations about people's lives and identities can become defining "truths", with the effect of potentially limiting the directions available for people to choose in their lives. A structure of rehabilitation goal setting regularly influenced by reflecting and exploring the individual's pre- and post-rehabilitation selves promotes a sense of personal agency to live a range of possibilities, and avoids iatrogenic impact through fostering dependence on rehabilitation professionals.

The classification of rehabilitation goals across both conceptual and temporal dimensions illustrates the context of the person's rehabilitation journey following brain injury. A narrative approach to goal setting seeks to place goals within the reference frame of the person's past and their envisioned or desired future, thereby moving goal setting from beyond the rehabilitation setting. An example of the importance of respecting and taking notice of the individual's needs and perspectives without imposing ideas on them is described by Linda Kat (Kat, Schipper, Knibbe, & Abma, 2010), in which she describes one of her "helping hands" during her rehabilitation journey as "having someone listening to my story patiently in a quiet environment" (p. 340). This enabled a recognition of the valued aspects of her life, rather than solely focusing on improving function or maintaining independence; "Seeing my daughter, talking to friends on the phone, sitting outside watching birds – these are the things in life I have come to value and that make me happy" (p. 340).

Goal setting begins with the rehabilitation professional listening to the person's narrative of the brain injury and its impact on his or her life. This requires appreciating the nature and importance of narratives following brain injury, being accustomed to hearing other people's stories, being able to reflect honestly on one's own narrative and assess preconceived ideas and biases, and being aware of the literature on narrative and disability (Franits, 2005). Hearing the service user's narrative should include not only factors typically assessed as part of an initial assessment for a period of rehabilitation, such as medical factors and psychosocial background, occupational history, family, interests, and expectations, but also an assessment and validation of the individual's internal resources and coping strategies. The rehabilitation professional thereby respects that the person has personal or local knowledge, and skills and abilities that they can tap into to address barriers and difficulties.

Professional focus upon personal deficits alone emphasises one's failures or weaknesses rather than one's accomplishments and strengths. Indeed, exclusive therapist focus on an individual's impairments has been found to contribute to a narrative of "self-as-damaged-goods" (Kovareky, Shaw, & Adingono-Smith, 2007). Adaptations to the emphasis of this information-gathering process are made based on an understanding of the individual's rehabilitation journey and the context of the rehabilitation service. For example, familiar physical, social, and emotional environments in community-based rehabilitation can elicit personally meaningful reflections that might not be identified in an acute hospital ward or rehabilitation unit.

Seeking a narrative of coping and personal abilities is a move away from the traditional assessment of problem-saturated descriptions of life following brain injury, building a compelling narrative about a self-efficacious individual who is capable of successfully navigating his or her own journey through rehabilitation and beyond. In this regard, rehabilitation following brain injury has recently been influenced by the "recovery" movement, initially developed by service users in psychiatric services, in which self-management strategies that empower individuals to take control of their own lives are valued.

The Wellness Recovery Action Plan (WRAP) (Copeland, 2002) is a popular example of the recovery approach, in which the service user identifies actions, thoughts, and behaviours that, for them, are associated with staying well, happy, and in control. These calibrated personal coping strategies, termed "wellness tools", are documented in a written plan that includes daily maintenance, triggers and how to avoid them, early warning signs and how to avoid them, and a crisis plan. In addition, the plan documents whom the individual wants involved in providing support, and whom he or she does not want involved, for each of the action plan strategies. This recovery approach can be applied to a rehabilitation goal-setting approach following brain injury in order to structure interventions and in developing a person-centred risk management plan. In terms of empowerment, developing WRAP documents in the context of brain injury rehabilitation services privileges the narrative of service users as experts of their own rehabilitation.

Negotiating decision making and developing shared definitions

The practice of goal setting suggests a set of assumptions or a worldview that might not necessarily be shared by all service users or therapists. Hart and Evans (2006) comment that most people are not in the habit of setting goals prior to acquiring a brain injury, let alone afterwards. Bearing this in mind, it is important to develop a shared definition with each individual in order to achieve an effective goal-setting process. Negotiation of the process of goal setting should take place through continued explicit exploration of the level of desired service user involvement, or "person-centredness", at each stage of rehabilitation. For example, in an inpatient setting, the focus is often primarily upon activities of daily living, whereas in contrast, in the community, the emphasis is likely to be on social functioning and reintegration within the family and community. The process of rehabilitation, then, is a shared dialogue and negotiation, involving individual autonomous decision making, information sharing, and shared decision making, or consultation, depending on the service user's abilities and desired level of input into this process. This requires an optimistic and respectful, but tentative or curious, stance from the rehabilitation professional, using listening and therapeutic skills and considering how language is employed.

Reflecting on the use of language is an important tenet of narrative therapy, and there is a wide range of terms used to describe goal setting within rehabilitation. Language can blur, alter, or distort experience as we tell our stories; it can condition how we think, feel, and act, and can be used purposefully as a therapeutic tool (White, 1995). Language is relational, and cognitions, emotions, and actions all need to be understood in context. This means that responses to difficulties following brain injury might themselves become cues and exacerbate the problem. For example, if service professionals reinforce or validate an internalising or disempowering account of disability to the individual and his or her family, this will directly contribute to a narrow description of life following brain injury. (See Chapter Six, "Narrative practice on the context of communication disability: a question of accessibility", in relation to working with communication impairments following acquired brain injury.)

Goal setting within an interdisciplinary or transdisciplinary rehabilitation team approach

Physical, sensory, cognitive, emotional, and behavioural functioning might become altered following brain injury, and often a large range of professionals are involved in addressing these different facets of human experience. This can have implications for the process of goal setting. When only a single professional discipline is involved with a service-user, a more formal goal-setting process might not be needed, although the principles and processes of goal setting can be applied in an adapted format. However, medium-term or long-term goals described within the WHO *ICF* activity or participation categories rarely involve one discipline (e.g., see "Case example 1", below).

Although there is no consensual definition of interdisciplinary and transdisciplinary practice (e.g., Lawrence, 2010), interdisciplinary team working is typically described as the clinical practice of a group of healthcare professionals working in co-ordination towards a common goal for the service user. Transdisciplinary team working involves a clinical team co-operating across disciplines, often developing creative and flexible working practices based on the individual's rehabilitation goals and their specific personal and contextual circumstances. This might involve going beyond the currently available evidence base and national guidelines to develop innovative and creative practice, based around the needs and hopes of the individual at the centre of rehabilitation. In this way, the multi-disciplinary team unite in goals that are led by the service user, the driver of the rehabilitation process. Interdisciplinary and transdisciplinary goals are achieved when this approach leads to unique and collaborative interventions, based on the shared skills and expertise of all involved in the rehabilitation team, and, in particular, the service user themselves.

Case example 1: Transdisciplinary approach to goal setting

Christian, a twenty-two-year-old man, experienced a severe traumatic brain injury after being hit by a car as a pedestrian. Following treatment in hospital, he was referred to a residential acquired brain injury rehabilitation service to address the barriers to his achieving his goals on discharge. He had severe difficulties with understanding and expressing language, such that he was reliant completely on gesture and drawing. In addition, he had problems in focusing his attention on what he was doing, as well as thinking through decisions effectively and finding good solutions to problems he encountered. However, neuropsychological assessment identified strengths in his ability to manipulate and work with real-world objects. He also had performed well in memory assessments, and could learn well from experience.

Christian and his family were proud farmers who emphasised the importance of family support and working with the natural environment. Together, they identified long-term goals for him of returning to living and working on their farm. Rehabilitation goals aimed to address the "activity limitations" to achieving this long-term goal. Family information-sharing sessions were held regularly, in order to identify any discrepancies in different people's expectations, or between goals and barriers; accordingly Christian and his family were incorporated as core members and directors of the rehabilitation team.

Individualised Makaton signs were developed with the speech and language therapist, and cognitive rehabilitation strategies and behavioural interventions were transferred to a vocational placement at a chicken farm, close to the rehabilitation unit, identified with the occupational therapist. This enabled rehabilitation interventions to be applied in a personally valid and ecologically valid environment, accounting for Christian's personal strengths and wishes.

Targeting intervention at goal level

As outlined above, rehabilitation goals can be described on dimensions of both different conceptual and temporal levels, in which the aim for the rehabilitation process is to link each individual's personally relevant future hopes and values with more immediate SMART goals. Conceptualised through the WHO *ICF* (2001), more proximal goals, which are typically the main focus in the acute stages of recovery, are often aimed at the impairment and activity components of functioning through a "bottom-up" approach to goal attainment. Interventions in neuropsychological rehabilitation addressing proximal goals consider whether a "restitutive" or a "compensatory" approach is required, that is, whether interventions should be aimed at improving impaired function (e.g., physiotherapy exercises, cognitive rehabilitation exercises) or developing alternative strategies to accommodate impaired function (e.g., use of compensatory external aids and systems, establishing adapted routines). For example, goal management training (GMT) (Levine et al., 2000) aims to prevent goal failure through implementation of a structured intervention.

Interventions seeking to achieve proximal rehabilitation goals are not directly informed by narrative approaches. However, proximal goals can serve as markers of progress towards goals that reflect a person's preferred self-narrative. For people with brain injury and significant cognitive impairment, such regular feedback can be effective in allowing the individual to experience a sense of the gap between their current situation and their goal reducing. Narrative approaches emphasise the importance of ensuring that rehabilitation goals adequately represent the person, and making sure that rehabilitation clinicians do not presume to know more about people's lives than the people do themselves. Subsequently, interventions aimed at supporting individuals to set higher-order, personally meaningful rehabilitation goals, through identifying and thickening preferred self-narratives, have been receiving increasing application in recent years (e.g., Kangas & McDonald, 2011; Ylvisaker & Feeney, 2000). Such interventions can be considered within the contextual factors and the participation components of the WHO *ICF* (2001) through a "top-down" approach, primarily aiming to enable the service user to identify a meaningful, higher representation of what is important to them as a basis for driving their goals. Congruent with narrative therapy, these interventions focus on contextual behaviour and flexible skills, and emphasise the constructs of personal values and relationships.

Goal-setting interventions

Setting higher-order goals

Narrative approaches view the goal of intervention as being constructed by the service user and therapist in a social context, building upon what works rather than "solving" narrowly defined problems. This involves making sense of how experiences tie into a person's life story. As applied to rehabilitation following brain injury, it has been my experience that achievable goals are situated in the context of broader personal narratives or values; these latter higher-order constructs provide us with directions in which our lives can move. Goals are achieved along the journey, whereas higher-order self-narratives are an ongoing process. In narrative therapy, and other congruent psychotherapeutic approaches, these higher-order constructs are not fixed truths, but are fluid and elaborated in an ongoing way by the individual.

Case example 2: Rehabilitation goals as directed by personal narrative

Judy, a forty-five-year-old woman, experienced a traumatic brain injury after being involved in a road traffic accident. She experienced difficulties with her abilities to plan, organise, and prioritise, and difficulties with self-monitoring and error-checking. Following discharge from rehabilitation back to her home in a fairly isolated rural location, she required support in order to structure her day and organise her activities. She was unable to return to her work as a homeopath and did not return to driving.

Judy was referred to the local community acquired brain injury rehabilitation team six years after her injury, with the reason for referral stated as to increase her level of independence. Goals were set with the rehabilitation team around developing compensatory aids, including files and diary systems. Discussion also took place around the possibility of moving home nearer to the local town, as this would enable her to access public transport, as well as providing her with more convenient access to shops and social opportunities. However, in discussion, Judy identified personally important narratives including "spontaneity", "creativity", and being "a roamer", and "a free spirit". This exploration revealed that her current accommodation, and the lifestyle it encompassed, was more consistent with this life story, despite providing some barriers to the achievable goal of increased independence.

Identity-orientated approaches to goal setting

Approaches to setting goals based on the identification of personally salient, higher-order constructs have focused on the reconstruction of a sense of personal identity (e.g., McPherson, Kayes, & Weatherall, 2009). Identity in this frame refers to the multiple ways that individuals may perceive themselves, and the feelings associated with these self-narratives. Based on this definition, other theories have used the term "self" as synonymous with "identity". For example, Hayes, Strosahl, and Wilson (1999) describe the "conceptualised self" as our historical view of ourselves, with a loss of sense of self after brain injury representing a crisis in the conceptualised self (Myles, 2004). One could interpret this as closely related to the narrative approach, with the brain injury leading to an interruption of self-narrative.

However, the notion of "identity" in narrative therapy tends to be replaced with the notion of "subjectivity", because narrative approaches adopt social constructionist viewpoints that do not assume that people's identities are primarily stable and singular, but, instead, that they change and are often contradictory (e.g., Gergen, 2001). In working with service users on the development of identity maps, or documenting a preferred narrative, narrative therapy approaches seek to emphasise that these representations of identity are fluid and flexible, as well as pluralistic and multidimensional.

"Metaphorical identity mapping" (MIM) (Ylvisaker & Feeney, 2000) is an example of an approach that draws on the reconstruction of identity following brain injury and has been applied to goal setting termed "Identity-orientated goal training" (IOGT) (McPherson, Kayes, & Weatherall, 2009). MIM involves developing preferred narratives around an admired individual, for example, an adventurer, a philanthropist, a family member, or a fictional character. Alternatively, a person can be invited to create a generic map focused on a set of appealing characteristics. This embodiment of qualities or attributes that the service user admires then functions as an external reference point from which he or she can identify higher-order values of personal importance, which can then be used as a basis for forming lower-order, concrete SMART rehabilitation goals (see Ylvisaker, McPherson, Kayes, & Pellett, 2008).

In developing identity maps, MIM incorporates the narrative therapy approach of creating therapeutic documents in order to record particular "knowledges" of preferred identities and skills. These identity maps can then be used to discuss preferred stories with others in the person's family or community, in accordance with the narrative therapy practice of "re-membering" (White, 1995). This includes sharing information with the rehabilitation team as part of the goal-setting process. However, consistent with narrative approaches, these identity maps should retain subjectivity and be viewed as a preferred narrative, or one perspective on identity within a particular context. Indeed, rather than being considered as a definitive statement, identity maps may be the start of a process, and used as a basis for accessing different perspectives on the problem within the family and rehabilitation team.

Identity, or sense of self, is often shattered by the effects of the brain injury on the individual's abilities and roles, and the effective reconstruction of a coherent and valued sense of self is central to the rehabilitation process. In order to compensate for the acquired difficulties following brain injury, the use of a hero or an admired individual as an external reference point, as in MIM, can be useful in supporting the identification of preferred narratives. However, the difficulty with this approach is that by utilising a reference point that is external to the individual, the values elicited might be seen as "other" to themselves and might not be applied to their own self-narrative. The role of the rehabilitation therapist is to facilitate the individual to incorporate these values or preferred stories into his own sense of self. Narrative therapy techniques can be useful here; for example, supporting the service user to identify "unique outcomes" in which her recent actions can be seen to reflect the values embodied by the identified admired individual. Another example of a useful narrative technique is inviting the service user to take a position: if she had access to the same circumstances as the admired individual, would her goals and actions also reflect these values? If the admired individual had the same circumstances as the service user, how would his goals and actions then reflect these values? Despite the use of such narrative therapy techniques, the requirement of abstract thinking for such approaches might not be effective for all individuals, particularly those with poor self-efficacy, and alternative interventions for identifying personally important values might be required.

Standardised assessment tools

The negotiation of higher-order goals with service users can, at least initially, be challenging and time consuming, and studies have found that clinicians can struggle to make goals that are relevant to the lives of people outside of the context of the rehabilitation environment (e.g., Levack, Dean, Siegert, & McPherson, 2011). In recent studies of interventions aimed at supporting the practice of setting higher-order goals with brain injury rehabilitation service users, some clinicians expressed concern about applying concepts that were markedly different from their traditional practice methods, for example, physiotherapists predominantly using physical intervention (e.g., McPherson, Kayes, & Weatherall, 2009). Ylvisaker, McPherson, Kayes, and Pellett (2008) found that identity-orientated goal setting appeared to require a "mind shift" for some clinicians and demanded clinical skills that were not uniformly distributed among rehabilitation professionals.

Problems with informal or non-structured assessment approaches have been identified, and it has been argued that resultant goals can be vague or lacking in meaningful origins (e.g., Neistadt, 1995). Consequently, in order to support the identification of higher-order goals and in aiming to develop a more structured systematic approach to goal setting in clinical practice, questionnaires have been developed assessing concepts including participation goals (e.g., Canadian

Occupational Performance Measure: Law et al., 1990) and personal values (e.g., Valued Living Questionnaire: Wilson, Sandoz, Kitchens, & Roberts, 2010).

Standardised tools such as questionnaires can provide theoretically driven instruments for supporting the identification of higher-order long-term goals, personally important values, or preferred narratives. However, consistent with narrative approaches, such quantitative tools should be applied and interpreted with caution. The domains represented in structured higher-order goal questionnaires are inherently restricted and restrictive, and their thin descriptions might not reflect the most important domains in some individuals' lives. This is reflected by the difficulty of establishing construct validity of higher-order, or more abstract, goal questionnaires, due to the individuality of self-narratives, and the subsequent lack of established criterion gold-standard measures (e.g., Bellack et al., 2007). Furthermore, consistent with the narrative concept of subjectivity (i.e., multiple narratives of self which are flexible over time), temporal consistency of higher-order goal questionnaires has been found to decline with longer intervals (e.g., Wilson, Sandoz, Kitchens, & Roberts, 2010), reflecting the dynamism and fluidity of self-narratives or personal identity. A further difficulty found with such self-report questionnaires is the potential confounding factor of social desirability, as the items are typically face valid and can lead responses in the direction of "desirable" higher-order goals, for example, regarding concepts of altruism (Conrad, Doering, Rief, & Exner, 2010).

Consistent with narrative philosophy, standardised assessments cannot be viewed as tools with which to generate narrative data, unless used as semi-structured interview schedules to gather rich qualitative data. However, it has been argued that the format and task-orientated nature of some interview-based assessments can, in fact, negate the service user's narrative (Kielhofner & Mallinson, 1995). In clinical practice, it is clear that questionnaires are simply one way to obtain information about a person's wishes and expectations; in individual rehabilitation, a more ideographic way of obtaining information about a person's life goals is recommended. Klonoff (2010) describes helpful non-standardised techniques of eliciting meaningful self-narratives, including looking at photograph albums, autobiographical essays, or discussing sources of inspiration from before the injury. Such techniques can also be helpfully applied in order to identify pre-injury self-narratives with service-users who lack the skills to contribute formally to the goal-setting process.

Overcoming challenges in goal setting

A number of challenges exist in supporting people to set rehabilitation goals following brain injury. Commonly cited obstacles include low motivation of the service user to engage in the rehabilitation process, or goals deemed by rehabilitation professionals to be unrealistic. Difficulties in the rehabilitation process have been described in working with service users who present as agitated or defensive during enquiry about life after brain injury. However, Playford, Siegert, Levack, and Freeman (2009) found that, in discussion about rehabilitation goals, expressions of dissent by service users typically led to the provision of clinical reasoning or, less frequently, some minor modifications by clinicians to the disputed goal, emphasising that we need to develop structures for negotiating goals as well as setting goals. Although an important aspect of the rehabilitation process is educating service users as to realistic goals within the environment and time point on the rehabilitation continuum, rehabilitation should be viewed as a process of sharing information, not simply providing information.

Lack of agreement in goal setting through "unrealistic" rehabilitation goals is often conceptualised by rehabilitation clinicians as due to poor self-awareness on behalf of the service user. However, it is recognised that self-awareness is a complex, multi-modal construct that has been defined as "the capacity to perceive the 'self' in relatively objective terms while maintaining a sense of subjectivity" (Prigatano & Schacter, 1991, p. 13). It involves a continual interaction of thoughts and feelings, and reflects the highest level of organisation and integration of brain structures (Prigatano & Schacter, 1991). Distinctions are made between "organic unawareness", or "anosognosia", and the denial of deficits as a psychological defence mechanism to suppress or avoid a truth that threatens self-image. However, recent neuro-psychodynamic accounts have described that, typically, both motivational and deficit perspectives can apply in the context of individuals' abilities to manage powerful negative emotions following brain injury (e.g., Turnbull & Solms, 2007). This is particularly relevant if the individual had developed only an "immature" identity or narrow description of self at the time of the injury. Indeed, it has been found that loss-of-self narratives are common following brain injury, typically involving comparisons of current self to prior self, or to others without injury (e.g., Nochi, 1998).

Thickening self-narratives following brain injury can enable the identification of rehabilitation goals that represent personally meaningful directions for the service user. These discourses can then be shared and understood by all stakeholders in the rehabilitation process, and can address the lack of fit between expectations and outcomes. Addressing such discrepancies enables the rehabilitation team to meet the challenges these dilemmas present in effective goal setting and outcome. Nochi (2000) identified five categories of effective reconstructed self-narratives following brain injury:

1. The self as better than others (i.e., "Things could be worse").
2. The grown self (i.e., "The injury has improved me in some way").
3. The recovering self (i.e., "I continue to get better").
4. The self living in the here and now (i.e., "I won't compare myself to others or to myself before my injury").
5. The protesting self (i.e., "The problem is with those who judge me, not with me").

Ylvisaker, McPherson, Kayes, and Pellett (2008) comment that this study illustrates the possibility of identifying new and helpful preferred self-narratives after serious injury, and highlight the individual variability of alternative discourses. It is argued that the goal of rehabilitation is not to become "normal"; instead, the goal is to embrace the human vocation of becoming more deeply, more fully, human (Deegan, 1996).

This case study illustrates that the content of self-narratives, including confabulations, are not emotionally neutral, but are likely to create a narrative about the world that is more positive for the individual. It has been suggested that there may be an iatrogenic impact of rehabilitation services at times in emphasising the narrative of "returning to normal" by privileging and focusing on impairment-based or activity-based SMART goals, with short time frames for goal achievement (e.g., Levack, Dean, Siegert, & McPherson, 2011). A dominant narrative of the pre-injury self can potentially lead to unsuccessful striving to retrieve previous abilities, or return to previous roles, with a slow erosion of self-esteem and self-efficacy in the face of persisting difficulties.

"Absent but implicit" self-narratives, directing effective rehabilitation goals, can be identified by working within the individual's "zone of proximal development" (Vygotsky, 1978), that is, not challenging to the point of disengagement and therapeutic rift, but being challenging enough to create space for change.[1] Specifically relating to working with people following brain injury, Prigatano (2000) describes the difficulties preventing psychotherapists entering the "phenomenological field" of their service users. This requires clinical skill in order to negotiate and achieve a balance between hope and acceptance. Brandstädter and Rothermund (2002) conceptualised this balance as reflecting a two-process goal-setting framework, including an "assimilative mode" and an "accommodative mode". The assimilative mode involves supporting people to experience progress in personally important goal domains, while the "accommodative mode" involves supporting people to abandon or substitute unhelpful goals, or to consider the wishes and expectations of others, including family members and those important to the service user.

Congruent with the principle of working within the service user's phenomenological field, Gracey, Evans, and Malley (2009) developed a model of change in brain injury rehabilitation called the "Y-shaped" model. This model can be applied during the goal-setting process to address discrepancies between the service user and others (e.g., family members, rehabilitation team) holding different views about the nature of difficulties or needs. The resolution of this explicit discrepancy is depicted in the converging lines of the "V" at the top of the "Y", enabling the development of collaborative rehabilitation goals.

In supporting this process of adjustment and therapeutic change, the setting of carefully identified and personally meaningful goals can itself represent a practical form of psychotherapy throughout rehabilitation. In addition, difficulties with mood and self-awareness can be managed by incorporating their impact into the goals themselves, using learning rather than performance-based outcomes (Hart & Evans, 2006). For example, "I will discover X ways of coping with feeling down". However, in some circumstances, barriers to an adaptive reconstruction of a future positive self presented after brain injury mean that, prior to the goal-setting process, more explicit psychotherapy might need to be offered. Formal psychotherapy may be usefully employed in order to address issues such as supporting adjustment, addressing psychological distress, or working with family systems (e.g., Klonoff, 2010).

Conclusion

Goal setting is a key aspect and central tenet of brain injury rehabilitation, and narrative approaches reflect that multiple perspectives are necessary for a person to be supported to be the person they want to be. In his seminal work with survivors of brain injury, Goldstein (1939) described the motive to aim towards "self-actualisation" as the process of seeking to maximise one's abilities and determining the path of one's life. Narrative approaches stress the importance of "self-actualisation", not as an achievable entity or defining truth, but, rather, as the participation in a journey towards horizon destinations. It is the journey towards these elusive and shifting objectives that facilitates compelling personal narratives of one's existence. Narrative approaches to brain injury guide the inclusion of these principles in the goal-setting process by empowering the service user to take control of rehabilitation, and to apply their skills and strengths to their own recovery and beyond.

Note

1. "Proximal" here refers to the nearness between the therapist's and the service user's positions and perspectives, rather than in the temporal sense described previously, relating to long-term and short-term goals.

References

Bellack, A. S., Green, M. F., Cook, J. A., Fenton, W., Harvey, P. D., Heaton, R. K., Laughren, T., Leon, A. C., Mayo, D. J., Patrick, D. L., Patterson, T. L., Rose, A., Stover, E., & Wykes, T. (2007). Assessment of community functioning in people with schizophrenia and other severe mental illnesses: A White Paper based on a NIMH-sponsored workshop. *Schizophrenia Bulletin, 33*: 805–822.

Brandstädter, J., & Rothermund, K. (2002). The life-course dynamics of goal pursuit and goal adjustment: a two-process framework. *Developmental Review, 22*: 117–150.

Cathers, R., Fryer, S., Hollingham, K., Hyde, S., & Woolridge, S. (2011). Re-audit of the utility and application of client-centred goal planning in the Cumbria Community Acquired Brain Injury Rehabilitation Team (CCABIRT) service pathway for clients discharged in 2010. *The Cumbria Partnership Journal of Research, Practice and Learning, 1*: 35–39.

Collicutt McGrath, J. (2007). *Ethical Practice in Brain Injury Rehabilitation.* New York: Oxford University Press.

Conrad, N., Doering, B. K., Rief, W., & Exner, C. (2010). Looking beyond the importance of life goals. The personal goal model of subjective well-being in neuropsychological rehabilitation. *Clinical Rehabilitation, 24*: 431–443.

Copeland, M. E. (2002). Overview of WRAP: Wellness Recovery Action Plan. *Mental Health Recovery Newsletter, 3*: 1–9.

Deegan, P. (1996). Recovery as a journey of the heart. *Psychiatric Rehabilitation Journal, 19*: 91–97.

Department of Constitutional Affairs (2005). *Mental Capacity Act 2005 Code of Practice.* www.opsi.gov.uk/acts/acts2005/related/ukpgacop_20050009_en.pdf (accessed 1 August 2011).

Department of Health (2005). *The National Service Framework for Long-term Conditions.* London: Department of Health. www.dh.gov.uk/prod_consum_dh/groups/dh_digitalassets/@dh/@en/documents/digitalasset/dh_4105369.pdf (accessed 1 August 2011).

Department of Health (2011). *A Simple Guide to Payment by Results.* London: Department of Health. www.dh.gov.uk/en/Publications andstatistics/Publications/PublicationsPolicyAndGuidance/DH_128 862 (accessed 1 December 2011).

Doran, G. T. (1981). There's a S.M.A.R.T. way to write management's goals and objectives. *Management Review, 70*(11): 35–36.

Franits, L. E. (2005). Nothing about us without us: searching for the narrative of disability. *The American Journal of Occupational Therapy, 59*: 577–579.

Gergen, K. J. (2001). *Social Construction in Context.* London: Sage.

Goldstein, K. (1939). *The Organism: A Holistic Approach to Biology Derived from Pathological Data in Man.* New York: Zone Books, 1995.

Gracey, F., Evans, J. J., & Malley, D. (2009). Capturing process and outcome in complex rehabilitation interventions: a "Y-shaped" model. *Neuropsychological Rehabilitation, 19*: 867–890.

Hart, T., & Evans, J. (2006). Self-regulation and goal theories in brain injury rehabilitation. *Journal of Head Trauma Rehabilitation, 21*: 142–155.

Hayes, S. C., Strosahl, K., & Wilson, K. G. (1999). *Acceptance and Commitment Therapy: An Experiential Approach to Behavior Change.* New York: Guilford Press.

HMSO (2000). *Adults with Incapacity (Scotland) Act 2000.* London: HMSO. www.legislation.gov.uk/asp/2000/4/pdfs/asp_20000004_en.pdf (accessed 1 August 2011).

Holliday, R., Cano, S., Freeman, J. A., & Playford, E. D. (2007). Should patients participate in clinical decision making? An optimised balance block design controlled study of goal setting in a rehabilitation unit. *Journal of Neurology, Neurosurgery, and Psychiatry, 78*: 576–580.

Kangas, M., & McDonald, S. (2011). Is it time to act? The potential of acceptance and commitment therapy for psychological problems following acquired brain injury. *Neuropsychological Rehabilitation, 21*: 250–276.

Karniol, R., & Ross, M. (1996). The motivational impact of temporal focus: thinking about the future and the past. *Annual Review of Psychology, 47*: 590–620.

Kat, L., Schipper, K., Knibbe, J., & Abma, T. A. (2010). A patient's journey: acquired brain injury. *British Medical Journal, 340*: c808; www.bmj.com/content/340/bmj.c808.full (accessed 1 August 2011).

Kielhofner, G., & Barrett, L. (1998). Meaning and misunderstanding in occupational forms: a study of therapeutic goal setting. *American Journal of Occupational Therapy, 52*: 345–353.

Kielhofner, G., & Mallinson, T. (1995). Gathering narrative data through interviews: empirical observations and suggested guidelines. *Scandinavian Journal of Occupational Therapy, 2*: 63–68.

Klonoff, P.S. (2010). *Psychotherapy after Brain Injury: Principles and Techniques.* New York: Guilford Press.

Kovareky, D., Shaw, A., & Adingono-Smith, M. (2007). The construction of identity during group therapy among adults with traumatic brain injury. *Communication and Medicine, 4*: 53–66.

Kuipers, P., Foster, M., Carlson, G., & Moy, J. (2003). Classifying client goals in community-based ABI rehabilitation: a taxonomy for profiling service delivery and conceptualizing outcomes. *Disability and Rehabilitation, 25*: 154–162.

Law, M., Baptiste, S., McColl, M. A., Opzoomer, A., Polatajko, H., & Pollock, N. (1990). The Canadian Occupational Performance Measure: an outcome measure for occupational therapy. *Canadian Journal of Occupational Therapy, 57*: 82–87.

Lawrence, R. J. (2010). Deciphering interdisciplinary and transdisciplinary contributions. *Transdisciplinary Journal of Engineering & Science, 1*: 125–130.

Levack, W. M. M. (2009). Ethics in goal planning for rehabilitation: a utilitarian perspective. *Clinical Rehabilitation, 23*: 345–351.

Levack, W. M. M., Dean, S. G., Siegert, R. J., & McPherson, K. M. (2011). Navigating patient-centered goal setting in inpatient stroke rehabilitation: how clinicians control the process to meet perceived professional responsibilities. *Patient Education and Counseling, 85*: 206–213.

Levine, B., Robertson, I. H., Clare, L., Carter, G., Hong, J., Wilson, B. A., Duncan, J., & Stuss, D. T. (2000). Rehabilitation of executive functioning: an experimental–clinical validation of goal management training. *Journal of the International Neuropsychology Society, 6*: 299–312.

Locke, E., & Latham, G. (2002). Building a practically useful theory of goal setting and task motivation. *American Psychologist, 57*: 705–717.

Markus, H., & Nurius, P. (1986). Possible selves. *American Psychologist, 41*: 954–969.

McPherson, K. M., Kayes, N., & Weatherall, M. (2009). A pilot study of self-regulation informed goal setting in people with traumatic brain injury. *Clinical Rehabilitation, 23*: 296–309.

Myles, S. M. (2004). Understanding and treating loss of sense of self following brain injury: a behavior analytic approach. *International Journal of Psychology and Psychological Therapy, 4*: 487–504.

Neistadt, M. E. (1995). Methods of assessing clients' priorities: a survey of adult physical dysfunction settings. *American Journal of Occupational Therapy, 49*: 428–436.

Nochi, M. (1998). "Loss of self" in the narratives of people with traumatic brain injuries: a qualitative analysis. *Social Science and Medicine, 46*: 869–878.

Nochi, M. (2000). Reconstructing self-narratives in coping with traumatic brain injury. *Social Science and Medicine, 51*: 1795–1804.

Playford, E. D., Siegert, R., Levack, W., & Freeman, J. (2009). Areas of consensus and controversy about goal setting in rehabilitation: a conference report. *Clinical Rehabilitation, 23*: 334–344.

Prigatano, G. (2000). A brief overview of four principles of neuropsychological rehabilitation. In: A. L. Christiensen & B. Uzzell (Eds.), *International Handbook of Neuropsychological Rehabilitation* (pp. 115–125). New York: Kluwer Academic/Plenum.

Prigatano, G. P., & Schacter, D. L. (Eds.) (1991). *Awareness of Deficit after Brain Injury: Clinical and Theoretical Issues.* New York: Oxford University Press.

Siegert, R. J., & Taylor, W. J. (2004). Theoretical aspects of goal-setting and motivation in rehabilitation. *Disability and Rehabilitation, 26*: 1–8.

Threats, T. T., & Worrall, L. (2004). Classifying communication disability using the ICF. *Advances of Speech Language Pathology, 6*: 53–62.

Turnbull, O. H., & Solms, M. (2007). Awareness, desire, and false beliefs: Freud in the light of modern neuropsychology. *Cortex, 43*: 1083–1090.

Vygotsky, L. S. (1978). *Mind in Society: Development of Higher Psychological Processes.* Cambridge, MA: Harvard University Press.

White, M. (1995). *Re-Authoring Lives: Interviews and Essays.* Adelaide, Australia: Dulwich Centre Publications.

Wilson, B. A., Evans, J. J., & Gracey, F. (2009). Goal setting as a way of planning and evaluating neuropsychological rehabilitation. In: B. A. Wilson, F. Gracey, J. J. Evans, & A. Bateman (Eds.), *Neuropsychological Rehabilitation: Theory, Model, Therapy and Outcome* (pp. 37–46). Cambridge: Cambridge University Press.

Wilson, B. A., Rous, R., & Sopena, S. (2008). The current practice of neuropsychological rehabilitation in the United Kingdom. *Applied Neuropsychology, 15*: 229–240.

Wilson, K. G., Sandoz, E. K., Kitchens, J., & Roberts, M. E. (2010). The Valued Living Questionnaire: defining and measuring valued action within a behavioral framework. *Psychological Record, 60*: 249–272.

World Health Organization (2001). *International Classification of Functioning, Disability and Health.* Geneva: WHO.

World Health Organization (2010). *International Statistical Classification of Diseases and Related Health Problems* (10th edn: *ICD-10*). Geneva: WHO.

Ylvisaker, M., & Feeney, T. (2000). Construction of identity after traumatic brain injury. *Brain Impairment, 1*: 12–28.

Ylvisaker, M., McPherson, K., Kayes, N., & Pellett, E. (2008). Metaphoric identity mapping: facilitating goal setting and engagement in rehabilitation after traumatic brain injury. *Neuropsychological Rehabilitation, 18*: 713–741.

CHAPTER FOUR

Narrative therapy and trauma

Maggie Carey

Introduction

For most people, experiencing a brain injury is traumatic, and for many the injury itself has occurred through traumatic circumstances. A narrative response to trauma explores the "sense of self" that has been traumatised or "injured" through the trauma. Trauma can subordinate a preferred story of self and disconnect people from a sense of having any agency in their lives. It can have the effect of escalating hopelessness, despair, and emptiness. Being able to use this distress or emotional pain as entry points to a preferred story of self can provide alternative places to stand in relation to the effects of the trauma. Rather than stay "stuck" in the single-storied account of loss and emotional pain, we can invite people to step into these different territories of self that have been subjugated. A narrative approach centres on creating opportunities for people to experience a reinvigoration of the very thin stories about their "sense of self" that are a consequence of the trauma, and to pick up on the ways in which they have been responding to what has happened. This can then be richly storied in order to develop a sense of being more able to navigate one's own life. This chapter will bring together the breadth of literature on narrative therapy and trauma. It will highlight links between philosophy, theory, and practice, with a particular emphasis on the philosophical work of Jacques Derrida and a focus on the practice known as the "absent but implicit".

How do we think about emotional/psychological trauma as distinct from the physical trauma of acquired brain injury?

One way of thinking about emotional or psychological trauma as a result of acquired brain injury is to see it as a *loss of the self that one once experienced before the injury.* Family, friends, work colleagues are no longer responding to the person that they knew before the accident or the event that caused the injury. More often than not, they are responding to some diminished sense of who the person was and this loss of the sense of one's self can be heard in the phrases "This is not the son we once knew", or "I want my old life back". The loss of the self that was once known and familiar is significant and can be devastating, and it can be experienced as a trauma in and of itself. In some situations, the loss can be compounded by the brain injury occurring as a result of traumatic circumstances such as those resulting from violence or abuse. In such circumstances there can be a violation of dearly held beliefs and values of how life is meant to be, or of what people can inflict upon each other, that can occur alongside the physical violation to the body.

The significant negative impact upon the sense of "who I am" is echoed in the questions and thoughts that press into everyone's consciousness: "What sort of life am I destined for? How might I live? What's the best I can expect now?" The insistence of these thoughts seem to carry with them an ever-present theme of what sort of directions life can now take for the person with the injury, and for those around them, and how much influence can be exerted over this.

A narrative approach responds to these questions of "what can I do now . . . what's to become of me/us?" with the appreciation that all of us desire to have a *sense of agency* or influence in our life. Broadly, the intention of therapy is to facilitate people to not stay stuck or constrained by the circumstances or situations or accounts of themselves that are negative and limiting. In the situations in which people live with a brain injury, the constraints are clearly magnified to an extent that the possibilities for influence and agency are generally submerged in either an ocean of resignation and acceptance, or drowned in frustration, anger, and defeat.

The sense of what is meant by this term "agency" can be elusive at the best of times. Michael White (2005, 2007) proposed that in order to have a sense of agency it is necessary to feel that we are having some say over the direction that our life is taking, that we are able to direct our lives in line with what we value in life, to act in accord with our beliefs about what's important to us. This can appear initially as problematic in the circumstance of brain injury, as this is the key thing that has seemingly been taken away—the power to influence the direction of one's own life. Understandably, the more immediate thoughts of the person who has an acquired brain injury is that they are now, and possibly will forever be, a passenger in life, always at the whim and mercy of others.

As narrative therapists, we appreciate that the sense of agency that we are looking for is not to be found in stories of self that are about what has been lost or about what is no longer possible for that person, even though a focus on these experiences is what is often most pressing. While it is important and necessary to acknowledge and appreciate the experience of loss, the sense of personal agency that we want the person to discover is to be found in the stories that sit outside of this "problem" account.

A principle understanding of the narrative approach is that there are always stories of self that are outside of the problem's domain and that these get submerged by the experience of trauma, be it the trauma of loss of self or the trauma of the circumstances in which the injury was acquired. These "alternative" or "preferred" stories (Morgan, 2000; Russell & Carey, 2004; White, 1995, 2007) have as their themes what the person intends for life, what matters to them, what they give value to, and what is right for them in how they aspire to live their life. These themes are not so vulnerable as to be totally lost because the physical body can no longer be part of them in the way that had previously been anticipated. People still have stories of self that go on being significant to them and still hold hopes and dreams of getting to experience life in directions that they desire.

Personal agency is based on the understanding that if we have not had the chance to develop some ideas about "who we are" and "what we are on about", then we will not have a sense of being able to steer our lives in directions that work for us. We will, instead, have an experience of not going anywhere and the problem story of loss, damage, and diminishment will continue to direct the course of life. In order to get to where we want to go, we need to be able to draw on certain skills and know-how in being able to move in a particular direction. The stories that can be developed (that are different to the problem accounts) also have within them the skills and know-how required to live according to the things that the person holds dear. It is this combination of connecting with the themes of what is important, plus a drawing out of the skills or know-how involved in living our lives in line with what we give value to, that brings about a sense of agency.

In responding to the trauma of acquired brain injury, we are looking for pathways and opportunities to construct a different sense of self to the problem saturated one. We are on the lookout for openings to other territories of self and when we find them we can then invite the person to move through these openings to explore the landscape that lies beyond.

What sense of "self" is being traumatised?

When we say that someone has lost his way or lost himself through what has happened, what is that "self" that we are referring to that has been lost? The common ways that are available to us of conceiving of self have largely come about through the pursuits of Western psychology and its influence on how we think about a sense of identity. What follows is a selective potted history that locates some of the different ways of thinking of self, as metaphors that were created in particular times and contexts. It is important to acknowledge that throughout the history of different ways of working, the intention has always been to help in reducing suffering. This exploration is not intended to diminish the different approaches to doing this or imply in any way that these ways of working have not been useful. It is also important to acknowledge that the narrative approach is also clearly a metaphor of identity. Rather, the intention here is to look at the ideas of self as metaphors that have particular cultural and historical locations, and to appreciate that there are consequences in practice to the take up of any of these metaphors of self. One consequence that does not fit with a narrative approach is the placing of the therapist as expert on the meanings that are to be made of a person's experience.

Metaphors of self and therapeutic responses that come from these

Many "modernist" assumptions of self have their origins in the structures laid out by Freud at the beginning of psychology with the id, the ego, and the superego spelling out an individual structure of self that resides at the core of our being. As a response to emotional or psychological trauma, there is the idea that things get repressed and the "depth psychologies" engage in digging through the layers of repression to bring to the surface what has been pushed down into the unconscious. Another common metaphor of self is of a machine that has broken down. It is as though we are a car that needs a "mechanic of the soul" to lift the bonnet, work out what has malfunctioned and fix it. Seeing the self as a functioning system or structure is an aspect of this, where the system has been damaged or broken or interrupted by the trauma and so has become dysfunctional. Problematic behaviour is seen as a manifestation of this dysfunction and the task is to be made functional again.

Thinking of ourselves as an emotional system that comes under pressure through experiences of trauma is another metaphor of what makes us tick. Psychological pain and distress are seen as substances stored under pressure, as if in a pressure cooker, and evoke the need to discharge emotions, to get things out of the system, to let off steam and release the pain. While these ways of conceptualising the self were generally deficit based, in the latter part of the twentieth century there was a move toward seeing the self as composed of personal qualities and attributes such as strength, courage, determination, resilience, or personal resources. In this conception of self, it is almost as though there are containers of these qualities inside us where the level of, for example, self-esteem or self-image becomes depleted by the trauma. The task of the therapist is to focus on the person's strengths and resources and to raise his levels of what has been depleted.

All of these understandings are shaped by universal truths or norms (normal recovery from trauma; normal adjustment to loss; normal boundaries) and the therapist is charged with re-establishing these norms. These expressions of taken-for-granted truths constitute our lives and identities and locate us on the spectrum of normality/abnormality.The self is seen as an individualised entity with no accounting for the social and relational context of life or of the way in which this shapes our sense of who we are. These approaches also place the therapist at the centre of the assessment, intervention, and treatment as the expert on knowing what meanings the person is making of her own life's experience.

So what constructions of self as a consequence of emotional or psychological trauma fit with the understandings outlined above? Often, it is of a shattered or damaged self; a fragile or weak self that is susceptible to life's vagaries. All too often, it is an individual and isolated self that must strive to make itself whole again or at least to achieve some sense of what would be considered "normal" in terms of acceptance of how life was going to be. So, what ways of working therapeutically do these understandings then evoke? The therapist's role is to engage in using his or her expert knowledge in re-building and repairing the shattered sense of self of the patient; to provide interventions or education or affirmation in order that the patient should achieve some level of "normative worth".

The following is an edited example that aims to highlight ways in which the narrative metaphor of identity offers a response to trauma that can contribute to a sense of agency rather than to one of fragility, damage, and vulnerability.

Katrina is a twenty-eight-year-old young woman who suffered what was referred to as "minor brain damage" four years previously through a violent assault in the city late one night as she was making her way home alone after being out with girlfriends. She was hit from behind with something hard and the fall to the pavement knocked her unconscious. She was in an induced coma for two weeks and after that was deemed lucky to have survived with only minor long-term damage. Rehabilitation followed and after twelve months she was told that she was "as good as she was likely to be" and that it was now time to "get on with her life".

The referral came to me through a job support agency and I did not have any more details other than what Katrina told me of her experience in hospital and in rehabilitation. The referring social worker had listed depression, lethargy, and low self-esteem as issues to be worked on in therapy and added that she felt that there was a "lack of acceptance" on Katrina's part as to what was now possible. Katrina herself added lack of patience and some memory loss to the concerns that she had. In our first consultation, I got a sense of how life was for Katrina.

> Most of my friends have dropped me maybe because I can't party the way I used to and besides I don't like going out at night even with others in a group.
>
> My Mum is really worried and nags me to make more of an effort with them. This gets me upset . . . and I think it's just so unfair that it happened and why did it have to happen to me?
>
> I can't remember what happened that night but I get this terrible fear sometimes and I can start to hyperventilate and have to get myself home as quick as I can.
>
> The social worker at the rehab centre said I have to give up and accept that I won't ever be the way I was, that I have to accept a "reduced life", and I just started swearing at him. I was so angry I wanted to smash him.
>
> I can't work at my old job [as a hairdresser] as I have good days and bad days and the boss isn't interested in the bad days and it's fair enough really, they need consistency.
>
> But really it's depressing and I just want my old life back. I feel like no-one understands.
>
> My life is so screwed, what's the point . . . I may as well give up.

As a therapeutic response, I could have followed the social worker's suggestion and engaged Katrina in the pursuit of "acceptance"; after all, the reality of her situation is that she cannot get her old life back. Or I could have "worked on" the depression and the panic attacks and given her some cognitive practices with which to combat the negative thought patterns. Being guided, however, by the narrative metaphor, offers some alternative pathways to pursue. The narrative approach has us interested in the effect of the trauma on Katrina's sense of who she is, on her sense of self. And "self" in this approach is seen as being constructed through the stories that we have about who we are. Our sense of identity comes from the meanings that we make of the social and relational experiences of life and it is through these stories that we come to have a sense of who we are. We are not born with these stories, but, rather, develop them, or have them developed for us, through what we are told about who we are and the meanings that we make of our experiences of life.

The story metaphor gives us an *intentional* self as opposed to a psychologised *internal state* self (White, 2004a). Stories are intentional in that some meaning is being got across; there is some purpose in the story. This is the nature of stories; that meaning is conveyed through them. There is also a discernment being made in telling *this* story rather than some other story because there is something that matters in this story; there is something of value or importance in this story that means it is the one that is told. In the narrative metaphor, in the themes of stories, there is the experience of value being *given to* something. In considering the themes as part of what makes a story, we can consider this whole landscape of what the story is about as a landscape of self or of identity. In these stories of self, the themes are the intentions and purposes, values and beliefs, hopes, dreams, principles, and commitments that people hold. The impact of trauma, then, is not about internal dysfunction and damage, but, rather, about what is happening to the things that we hold as important and precious in life and our sense of intentionality and aspiration. Narrative practice looks to reinvigorate the preferred stories of self that have been subjugated or made secondary through the influence of the trauma.

So, what are the pathways that we can use to get to these other stories? The pathway of "externalising" what is problematic, of getting some separation from the problem and finding a preferred story in relation to this, is one avenue that could be explored (Freedman & Combs, 1996; Russell & Carey, 2004; White, 2007). However, where there is an expression of distress or upset as a consequence of trauma, then even keeping things externalised can inadvertently open the space for the person to be taken back to that experience in a retraumatising way. The person could very easily end up on shaky ground if the influence of the trauma story becomes loud in the conversation. Listening for gaps in the story, or times when the person has done something that stands outside of what the problem story would predict, could be another way to approach the territory of the preferred story, but it is unlikely that these "moments of difference" or "unique outcomes" (White, 2007) could readily be evaluated as significant in face of the strength and persuasiveness of the trauma story. But there *is* a third pathway that is available to us that can provide a platform of solid ground on which to stand in order to explore the trauma story, and this is a pathway that is particularly useful when there is the expression of upset and emotional pain and strong negative affect. White (2000) referred to this pathway as the *"absent but implicit"* and it offers a way of responding to trauma that contributes to the exposition of stories of self that are rich in personal agency.

The absent but implicit as a pathway to different stories

The practice of the absent but implicit is captured in this statement that White made in referring to the work of Jacques Derrida: "It is not possible to talk about anything without drawing out what it is not. Every expression of life is in relation to something else".[1]

The notion of the "absent but implicit" is based on Derrida's ideas about how we make sense of things. Derrida talks about how we "read" texts and how the meanings that we derive from texts depend upon the distinctions we make between what is presented to us (privileged meaning) and what is "left out" (subjugated meaning: Derrida, 1978). The understanding that White drew from Derrida is that when we put words to our experience we are actually drawing a distinction between what it is that we are describing and what it is not; we are making a discernment between what we are describing as problematic and these other experiences against which this discernment is being made. For example, we determine an experience of light by it not being dark, cold by it not being hot, isolation by it not being connection, despair by it not being hope. In our therapeutic conversations, these "other" experiences can be thought of as preferred stories of self that have been made subordinate or been overshadowed by the main (problem or trauma) story.

When we first meet people, these preferred or subordinated stories (White, 2005) are not present in how their experience is being described, but they are implied. They are the out-of-focus background against which the expressed experience of the pain, distress, or despair is foregrounded; they are a backdrop that distinguishes and illuminates what is in centre stage. From a narrative perspective, we are always looking for ways to explore the stories that are different to the problem story and so it is the experience of what the problem is *not* that we are interested in exploring.

The absent but implicit is a practice of "double listening" (White, 2000) to both the story of what is it is that is problematic or trouble-some, and also to the story that is "beyond" the problem that is help-ing to make sense of how people are describing their problematic experience. When we meet people who have acquired a brain injury, the experience of loss, despair, or hopelessness is often what is present and is taking centre stage. Through considering what is "absent but implicit" in these expressions, we can open an exploration of the rela-tionship the person has with certain understandings of life to which they are giving value and that have sensitised them to making this discernment. What is it that is important to this person? What ideas of life is he giving value to that are implied by the way in which he is putting words to his experience?

When we keep to this understanding, that meanings are made in relation to other meanings that have already been described or cate-gorised in some way, we can open a pathway from the expression of what is problematic and to that which is on the "other side" of what is troublesome. If we hold to the understanding that for people to be describing their life in the way that they do implies there are other experiences that are "beyond" or on the other side of this problem account, then a wide field of possibilities for exploration opens up. As practitioners we can know that there must be some connection with, knowledge of, or experience of, something that will be in contrast to the problem.

A narrative response to trauma is interested in finding out what the person gives value to that has been violated or transgressed in some way (White, 2000). If the person with whom we are meeting is expressing distress or emotional pain as a result of the circumstance of acquired brain injury, then we can ask questions such as, "What does this upset speak to in terms of important beliefs or hopes about life that have been trodden on or compromised through the injury? What might these tears be a testament to in regard to what it is that you hold precious in life? What are the knowledges of life that you are keeping connected with that have not been given their rightful place? What have you lost touch with as a result of the trauma?" These lines of enquiry offer an entry point to preferred or subjugated stories that can then be developed into rich accounts of what has been trans-gressed by the trauma.

This is not about substituting a good story for a bad one and neither is it about highlighting the pain of the situation. Rather, it is about finding the story that can help to make sense of why this experience is so painful. It is then about creating space for this other story of what it is that matters to the person, of what she might stand for or hold as important commitments in life, and through this, developing another place to stand in this territory of self that is different to the problem one.

In relation to Katrina's comment, "My Mum is really worried and nags me to make more of an effort with my old friends. This gets me upset and I think it's just so unfair that it happened, and why did it have to happen to me?", we can ask Katrina what the upset is, telling us about what is important to her that has been violated in some way. What understandings of the world that she holds dear have been insulted, or compromised, or trodden on by the experience of what has happened? What has been put at risk, bullied, jeopardised, menaced, imperilled, dishonoured, debased, disrupted, encroached upon, infringed upon, contravened, or desecrated? This will take us in a very different direction from exploring the upset as an effect of what happened and to see it as a response to what happened, and a response that is based on the discernment of meanings that are backgrounding the upset and that can now be foregrounded.

In response to this line of enquiry, Katrina responded with a statement about how she had "wanted so much from life" and that this should have happened to someone who "didn't give a shit". This is what Katrina experienced as so unfair. She also spoke her mind about how "friends are meant to stick with you and not drop you when you're down" that clearly reflected some important principles around friendship and how you do friendship that we later explored. But I was initially struck by this comment about how she had "wanted so much from life". The "wanting so much from life" and the understandings and principles of friendship can be seen as expressions of what might be absent but implicit in the upset. I checked their significance with Katrina, asking if these were important considerations to her and, if so, whether it would be all right to ask some more questions about the importance of them? Katrina responded that yes, they were important and that she would be quite interested to explore them some more.

Developing the subordinate or preferred story

The absent but implicit is considered as an entry point to the preferred story, and from here the task is to develop a rich account of "wanting so much from life". In doing this, we are creating another place to stand than just the upset and the loss of what Katrina had anticipated would be her "damaged" life. The themes of what she gives value to are not lost through what has happened, and there is the opportunity for Katrina to recognise what is important to her and to see that she has skills and know-how in "doing" this sort of life. I asked questions to draw out this account of what Katrina holds dear in life: What's important to you in wanting so much out of life, like why does that matter to you? Katrina replied along the lines of "You have do things with what you've got; you don't just throw it away. You make the most of it."

These responses were not easily or quickly come to and required at times the careful "scaffolding" of what mattered to Katrina The practice of scaffolding conversations to develop knowledge about things that were previously not known is based on the work of Vygotsky, a Russian learning theorist (White, 2007). At times this involved Katrina making very small steps into new meanings through choosing from some possibilities I put before her.

Once the theme of "making the most of it" had been identified, it was possible to draw out some of the history of this theme in Katrina's life by asking if it had always been important to her. I was also keen to bring in the significant figures that were part of this story, keeping in mind the social and relational appreciation of how we are thinking of self. Who else would have known that "making the most of life" was something that mattered to you? What would they have seen you doing that would have told them that this was something that was something that was precious to you? What are the practices of, or the skills required, in "making the most of life"?

An account began to slowly unfold of a young girl who had grown up in poverty but who had had an ability to not let anything stop her from learning and participating in life. One thread of this account revolved around how, as a teenager, her one treat each week had been to attend an activities evening at a local youth centre. This had been an opportunity for Katrina to go out that did not cost anything and, while she had done her share of "goofing off" and "chilling out" with the other young people, she also made sure that she participated in the activities that were on offer. Katrina came to reflect that she had done this in a way that meant that she had not just been wasting time but had been "learning and trying things" that she might not otherwise have had the chance to do, things such as badminton, improvised drama, cooking, archery, and, one summer, abseiling. At times, this had invited ridicule from the other young people and comments about her sucking up to the youth workers, but she always managed to walk the line between being part of the group but also getting the most out of this one evening a week. On enquiring as to who might have known and appreciated this about her, we found that there had been one youth leader, Mandy, at this centre who would certainly have known that "getting the most out of life" was important to Katrina, as she had made comments to that effect that Katrina had completely forgotten about until this conversation. Katrina also thought that her mother would be someone who would not be surprised to hear her talking about the importance of this in her life.

Through this line of questioning, a fuller or richer account of self is placed into story lines. Together we unfolded many stories around this theme and found in these stories that there were particular skills that Katrina was employing in her pursuit of this approach to life: skills such as

- keeping an eye out for opportunities to learn something new;
- not worrying too much about what others might say;
- knowing that things can be difficult at first because they are new, but that it helps to hold your breath and just do it (a phrase of encouragement that Katrina remembered Mandy saying that helped her step over the edge of the cliff for her first abseiling experience);
- having a belief that it is all right to want to learn new things or give things a try;
- knowing that there are others who share the same ideas of what life is about;
- staying true to the understanding that what matters is "getting the most out of life".

Having developed the story of "getting the most out of life", the skills for how to do this and pointers to possible directions to take are now available to Katrina to use in her life in a ways that had not previously been available.

Another entry point for an exploration of the "absent but implicit" came from the statement "My life is so screwed, what's the point. I may as well give up." This came to be named as "despair" and again this expression of what was problematic opened the door for an enquiry through the following sorts of questions into what was absent but implicit in the despair:

What are you despairing of?

Being able to work and to look after myself.

What's important about that?

Independence—I was always the self-sufficient and strong one.

How have you managed to keep connected to the importance of this for you? What are some of the small ways in which you do independence now?

I won't let my mum drive me to appointments . . . it's something that I have to do on my own even though it means leaving home an hour earlier to get the bus. She says I'm pig-headed but this is one thing that I don't want to give in on.

What does it take to do that? What sort of ideas and beliefs about yourself do you have to keep close with you to do this? What effect does it have on you when you get yourself to an appointment? What other things do you do that are about independence?

What sort of independence is this? Is it different to the independence that you did before or is it the same? How did you learn the skills of this pig-headed type of independence?

In these conversations, questions are not asked as a barrage but rather as an unfolding enquiry that comes from curiosity as to what is the story of self that has been overshadowed by the trauma. As the story develops, Katrina starts to get more interested and curious for herself about this story that is so different to the "I am damaged forever and I must live a reduced life" one.

When there is only a single-storied account of a person's experience of life, the stories that are about personal agency and ability and about having knowledges and skills to respond to issues are subordinated by the problem description. By listening for the stories that have been relegated to the background, and bringing them forward, we open space for the preferred meanings to be available in ways that they have not been previously. Once we have found this opening, then we can use the practices of "reauthoring" and "rich story development" to reinvigorate the previously subordinated story of self.

While the hopes and plans for "getting the most out of life" are not going to be the same as they were before the attack, the theme itself is still present for Katrina and she is able to apply the skills involved in doing this sort of life in ways that fit for her. One thing she decided upon was to keep Mandy's voice with her whenever she felt like giving up and this made it possible to do some "stepping off" into new experiences that involved joining a group in her town for people who had experienced trauma or violence. This proved to be a door into new connections that are ongoing.

Pain and distress as testimony to what is held precious

At one point in our conversation, there was the opportunity to look at what was "absent but implicit" in Katrina's expressions of anger or frustration at the social worker saying that she had to give up and accept a reduced life. Through asking what it was that Katrina believed in that had been ignored or negated by these comments that could give rise to such anger and what was she refusing to give up on that was reflected in this rage, the story opened up of what Katrina was taking a stand for in responding in the way in which she had. Her anger and frustration became a testament to her belief that "everyone deserves a chance", "everyone needs to have hopes", and these themes linked in to her account of herself of "getting the most out of life". This was experienced by Katrina as "standing for the right of everyone to get the most out of life" and assisted her to take further steps in that direction.

Emotional pain and distress can be seen as a testimony to how important these conclusions of what matters in life are to us, and the degree of pain or upset can almost be seen as a measure of the significance of what it is that is held dear (White, 2005). So, rather than emotional pain being seen as an expression of weakness or damage or dysfunction, the pain or upset, or even despair and hopelessness, can be seen as expressions of how the person is holding certain understandings of life in high regard. The pain becomes a reflection of the strength of holding to these principles or understandings of life, or of standing for certain commitments in life and holding on to hopes and dreams. The stories and the skills and knowledges of holding to these hopes and dreams and commitments in life are still there and can be revitalised and become available for use.

Seeing responses to trauma rather than effects

Enquiring into what is absent but implicit as a reflection of what is given value to is one way of using the practice of double listening for the absent but implicit. There is also another pathway that we can consider. This is one that comes from the understanding that people are always *responding* to what is problematic or traumatic in their lives (White, 2005). Experiences of emotional trauma can often try to convince people that they did nothing in the face of what happened, or that in some way they are to blame for its occurrence, or even that they asked for it or that they deserved it. But people are never just passive recipients of what is dealt them, and even if the response is to think "this is not all right what is happening", this is a response. This key understanding, that people are always responding to trauma, offers us multiple pathways to stories of personal agency.

When a person has experienced trauma, they are often left with half memories of what took place in which any account of a response of personal agency has been erased (White, 2005). What is generally focused upon are the *effects* of the trauma—the experience of emotional damage or dysfunction as a consequence of what took place—and how these effects might be ongoing and how they should be dealt with. The construction of self as a "victim" of what happened is often associated with this way of looking at trauma and the person's responses to the trauma are rarely canvassed. Even the more active label "survivor" does not necessarily carry a sense of agency with it, as it can be all too easy to attribute surviving to luck or to external circumstances and so miss the opportunity to story and make visible the skills and knowledges that the person has used in responding to the events of the trauma. The focus on the person's *response* to the trauma and the skills and knowledges involved in making that response are the focus of a narrative enquiry.

The "absent but implicit" as an action

Having the understanding that people are always responding can support us, then, in seeing expressions of pain or distress, complaints, frustrations, or laments about life as active responses that are being made. We can hear how, in expressing what is problematic or upsetting, people are refusing to just go along with what has taken place. They are refusing just to be quiet about something that is not all right; they are making some form of a response that is an *active* response of protest or refusal or challenge or questioning of what is going on. These actions can then be seen to be based in having some skills or know-how in being able to take that particular action, otherwise they would not be able to do it. The skills that the person is employing are an expression of some intentional understandings he has for his life and those intentions will be shaped by beliefs about what he gives value to that has a history and that have significant other people who are part of that story of self.

White described a "map" of therapeutic practice that scaffolds the absent but implicit as an action (Carey, Walther, & Russell, 2009). This map is an orientation to practice that is particularly useful in those instances where people feel as though they are really stuck with just complaining about what has happened to them, or where people feel that they are passive recipients of what life is throwing at them and where they experience themselves as inactive in the face of what is happening. It can be useful in those circumstances where the person believes that she does not have the skills or does not know what to do to "get on" with life. It is a map in eight parts, described in the sections below.

The expression

We start with the way that the person expresses his experience of what is problematic or troublesome. We can listen for the expressions of distress, the concerns, laments, frustrations, and start to gather an account of the effect of this in people's lives. With Katrina, there was a clear lament and frustration at how her life was turning out; a sense of "not getting anywhere".

What the expression or complaint is in relation to

In order for Katrina see that she is taking action by raising her concerns and giving voice to them, there needs to be some appreciation of what she is *responding to* through her concerns and complaints. What is it that is going on in the context or situation of her life that is not all right with her, and that she is taking action against? We might need to enquire into what the situation or context is doing and what it is getting her to think about herself in order to make visible to Katrina what it is that she is up against. What are the forces that are at play that might be subjugating or marginalising her experience that she is taking a position on? What sorts of practices are people engaged in that are not all right with her? In response to this line of enquiry, Katrina identified a number of things that were going on.

> "I seem to get knocked back at everything I try. Like with my ex-boss saying he needed me to be on top of things every day, when I am good a lot of the time. A bit of understanding would go a long way. And my friends just wanting to see me as the 'party girl' me—it seems so shallow given what I've been through. And as for that social worker who expects me to just accept a reduced life . . . !"

Naming the response as an action

Having identified these things, we are now in a position to invite Katrina to name her response to them as an action. What is it that she is doing in response to what is going on; how is she responding to it? In a broad sense, the action can be seen as her taking a position on what is not all right, and so indicates some sort of a protest or challenge or questioning or a refusal to go along with something. We can ask what Katrina is refusing to go along with here. "What sort of action is this that you complain about the knock-backs, about your boss's lack of understanding, the shallowness of some of your friends, and the expectations from the social worker of you accepting a reduced life? How would you say you are responding to this?"

"Scaffolding" naming of the response as an action

This is, of course, a very unfamiliar way for Katrina to be looking at her experience, and so it is unlikely that she will easily see herself as being active through expressing her concern and complaints; it will then be difficult for her to name her response as an action. We can provide more of a platform for naming the response through using the

Derrida-inspired thinking outlined above and asking Katrina questions that will elicit "what it is by what it is not". Questions can be asked such as, "Are you happy to go along with the lack of understanding and the shallowness, or not? Are you there for these expectations or are you not there for them? It sounds as though you are not accepting of this situation; if you are not accepting of it, then what are you doing? What sort of a response are you making?"

Katrina was quite clear that she was not happy to go along with any of it, but was still not sure how she would name it as an action. Further scaffolding was employed that supported this step into meaning making through offering some possibilities. "Might this be a refusal or a protest or a resistance or a questioning of some kind?" From this, Katrina was able identify that it was a "refusal", and when I asked her to characterise this refusal through asking her what *sort* of refusal it was, she replied, "A pig-headed refusal." Links were made with the *pig-headed determination* that had been developed in previous sessions and this pig-headedness became a rich and very useful identity account for her.

Skills and know-how that are expressed in the action

The response is now named as an action of *refusal*, and from this point on we are in a different territory of story and the task becomes one of richly developing the subordinate or preferred story of "pig-headed refusal". In order for people to take any action in their life, they must be drawing on some previous history, knowledge, or experience, and so we can enquire into how it is possible for Katrina to take this action. How is it possible for someone to question or refuse the expectations of them? What are the skills that are at work here and what do they reflect about what Katrina knows about life? What is making it possible for her to refuse these expectations?

In response to questions about how she had been able to make that *pig-headed refusal* to go along with the expectations, the shallowness, and of the lack of understanding, Katrina spoke about her experiences from her childhood. Having been the only girl in a family of boys, she was often told that "girls can't do things". It came to light that she had never gone along with that idea and had learnt to do most things that the boys did and had even been chosen at times to play in the scratch games of football that were a regular feature in the local park. "I knew that if I didn't push for things it wouldn't happen" was her response to my questions about the skills involved in refusing to go along with things that are not all right.

Intentions that fit with using that skill or know-how

The story can be further developed through bringing our curiosity to asking about the intentions and purposes that are reflected in this skill or know-how. "What are your purposes in making this pig-headed refusal and in using your skills of *'knowing that if you don't push for things then they won't happen'*? In taking this action of refusal, what does it say about what you are wanting in life or what you intend for your life? When you think about not siding with shallowness, expectations, and lack of understanding, what purpose might that serve?" From this, there came a statement of Katrina's intent in this action of refusal: "I want to have as much of a life as I can. If it's a reduced life then I want it to be the fullest reduced life it can be."

What is given value to in these intentions

Drawing upon the appreciation of an intentional self as an aspect of developing the themes of the preferred story, it follows to enquire as to what it is that Katrina is giving value to through the intentions that she has identified. I asked questions along the lines of "These purposes or intentions of *'having as much of a life as you can, of having the fullest reduced life it can be'*, what do they say about what is important to you? What does this reflect about what life is about for you?" These questions around the values in life that were significant and precious to Katrina brought forward a stand that she has in her life that had not previously been so clearly elucidated; it was that "*Everyone deserves a chance to have a good life, no matter what.*"

Social and relational history

Once we have established what is being given value to, we can then go on to invite rich accounts of the social and relational history of that valuing (White, 1997). When people have experienced things that are traumatic, they can often have an experience of being cut off from a sense of self that flows through life. They can have feelings of just being stuck in life and that this is all there is. If we can find ways to have these accounts connected with other events and people in the past we can "resurrect a sense of continuity of self in the place of discontinuity" (White, 2004b).

In response to my questions about whether she had ever thought anything like this before, Katrina spoke about how there were children in her neighbourhood who had been even poorer than her family and how one of her brothers used to make up jokes about them being "stupid". Katrina had always found that this did not sit right with her and she never joined in. Sometimes she would find things to say about them, about what they had done that was good, even if this had to be a bit made-up or embellished.

I enquired as to who would have appreciated what she was standing for in doing what she did back then and after a while Katrina remembered her grade seven teacher, Ms Forrester. Ms Forrester was smart and cool and Katrina felt that she conveyed very clearly her belief that everyone deserved a chance no matter what, "*though she didn't come on heavy with it . . . you just knew*". Katrina spoke about an example of the sort of thing that Ms Forrester might have noticed Katrina doing that would have alerted her to knowing that Katrina stood for the belief that "*everyone deserves a chance to have a good life no matter what*". There was a time where some of the girls in the class were being "bitchy" and started leaving horrible notes on this particular girl's desk . . . she was new and was from India, and Katrina used to get to her desk first and take the notes and pretend that they were for her and that it was a joke and pretty soon the girls stopped doing it. "I haven't thought about that for years," Katrina commented.

Connections over time and into the future

Having developed a rich account of the social and relational history of the response, we can now invite Katrina to connect these actions over time. Pulling together the events from the past and putting them alongside the present action enables her to see that there is a solid foundation in the past for this action; she can come to appreciate that there is a long history to this way of responding, that it has not just come from this conversation. It becomes possible for Katrina then to be able to think forward into the future and have an appreciation of further actions that can be taken that are in line with these accounts of self. In this way, a sense of movement is implied and there is an experience of personal agency. A reflecting surface is created for Katrina to be able to see that she has done something about what is not acceptable to her and that she has the skills and know-how to do more.

To the questions of "What is it like to look at this past event in light of the theme of *pig-headed refusal* that we have been exploring? What is the link between these two times?" Katrina replied, "I have the right to a good life no matter what. If I listen to my ex-boss and that social worker, or think too much about those ex-friends, it will just drag me down. I have to push for what I want."

We then went on to look at how this could be put into practice in the coming months. This involved drawing out in detail what Katrina knew about the things that might attempt to take her off track and what she could have in mind as a counter strategy if this did happen.

Conclusions

This chapter has focused on the practice of story development as a response to the emotional trauma that can be associated with acquired brain injury and has explored some of the ways in which we can use the concept of the "absent but implicit" as an entry point to stories of self that have been subordinated by the trauma. In this way, emotional pain, concern, and distress can be thought of either as a pathway that is reflective of what is given value to, or can be seen as an active response to what has happened. In using either of these pathways, stories that can contribute to a sense of agency are then developed.

The experience of acquired brain injury is a trauma that can erase a sense of self and a sense of agency. Through careful story development, the narrative approach can contribute to an invigoration of the stories of self that have been subordinated by the trauma. This can then make it possible for the person who has experienced the injury to move in directions that are aligned with the continuing themes of what matters to them, and to live in ways that they recognise as fitting with what they give value to in their lives.

Note

1. Workshop notes, 2006. Small group intensive with Michael White, Adelaide.

References

Derrida, J. (1978). *Writing and Difference*. Chicago, IL: University of Chicago Press.

Freedman, J., & Combs, G. (1996). *Narrative Therapy: The Social Construction of Preferred Realities*. New York: W. W. Norton.

Morgan, A. (2000). *What Is Narrative Therapy? An Easy To Read Introduction*. Adelaide, South Australia: Dulwich Centre Publications.

Russell, S., & Carey, M. (2004). *Narrative Therapy: Responding to Your Questions*. Adelaide, Australia: Dulwich Centre Publications.

White, M. (1995). *Re-Authoring Lives: Interviews & Essays*. Adelaide, South Australia: Dulwich Centre Publications.

White, M. (1997). *Narratives of Therapist's Lives*. Adelaide, South Australia; Dulwich Centre Publications.

White, M. (2000). Re-engaging with history: the absent but implicit. In: *Reflections on Narrative Practice*. Adelaide, South Australia: Dulwich Centre Publications.

White, M. (2004a). Folk psychology and narrative practice. In: L. E Angus & J. McLeod (Eds.), *The Handbook of Narrative and Psychotherapy: Practice, Theory and Research* (pp. 15–52). Thousand Oaks, CA: Sage.

White, M. (2004b). Working with people who are suffering the consequences of multiple trauma: a narrative perspective. *International Journal of Narrative Therapy and Community Work*, 1: 45–76.

White, M. (2005). Children, trauma and subordinate storyline development. *International Journal of Narrative Therapy and Community Work*, 3 & 4: 10–21.

White, M. (2007). *Maps of Narrative Practice*. New York: W. W. Norton.

CHAPTER FIVE

Exploring discourses of caring: Trish and the impossible agenda

Sarah Walther, Amanda Redstone, and Anette Holmgren

This chapter will describe developments in narrative practice that support people to position themselves preferredly in relation to the dilemmas and complexities of discourse, focusing specifically on a conversation about the discourses of being in a caring role. We will describe how the Context and Discourse Map, often referred to as the Shoulds to Coulds Map, offers a conversational framework to structure explorations of the effects of normative ideas about "being a good carer" and invites people to make their own evaluation in relation to these ideas. Such conversations explore possibilities for action and caring practices that extend beyond the shoulds of discourse and seek to honour what it is that people give value to in their lives.

Why are we so interested in talking about discourse and normative ideas?

We are a group of narrative therapists who meet to share and develop ideas in relation to narrative therapy and practice. Anette lives and works in Denmark, where she is a co-director of Dispuk. Sarah and

Amanda are Directors of the Institute of Narrative Therapy (INT) in the UK and members of the INT teaching faculty. Amanda works in Devon as a counsellor with families, individuals, and children; Sarah is employed as a narrative therapist in East Lancashire Hospital Trust Child and Adolescent Mental Health Service.

Narrative therapy locates concerns in context and offers a therapeutic response to address the effects of modern power. However, we have found that it is sometimes difficult to explore the influence of dominant discourse and culture in the lives of the people we meet, including those of people who are in the role of carers.

Narrative therapy is particularly concerned with exploring the influence of discourse as it holds an assumption that the stories we tell and that are told about us shape our lives and have real effects on our actions, relationships, and the way we think about ourselves: our identity (White & Epston, 1990). These stories do not just appear from nowhere, rather they are part of a bigger story context: a cultural, social, and historical context which holds particular sets of ideas about what people *should* be doing and how they *should* be living their lives. These normative expectations are located within a particular culture, time, and place. They differ between contexts and reflect what is valued in human behaviour, in our society, at any given time. Yet, despite this, these *shoulds* are usually understood and presented as truths.

White (2002) drew on the work of the philosopher Foucault to describe how these normative ideas have become so commonplace that they are virtually invisible. They are carried in our heads and influence our actions and sense of self in relation to what is "normal" for virtually every aspect of life, be it cultural, spiritual, or physical, and in aspects such as sexuality, mental health, and ability. Are we brave enough? Have I grieved properly? What should I look like? Am I coping well enough? How happy should I be? These ideas combine to form a set of complex discourses about how we should be living our lives as normal, adequate, and successful people.

When people experience an acquired brain injury, a whole new range of discourses comes into play in their lives. These discourses are not just in relation to themselves and their own competencies as workers, partners, etc., but also about their relationships and the skills and competencies of the people with whom they share relationships: friends, children, parents, and partners. These friends and families also have to negotiate the conflicts, dilemmas, and complexity of these additional discourses; how can they continue to be a good friend or family member to a person who now has additional caring needs?

An introduction to Trish

Trish was referred to me (Amanda) by her doctor, who described her as a very distressed and anxious woman. In my first meeting with Trish, she agreed with her doctor's description; expressing a sense of failure as a wife, mother, and carer. Trish's husband, Jon, had sustained a brain injury as a result of a severe asthma attack thirty years ago and afterwards struggled to discern complexities in social interaction. This could lead to what Trish described as "inappropriate behaviour", causing Trish to feel that she had to be constantly vigilant and "controlling". She expressed resentment, frustration, and anger in relation to her perception of what her family needed from her: "I shouldn't be feeling like this about my family, a wife shouldn't feel like this about her husband."

How do we end up not feeling good enough?

Foucault proposed that notions about successful living practices are implied not only in how we act, but also in how we go about knowing things, and especially in how we go about knowing ourselves and each other. As we constantly give each other feedback and make comparisons that reinforce normative ideas, we all both receive and engage in judgements about each other's and our own performance in relation to sets of norms. Trish's ideas of what she should or should not be doing, her conclusion that she was a failure as a wife, mother, and carer, can only have been arrived at in the context of relational and contextual experiences. These experiences or episodes of life may be so everyday and so small that they are hardly noticeable. It is only when we ask about specific instances that we can begin to appreciate how everyday and small episodes of life both shape and are shaped by a multiplicity of broader normative ideas.

Trish related an account of a recent social occasion she had attended with her husband, Jon, during which she had spent the entire evening worrying that he might drink too much and "make a spectacle of himself". These worries were based on Trish's knowledge that alcohol exacerbated the level of disinhibition that Jon sometimes experienced. Friends were offering Jon alcoholic drinks and when Trish had asked them not to do this, they had told her that she was a "spoilsport and should let him have some fun". Trish expressed a sense of distress, confusion, and frustration at the dilemma she faced: how should she care for Jon without seeming unfair or unkind, or being seen as a spoilsport? She was left feeling ashamed and guilty, and asking herself whether she should have responded differently.

Trish's confusion reflects the multiplicity of discourses she is up against in this situation. How to be a good enough carer, wife, and partygoer all at the same time? If she manages to work out how to be the perfect partygoer, will she also be able to be the perfect carer? If she tries to be the perfect carer, will she be a party spoilsport? This is not just a dilemma for Trish; all of us are constantly trying to negotiate our way through the demands of complex, multiple, and often conflicting sets of ideas about what we should be doing in any situation. It is almost inevitable that we will experience some sense of failing to do what we should be doing (White, 2002).

The practice challenge: moving from the "should" of discourse to the "coulds" of living

The effects of these normative ideas can seem ubiquitous, omnipresent, and overwhelming. However, Michael White drew on the work of Foucault not only to describe the effects of normative ideas, but also to offer a way to shape hopeful conversations about this (White, 2002). By understanding our history and the effects of our history on how we live, we can choose to make changes. We can begin this by making discourse visible through a deconstruction of historically given practices. We can ask about where these normative sets of ideas, expectations, and shoulds come from and think about how they remain so powerful. If we can explore these questions, then we can decide the extent to which these practices and ideas are useful or not. We can ask people to evaluate the effects of these normative ideas on their lives and to explore additional options for living. In doing so, we can support a move from the "shoulds of discourse" to the "coulds of living".

In practice, however, it can be difficult to invite people into conversations about discourse. The influence of non-structuralist ideas about relationships and the self has always been reflected in the way in which narrative practice includes categories of enquiry that make visible the contexts in which people experience problems. However, the effects of our historical legacy are profound and saturate our ways of speaking, thinking, and living. It is, therefore, not surprising that many of us have found it a challenge to scaffold therapeutic conversations which consider and evaluate the implications of wider context and discourse. There are a number of reasons why this might be the case, such as the dominance of structuralist understandings of identity, our position as therapists, the immediacy of experience, and the location of hopes and dreams within normative discourse.

The dominance of structuralist understandings of identity: our position as therapists

The distinctions between structuralist and non-structuralist ideas about identity have been well documented elsewhere (e.g., White, 2001). In brief, structuralist ideas inform an understanding of an identity as a core and fixed entity and draw on a surface–depth metaphor to describe how the problems people experience are a surface manifestation of an underlying structural disorder, requiring expert assessment, identification, and remedy. In contrast, non-structuralist notions of identity emphasise intention and agency. They invite us to consider the actions, hopes, dreams, and wishes of people in relation to what it is they give value to.

Whatever our theoretical/philosophical orientation is, many of us are living and working in contexts in which the dominant discourse about understanding lives and identity is a structuralist one. Therefore, it is often unfamiliar to think about the effects of broader contexts and discourse in our lives. This is not just the case for the people who access the services in which we work; it is also the case for ourselves as practitioners. We all live in discourse, so we all participate in the reproduction of dominant ideas. This participation includes those of us who practise in the fields of mental health, education, and social care and hold particular positions of power in relation to the people they work with.

At its most visible, the influence of normative ideas in mental health can be traced in the development of formal social, psychiatric, and psychological questionnaires which assess people's performance in relation to a range of norms: defining which of our personal skills are considered strengths or resources, which of our relationship practices are valued as healthy, and, of course, which of these skills or relationship practices are deemed to be unhealthy.

In less visible ways, the advice we offer and the questions we ask as workers often reflects particular ideas about what is normal and what is not. Trish's dilemma about what to do at the party could be understood as an invitation for the therapist to problem solve: how could she be both the perfect carer and the perfect partygoer? However, if we step into this, then, despite our best intentions, and perhaps because of our best efforts to do what we consider to be most helpful, we might inadvertently reproduce dominant discourses and normative expectations. These discourses and expectations can result in marginalising other perspectives and further invite a sense of failure in those people who do not meet those expectations. As Foucault neatly states: "People know what they do; they frequently know why they do what they do; but what they don't know is what what they do does" (Foucault, 1982, p. 187).

If the therapist responds to Trish's dilemma by offering advice about how she should resolve it, but Trish still does not experience herself as a perfect wife, carer, and mother, then Trish might conclude that she is now also a failure in following advice properly.

In practice, if we wish to avoid this reproduction, then we need to be vigilant in noticing the effects of these discourses on our work and the people with whom we work. Orientations to therapy that are informed by non-structuralist thinkers, such as Foucault, have led to therapeutic practices that invite practitioners to adopt a decentred position to their role. This decentred position privileges the life expertise and preferences of the person who is consulting the therapist, rather than the expertise and preferences of the therapist herself. As therapists attempting to take a decentred position, we can ask ourselves what our own ideas are about what sort of carers, wives, or partygoers people should be. While we cannot be neutral in relation to these ideas, we can acknowledge that we cannot be neutral and can instead think about the effects our own sets of "shoulds" might have on our work.

This philosophical orientation also seeks to expand the options in people's lives through an interest in multi-storied possibilities of "becoming" rather than single-storied definitions of "being" (Walther & Carey, 2009). In relation to Trish's experience, we are interested in exploring the multiple positions that she might take to the dilemmas she faces, rather than keeping our conversations reduced to the very narrow choice currently available to her: being *either* a good carer *or* a good wife.

The immediacy of experience

A further consequence of the dominance of structuralist understandings about identity is that the people we meet with often hold structuralist understandings of their predicament. They situate their problems and distress within more immediate (often internal) contexts: relationship dynamics, inherited traits, intrapsychic process, etc. It may appear both unfamiliar and disrespectful to the people we are consulting with if we invite conversations about the effects of wider context without first honouring the local immediacy of their experience of the concern. Therefore, we need to carefully scaffold conversations which support alternative broader explanations.

Explorations of immediate experiences of concern are not only respectful, but also enable us to gain a good understanding of the specific local effects and practices of broader discourses. This is important, as we do not inhabit "big contexts" or "broader history" directly; rather, their effects are mediated in the local contexts in which we live (May, 2006); while there will be some broader contextual ideas about how to be a good carer, more specific expectations of exactly how to behave in the carer role will differ according to local contexts, including cultural influences and traditions developed in neighbourhoods and families. This means that each of us has a unique and complex history, which is not reducible to a universal, essential history of broader context. As people recount this complexity, they can begin to appreciate that they are more than an inevitable outcome of history or of internal structures, and can consider their options for agency in relation to change.

In therapeutic practice, this implies that we need to begin by asking about the local context in which people live and about the practices that they engage in and that come to engage them. Trish's account of the party offers a foundation for naming the "shoulds" that might have been shaping her experience here. Without this foundation, it is likely that Trish would find it a very large jump to consider the issues and relevance of wider discourse.

The location of hopes and dreams within normative discourse

As we all inhabit the milieu of discourse, inevitably the hopes, dreams, and principles we hold as important reflect those discourses that are most normative and dominant. In addition, we hold sets of normative expectations about how these hopes and dreams should be lived out. Fisher (2008) has described these as the "prescriptions" for living that such discourses endorse.

Narrative therapy seeks to make visible how the distress of the people we meet may reflect a sense of failure in being able to live life according to the shoulds, or prescriptions, of normative discourse. However, we must find a way of having these conversations without implicitly constructing "normative" hopes, dreams, or ways of being as undesirable or negative. If we did not take care to do this, then our conversations might constitute a reproduction of the very same practices of evaluation and marginalisation we are attempting to address, and this would be inconsistent with our intention to adopt a decentred position as therapists. Some of the ideas that Trish holds in relation to caring practices will be normative and will also be cherished, precious, and important to her. It is important that we honour this and ensure we are consulting her about which of these ideas she wishes to go forward with and which she wishes put to one side.

This is different from structuring a conversation that invites a *refusal* of normative expectations and prescriptions of discourse. A person may, of course, choose to construct their position in this way and at times this can be a helpful direction to take (White, 2002). However, the enquiry we are describing is about creating a conversational space in which a person can make his own evaluation of normative expectations and prescriptions and then explore additional, perhaps less prescribed, ways of living that are also helpful to him: other options, possibilities, or actions that a person could take up in his life more. These conversations seek to support people to move from "shoulds" to "coulds" in relation to how they live their lives.

Considerations for practice

The discussions above present a number of considerations for us as practitioners.

- How can we invite people to consider context, discourse, and the effects of these in their lives?
- How can we make discourse visible, but also respect the immediacy of people's experience?
- How can we respect the ways in which people's hopes and dreams are situated within dominant discourses?
- How can we address the marginalising effects of the practices of power and promote possibility and difference?
- How can we invite an evaluation of these effects without privileging alternative responses to discourse as "good" and diminishing normative responses as "bad"?
- How can we then reconnect people with a sense of agency in their lives, so that they can consider which living practices most reflect their hopes, dreams, and what is important to them?

Trish and the impossible agenda

As Trish began to talk about her dilemmas in working out what she should be feeling or doing as a wife, carer, and mother, I (Amanda) considered this an invitation to enquire more about the exact ideas that Trish held about what a mother or wife *should* feel like and to consider the effects of these *shoulds* in shaping her experience.

In hearing about the party, I began to get a good understanding of how events could leave her with a sense of frustration and failure. Having established this understanding, it was possible to ask Trish whether she thought that other wives or carers might ever experience similar feelings of shame, guilt, and frustration. Trish thought that they would and began to wonder how it was that so many people could end up feeling this way. She reflected on her own experience, speaking about her childhood in rural England during the 1960s and her early married life in Norway. Trish described the ideas she had learnt in these contexts about being a good wife, mother, and caring person, and then began to list exactly how she should have been fulfilling this: for example, "Wives should always stick up for their husbands. Also a caring person is always understanding, about everything."

Trish then went on to fill two pages with prescriptions about what wives, carers, and mothers should be doing. She also listed what was promised if all of these prescriptions were followed to the letter. At the end, Trish shook her head and said, "It sounds crazy to say it, but I thought that if I did all these things then everyone would be happy, have no worries, and think I was a really nice person. But this is an IMPOSSIBLE agenda! I could never do all these things all the time!"

When Trish was asked about how much of the impossible agenda fitted with her own preferences in relation to caring and being a wife and mother, she selected some ideas that were important to her and that she wished to continue with. However, she also expressed a realisation that she could not fulfil any aspects of the impossible agenda twenty-four hours a day. Trish also spoke about some ways of being a wife and mother that were not on the list, but which were equally important to her, such as "taking time" for herself and being more relaxed about her husband's behaviour.

At the end of the conversation, Trish thought that keeping the impossible agenda in mind would make a big difference to her week, in that she might be kinder to herself when situations arose that would otherwise invite self-criticism. In subsequent meetings, I drew on other narrative practices to further describe Trish's preferred sense of herself as a caring person and to make visible the skills associated with this.

It was not the intention of these conversations to eradicate the impossible agenda, as, of course, this would in itself be setting an impossible agenda for the work. Trish remains vulnerable to the impossible agenda's invitations to self-criticism, but now has many more options for how to respond and many more ideas for how to develop her preferred ways of living. The range of possibilities for action available to her has expanded from the shoulds of discourse to the coulds of living.

Narrative maps and scaffolds

As practitioners, it is our experience that these conversations do not happen by accident; rather, they require planning, practice, and the development of skills. Holding a decentred orientation to practice is useful, but only if we can also be influential in scaffolding conversations that support people to think about new possibilities. Narrative practice offers a series of frameworks or maps to support the scaffolding of therapeutic conversations that are congruent with the broader orientations that inform the practice. The conversation with Trish was guided by a two-part map, the Context and Discourse Map, which we have developed to support our work (Walther, in press).

The Context and Discourse Map is a conversational framework that can be useful in rendering discourses and normative expectations visible. It can also be a way to invite people to name their own position on those discourses and expectations. In doing this, we are not inviting people to step away from their dreams or give up on their hopes; rather, we are constructing opportunities to stand in a place of more possibility. In other words, we are inviting people to move from the shoulds of discourse into the coulds of life. For this reason, we have found that people often refer to this particular framework as the "shoulds to coulds map".

The Context and Discourse Map: from the shoulds of discourse to the coulds of living

Points of entry

As we hear the accounts of life that people bring to conversations, we can adopt a listening position that is sensitive to people's experiences of aspiring to the normalising expectations of their cultures. We might listen for

- times when people describe an evaluation or conclusions about themselves or someone else;
- times when people speak of shoulds, coulds, and expectations.

Part A: Locating the problem in context and discourse

The three categories of enquiry in part A of this map aim to support a consideration of how problems can be located in context and to make visible and name the discourses which operate in these contexts.

1. *Locating the concern in immediate context.* A range of questions to elicit a full description of the *specific and local context* in which the concern occurs. In the responses given, we can start to listen for the discourses that might be operating in the context described. Questions may include:
    - Can you tell me about a time you have had this experience of feeling that you should have been a better carer?
    - Where was it? What was happening?
    - Who was there? How did they respond?
    - When else is this most likely to happen?

2. *Locating concern in the broader context.* This category of enquiry seeks to locate the experience in the *broader context* of people's cultures. This assists people to get some distance from the immediate experience, moves it from internal to external, and links the person to others with shared experience. We can also invite the person to consider how differences in experience might be connected to issues of gender, cultural heritage, age, etc. Examples of questions could be:
    - Do you think other people have a similar experience of not feeling that they are being a good enough carer ever?
    - Who else is most likely to also experience this? When? Where?
    - Would they experience this differently or at different times? Why?

3. *Naming and making visible the discourse(s) operating in contexts.* These questions begin to develop externalising conversations which make discourses more visible as ideas about living rather than truths about living:
    - Why do you think some people in particular might end up feeling this way?
    - What would you call what's going on here?
    - What name would you give to this?

Part B: From the "shoulds" of discourse to the "coulds" of living

Once particular discourses have been made visible and named, the effects of these discourses in people's lives can be explored. This brings forward a range of possibilities for expressing what it is that people give value to.

1. *Making discourse prescriptions (what you should be doing) visible.* This category of enquiry assists people to make visible the ways in which normalising ideas can shape how they live their lives and reflect on their relationship with them. We can explore this by asking questions such as:
    - Does this put forward some ideas about what people like you *should* be doing in such situations then?
    - What are these ideas? Where do they come from? How do you know about them?
2. *Making discourse promises visible.* These questions support people to consider how discourse engages us all in the forming of our hopes and dreams:
    - If you did manage to do all these *shoulds,* what are you promised as a reward?
3. *Making the discourse small print or "ps" visible.* An invitation to consider whether the promises of discourse are always met:
    - Does this (discourse) always deliver on its promise?
4. *Inviting an evaluation of the effects of discourse in relation to a person's preferred identity.* This category of enquiry supports people to take a position on the effects of discourse in their lives and how this fits with their preferred ways of living. These questions find ways to honour what it is that people give value to in life, including those dreams, hopes, and wishes that are associated with dominant discourses. Questions reflect a position that discourses and prescriptions are not necessarily good or bad, but that the effects of them on our lives can be evaluated as preferred or not preferred:
    - What do you think of all this?
    - In what ways has this made it harder or easier to keep going with the things that are important to you?
    - How much of this fits with *your* ideas about how you prefer to go about life and what is important to you in life?
    - How much is different or the same?
5. *Bringing forward the coulds of living.* This is a range of questions to explore possibilities for action that extends beyond the shoulds of discourse and which promote multiple coulds of living:

- How else do you express what is important to you?
- Are there other ways, as well as or different to these ideas about what you "*should*" be doing, in which you keep going with what is important to you?
- What would you call these ways of being in the world?
- Can you give me an example of this?

6. *Naming what this makes possible/problem solving stage.* This final category of enquiry is based on an understanding that when people are standing in a place of preferred meaning and identity, then they have more of a foundation from which to take preferred actions in the world: people will be more able to problem solve when they are connected to their preferred values and beliefs. Questions may include:

- If you were to keep all these ideas in mind, what difference would this make?
- What ideas do you now have in relation to the problem/discourse/prescription?
- What might this make possible for you in relation to work/home life/relationships/how you think about yourself?

How might the Context and Discourse Map be helpful?

Conversations that begin with an expression of a concern or problem can take many paths and the Context and Discourse Map is just one possible way to explore problems in relation to dominant sets of normative expectations. In presenting this map, it is not our intention to narrow the possibilities for practice by suggesting a "correct way" to undertake these explorations. To do so would be incongruent with the ideas that inform our preferred way of working. Rather, we are presenting these ideas to expand possibilities for ourselves as workers, and for those people who meet with us.

We might choose to follow this pathway on first hearing about the problem that the person wishes to talk about, or we might follow this line of conversation at some later date. We might choose to follow the whole map or to select some aspects of it. We might include categories of enquiry from this map as a foundation for addressing experiences of personal failure or for exploring what is "absent but implicit" in people's concerns.

This map can be a way of addressing any of the multiple discourses that exist about people with acquired brain injuries and those who love them or work with them. We have used this framework to structure shared conversations in group work as well as with individuals, couples, families, professional networks, and young carers.

In conclusion, this map, as with all narrative maps, is not intended to be prescriptive and there are multiple ways to use the ideas presented in this chapter. This framework may simply invite us to be mindful of the principles of narrative therapy, and to honour its origins as a response to the effects and practices of power.

References

Fisher, A. (2008). *Notes Taken From Teaching*. Dispuk, Snekkersten, Denmark.

Foucault, M. (1982). *Beyond Structuralism and Hermeneutics*. Chicago, IL: Chicago University Press.

May, T. (2006). *The Philosophy of Foucault*. Buckinghamshire: Acumen.

Walther, S. (in press). *Possibilities in Narrative Therapy and Practice*.

Walther, S., & Carey, M. (2009). Narrative therapy, difference and possibility: inviting new becomings. *Context, 105*: 3–8.

White, M. (2001). Folk psychology and narrative practice. *Dulwich Centre Journal, 2*: 1–34.

White, M. (2002). Addressing personal failure. *International Journal of Narrative Therapy and Community Work, 3*: 33–76.

White, M., & Epston, D. (1990). *Narrative Means to Therapeutic Ends*. New York: Norton.

CHAPTER SIX

Narrative practice in the context of communication disability: a question of accessibility

Rozanne Barrow

The following quote gives some insight into my personal view on where narrative sits within my professional identity: "Storytelling offers one way to make sense of what has happened and this makes stories essential to practice" (Mattingly, 1998, p. 6). Recently, a friend told me that during a stay in hospital, not one member of staff introduced themselves to him by name. This led to a discussion about the role of introducing oneself and how this carries an important submerged message; a message of welcome that conveys to the recipient "you are worthy of knowing me as a person". This ritual of introduction is what Frank (2004) refers to as a "moral moment"—an occasion to respond to another at a human level. Due to the very nature of the impairment, people with communication disability may be at greater risk of not being responded to on such occasions. Failure to respond to a "moral moment" has the potential to have a dehumanising effect on both the individual and the encounter. Introducing oneself is the first step toward placing a healthcare encounter on a partnership footing and so paves the way for effective collaborative work. Good narrative practice is about partnership, as a narrative perspective differs from a biomedical perspective in that the main character of the healthcare encounter is the *person* with the brain injury rather than the symptoms of the brain injury.

The focus of this chapter is on ways to make a *narrative approach to practice* accessible for people with communication disability. While I may allude to techniques used in narrative therapy, I am not a trained narrative therapist. I begin this chapter by introducing and situating myself within the context of this book. I go on to give an outline of my understanding of what I refer to as a *narrative approach to practice* and its contribution to working with people with acquired brain injury and, in particular, those with communication disability. Given the assumption that language is what brings narrative to life, I go on to summarise some of the potential issues and challenges in applying a *narrative* approach with this group. The essence of the chapter centres on exploring how to make *narrative* accessible for people with communication disability. In particular, I draw on what others and I have learnt from people with aphasia (impairment in the ability to process language) about the challenges of engaging in life again in the context of brain injury. At the conclusion of the chapter there are "reflective boxes" in which I pose a number of questions for us to consider when working with people with communication disability.

Situating myself in context

I am a practising speech and language therapist working in a hospital context primarily with people with communication disability as a consequence of brain injury. Currently, I work in Ireland, but in the past I have worked in the UK and in New Zealand. My research background is principally in qualitative research exploring the experience of living with aphasia. Qualitative research has parallels with a narrative approach to practice. Both are driven by a desire to understand the contextualised perspectives of individuals and both assume that knowledge is jointly created within a dynamic state of flux. I am an avid tennis player and I love dance. I believe that these also resonate with narrative practice. Each is co-constructed and the satisfaction and joy in taking part relies on the skills and experience of all involved. Similarly, a narrative approach to practice requires that both people work together to explore and co-construct a way to manage a particular situation at a particular point in time in a way that feels comfortable for the individuals concerned.

For me, a narrative approach to practice means practice that is guided by the person's story. This shapes how both the person and the practitioner work together in bringing about a "revision" of that story in the context of the past and incorporating the future.

Setting the narrative context

Listening well is our most important clinical tool. This was highlighted by Arthur Kleinman when he stated that "Each patient brings to the practitioner a story. That story enmeshes the disease in a web of meanings that make sense only in the context of a particular life" (Kleinman, 1988, p. 96). Yet, all too often in the busyness of contemporary healthcare, listening well takes second stage, as it does not feel enough like a clinical action (Charon, 2006). Both Hippocrates (460–370 BC) and Plato (428–348 BC) attributed great importance to listening to their patients. However, they differed in what they valued from listening. Hippocrates valued listening as a means to gain enough information to cure the person. He is acknowledged as being a significant influence in what we now refer to as Western medicine. Plato's listening, on the other hand, focused more on open dialogue with the patient in order to gain information about their ideas and resources that they could use in solution making: he presumed that the patient held valuable knowledge (Duchan, 2011). Perhaps Plato is the ancient founder of what I refer to as a narrative approach to practice.

Charon (2004) advises that the skills required for narrative practice include the ability to "recognize, absorb, interpret, and be moved by the stories one hears and reads" (p. 862). In this way we enter into a relationship with the person, thereby lifting the encounter from merely the gathering of data (Frank, 1998). Narrative is a meaning-making tool that allows a person to maintain and renegotiate their identity after a life-altering event such as an acquired brain injury (Shadden, Hagstrom, & Koski, 2008). It helps to uncover how disruption is experienced and how continuity is created (Becker, 1999).

Healing power of narrative

It is well documented that hearing a person's story is both therapeutic and empowering. People talk about their experience in order to find coherence through time and to contain and find meaning in it. In this way, narrative weaves disruption into the fabric of life (e.g., Becker, 1999; Gwyn, 2002; Mattingly, 1998). By witnessing and listening to the person's story, we implicitly value the individual and so bolster confidence (e.g., Charon, 2006; Swain, Clark, Parry, French, & Reynolds, 2004; White & Epston, 1990). It helps us to focus on *who* the person is in relation to *what* they want, rather than *how* they are (e.g., Gwyn, 2002; Nelson, 2001).

Many people come to us when they are in a "liminal space" (Mattingly, 1998), or what Becker (1999) refers to as "living-in-limbo". This refers to the in between time following a life-altering event when the person is not who he was, yet has not emerged as a new kind of person. A narrative approach to practice is well suited to supporting the person during this "revision" of his self-narrative while at the same time helping him to keep in touch with his multiple selves. Stories are a way of "re-drawing maps and finding new destinations" (Frank, 1995).

Cultural, public, and personal narratives

The social meaning of brain injury and disability influences how the person and others make sense of it and accommodate it into daily life (Swain, Clark, Parry, French, & Reynolds, 2004). Our experience of events is informed by, and integrated within, one or more cultural, social, public, and/or personal narratives (i.e., the stories we live by). This guides how we behave. Traditionally, Western society values those who are independent and who are able to walk, talk, hear, see, and who have mental agility. Indeed, our society is designed around people who have these abilities. Therefore, following brain injury, it is common to hear people talk about their "battle" to recover and many feel pressure to hide their disability in order to fit within a society that values people of "normal" abilities.

Many people, particularly those with "invisible" impairments such as aphasia, choose to conceal their difficulties so that they will not be judged as disabled. I remember one person telling me about how he would make a "judgement call" as to whether or not to "bluff" his way through an interaction when he was having difficulty in understanding what was being said. Consequently, there were times when he did not have access to important information for fear of revealing himself as disabled. Cant (1997) writes about his fear of being judged "less worthy" due to his difficulty in talking following a stroke. Similarly, Boazman (2003) reports how she used to draw attention to her previous occupation and status in order to strengthen her self-esteem and to reaffirm her sense of competence in the context of aphasia. The social model of disability advocates an alternative view, whereby people are *dis*-abled more by society than by the impairment (e.g., Shakespeare, 2006).

These narratives, often hidden, that we hold about brain injury, disability, and healthcare can influence the therapeutic event (e.g., Kleinman, 1988). They set the background tone, so, as practitioners, we need to reflect on our own constructions of brain injury and communication disability and the role they play in shaping how we practise (see Reflective box 1 at the end of the chapter).

Conceptual narrative frameworks

A number of frameworks surrounding illness and disability have emerged in the literature. Arthur Frank (1995) was one of the first to conceptualise illness within a narrative context. He identified three main illness narratives: *restitution*, when illness is viewed as transitory with a focus on remedy, *chaos*, when illness overwhelms as if life's map is lost, and *quest*, when illness is met head on and alternative ways of understanding illness are sought and incorporated into daily life. Other frameworks have since emerged. For example, Crossley (2000) identified a number of narrative types in her study of people living in the context of HIV positivity, and four main narrative types emerged in Mitchell, Skirton, and Monrouxe's (2011) study exploring narrative in people with aphasia. Both Crossley's and Mitchell and colleagues' narrative types resonate with Frank's illness narratives. Many people find such conceptual frameworks helpful in tolerating their illness experience (e.g., Weingarten, 2001). However, Frank (1995, 1998) cautions practitioners that such schemas can objectify the person and advises that they are useful only as listening devices for us to understand, rather than decode, what is heard.

Hydén (1997) proposes three types of illness narratives that differ conceptually from those proposed by Frank and others. First, he describes *illness as narrative*, which is the story the person tells about their illness experience; second, *narrative about illness*, where the narrative conveys information about the illness (common in the talk of health-care workers); and third, *narrative as illness*, when the difficulty in telling their story contributes to the illness experience itself. It is this third narrative type that places people with communication disability at particular risk, due to the inherent difficulties of having their voice heard. So, the very nature of the impairment brought on by brain injury can compound the person's sense of isolation and suffering.

Brain injury and communication disability

Communication abilities may be affected in many different ways following brain injury (e.g., aphasia, dysarthria, right hemisphere language impairment—see glossary for descriptions). For the purposes of this chapter, I am drawing primarily from working with people with aphasia. People with aphasia (sometimes referred to as dysphasia) know what they want to say but find it difficult to translate their thoughts into words as well as in interpreting spoken and written language. Jasvinder Khosa, a person with aphasia, explains, "I do not have the stamina to follow conversations. After a few minutes my ears, my mind, are exhausted . . . I cannot keep pace . . . At times, I'm very much an onlooker, not a player" (Khosa, 2003, p.12).

Risks associated with communication disability

Not only do difficulties in communication place people at three times greater risk of having a preventable adverse event (Bartlett, Blais, Tamblyn, & Clermont, 2008), but also the presence of communication disability significantly increases the likelihood of experiencing "high distress" following stroke when compared with those who do not have communication disability (Hilari et al., 2010). "Suffering arises not only from the experience of bodily disruption but also from the *difficulty of articulating that disruption*" (Becker, 1999, p. 39, my italics). As feelings of isolation have been found to be correlated with distress, Hilari and colleagues speculated that their findings reflected the subjective sense of isolation experienced by those participants with aphasia. Alan Hewitt, a person with aphasia, has reported that the social isolation of aphasia is profound and that most of his friends faded away following his stroke (Hewitt & Byng, 2003).

Feelings of well-being have been found to be directly related to the degree to which disability affects the person's sense of identity (Clarke, 2003). One's sense of self and the ability to manage identity change are particularly vulnerable for people with communication disability, as it is through communication and storytelling that we construct and negotiate our identity (Shadden, Hagstrom, & Koski, 2008). Sue Boazman, who has aphasia, views her ability to speak as a "reflection of my personality, the very core of my being and vital to my sanity" (2003, p. 34). It is crucial that people with communication disability have their voices genuinely heard in order to have "who they are" acknowledged and validated.

I believe that the presence of communication disability can jeopardise the goal-setting process as well as reduce opportunities for the person to engage in therapy due to the challenges of having their story heard. Therefore, given the risks associated with living in the context of communication disability, the importance of making a narrative approach to practice accessible is critical. Jasvinder Khosa, who has aphasia, points out, "People with communication disabilities need fair access to services. It is vitally important for us that service providers learn how to respect our needs and to make their services accessible. Otherwise we are lost" (Khosa, quoted in Parr, Wimborne, Hewitt, & Pound, 2008, p. 10).

If we, as practitioners, are not able to find out about the individual's experience of living with brain injury, then we will not be able to engage meaningfully with that person. It follows, then, that if we do not support communication appropriately to make the range of our services accessible, we risk discriminating against people with communication disability.

Making narrative practice accessible

Legislation around the world states that we must make every effort to ensure that information and communication is accessible so that people can avail themselves of different services (e.g., United Nations General Assembly, 2006). Therefore, we have a duty to do everything practicable to make a narrative approach to practice accessible so that people with communication disability can benefit. We need to be mindful that "People realize themselves through dialogue with others, *others can block that realization*" (Frank, 2004, p. 23, my italics).

It is through communication that we connect with others to share such things as information, humour, "a bit of ourselves". It is the foundation upon which relationships develop and grow and our identities are acknowledged and validated. The tone and style of interactions are shaped by many factors, such as degree of formality, the context, the relationship between the participants, the emotional backdrop, etc., as well as the actual purpose of the meeting. Most conversations have natural ebb and flow, as such things as rate of speech, tone of voice, and vocabulary used are mirrored while the turns are passed effortlessly between participants. Or, to draw on my love of dance, effective and/or enjoyable communication is like a well choreographed routine. It is the combined ability and skilled synchronicity of both partners working together that results in that sense of satisfaction and achievement. It might take a while to find the right timing and rhythm with a new dance partner, but it soon falls into place. Similarly, for communication to feel natural and effortless, each participant has to get a *feel* for the rhythm that makes up the ebb and flow of that conversation. It is this synchronised subtle timing that helps us to feel comfortable, confident, and free to reveal and be who we are.

The benefits reaped from a narrative approach to practice are underpinned by effective communication. When someone has a communication disability, the usual "rules" of conversation are altered. Both conversation partners need to work harder to establish a natural rhythm to communication that works best for them in the context of their combined abilities. In this section, I propose a number of techniques and tools that might be useful to consider when working with someone with communication disability. By *techniques*, I mean specific things to keep in mind, and by *tools*, I refer to things "out there" that might be helpful as ways into hearing the person's story. Neither the techniques nor the tools that I discuss are new; indeed, many of them may be familiar to you. They are not intended to be used "cookbook style"; rather, they should be weaved sensitively into the fabric of the conversation as a means to support the person to tell her story, to have it heard, and to explore her issues and concerns.

Techniques

The temporal rules that govern "normal" communication contribute to the social exclusion of people with communication disability and particularly those with aphasia (Parr, Paterson, & Pound, 2003). Turid deMare, a woman with aphasia, explains,

> . . . I'm feeling often that the voice, internal voice, it is in your head but I can't tell you, and I think a lot of certain things that I can't tell you, but it is there . . . the thinking comes from both of us . . . both of us have to think. (Penman & deMare, 2003, p. 97)

Therefore, many of the techniques central to supporting communication effectively can be corralled under one key theme: *time and timing*. It is the taken for granted timing of the flow of communication that can compound the experience of disability. An awareness of timing and pace, therefore, is one of the most important techniques in making narrative practice accessible for people with communication disability. Following her stroke, Jill Bolte Taylor (2008) found that the impatient communication style of her doctor dictated the pace of their conversations, resulting in neither of them being satisfied. "Caring begins by respecting the pace of those being cared for" (Frank, 2004, p. 139).

Attentiveness

Attentiveness and *being mindful* is particularly relevant when working with people with communication disability, as it helps us to tune in to the rhythm of communication. It emphasises the need for us to be in the present; it allows us to attend to the ordinary as well as the obvious (Epstein, 1999), and to make those minute online adjustments necessary to ensure conversational flow. Earlier, I mentioned my love of both tennis and dance; both remind me that if I pay too much attention to the different muscle movements necessary to play a specific shot or make a dance move, then inevitably the result is awkward and stilted. Similarly, if our attention to the timing and pace of communication becomes overly conscious and detailed, then the natural ebb and flow of conversation is lost. Being attentive and aware reminds us of the importance of absorbing and responding to *what* and *how* the person is communicating, rather than focusing too much on what we have to do.

Being in the present allows one to capitalise on the strengths and abilities of both communication partners. For example, people with aphasia skilfully and naturally use many techniques blended together to communicate what they want to say in the context of a compromised language processing system. We need to be attentive and attuned to both non-verbal and verbal aspects of communication (e.g., posture, facial expression, movement/stillness, tone of voice, rate of speech, gesture, eye gaze). How we frame questions and the words we select shapes how the person responds. Reflecting their choice of words and mode of communication can open up the space for them to feel comfortable and competent in the telling of their story. We need to listen "as an instrument of the speaker" (Charon, 2006, p. 58).

Being present in silence

Central to being attuned to timing and pace, as well as content, is respecting silence. Being present in silence provides an opportunity not only for reflection, but also for time-out from language overload. Therefore, it takes on even greater significance when communicating with people with aphasia, as it provides them with the processing space necessary to interpret what has been said, to retrieve words, and to formulate a response. For some, if their word search is interrupted too quickly by an eager conversation partner, the process is derailed, resulting in the need to restart the search, thus adding to frustration. Invariably, the person will give a subtle signal when they require assistance (e.g., going from averted eyes during the search to making eye contact). Being present in silence helps people with communication disability to feel genuinely listened to and part of the conversation, thus avoiding a feeling of being on "the edges of the conversation".

Use of questions

When someone experiences specific difficulties in saying what she wants to say, we might be lured into using closed and yes/no questions in an attempt to find out relevant information. However, over-directed interviewing might obscure the very issues we need to be aware of (Gwyn, 2002; Mattingly, 1998). While the use of both closed and yes/no questions are useful techniques to support communication, hearing a person's story is not a "tick-box" exercise. The importance of exploring whether there are other options other than those we place on the table, checking that our understanding or version of the story is the same as theirs, and "inviting" the person to correct us, are all integral parts of a narrative approach to practice. If structured directed interviewing is necessary to support the person to tell their story, then the way in which it is done is crucial. This means resisting a traditional biomedical "fix-it" role and putting on the radar to prevent over-directive questioning. This, together with an awareness of things such as our own posture and bearing, our use of silence, the rate of our speech, our tone of voice, and so on, allows the person to feel free to correct us and to add additional information.

Record of meeting

People with communication disability often find it harder to recollect what has been spoken about, making it difficult to reflect on what transpired during the meeting, to share this with others, and to consider their "story" of living with brain injury. Jotting down a summary of key points that were discussed and agreed for the person to take away can be a helpful reminder (Parr, Wimborne, Hewitt, & Pound, 2008). In this way, "pegs" are provided upon which the person can construct his story during the course of your work together and beyond.

Tools

The use of a variety of resources or tools can be helpful in supporting a person to tell their story and to engage in therapy. Lorenz (2010) comments that "Visuals—photographs, videos, drawing, or paintings—may enhance the ability of patients to talk about topics that are difficult to articulate or embarrassing" (p. 159). Here, I am placing tools under two main headings: "pen and paper" and "other resources". For them to be effective, they need to be meaningful for the individual concerned as well as being naturally introduced and sensitively woven into the fabric of the conversation and purpose of the meeting.

Pen and paper

The use of pen and paper by both the person and the practitioner can be invaluable to support communication, to elicit information that may otherwise remain hidden, to facilitate the goal-setting process, and to track change over time.

While reading and writing abilities can be affected following brain injury and, indeed, people have varying degrees of literacy prior to brain injury, they are, none the less, helpful in supporting the person to tell their story. The paper itself acts as a shared resource for the conversation, as it is the site upon which both the person and the practitioner can write a key word, the first few letters of a word, draw a diagram or picture, and list things. In this way, it becomes a live dynamic document that acts as a point of reference for what has been discussed, what is currently in discussion, and what might be discussed at a later time. This co-constructed paper "narrative", while making little sense to anyone other than those involved in its creation, becomes a useful tool for verification, as both parties can use it to check and recheck things that have been discussed and/or agreed. In addition, it acts as a resource to repair communication breakdown as well as to thicken the story, making it more real.

A person who is finding it difficult to say what he wants might be able to write a key word or the first letter of the word, thus providing a clue. The conversation partner can then ask questions around that clue to try to establish what it is the person is trying to communicate. Similarly, the practitioner may write a key word in order to verify what the person has communicated. In this way, an online co-constructed record is created that can provide a point of reference as the conversation proceeds.

Drawings and diagrams created as part of the conversation can also provide a way in to talk about the issues and concerns that the person might wish to discuss. I remember some time ago working with a young man following brain injury who had significant difficulties in both interpreting and expressing spoken language. However, he spontaneously drew to tell me about his experience of living in the context of aphasia and the meaning it held for him. His drawings were not what one would consider "works of art", but they were vibrant and alive and told his story in a rich and accessible way. Early on, the pages were dominated by a collage of diagrams, word fragments, and drawings that told of his feelings of isolation as compared with his people-filled life prior to brain injury. These discussions formed the basis of our work together as we explored options for him to re-engage with life again in the context of aphasia. Later, more hopeful stories appeared on the pages, depicting a life becoming filled with activities, albeit different from his life prior to injury. These seemingly random pages of conversations acted as a way in to goal setting, as well as a means to track change over time. Likewise, creating diagrams "online" to reflect the externalisation of a problem act as both a useful point of reference and a springboard to discuss goals and to thicken "unique outcomes" (see Barrow, 2011). Also, the Kawa River drawing technique can be used as a metaphor for life and can be another way to explore how a person has managed things in the past, in the present, and how they see the future unfolding (see Cheng, 2010; Iwama, 2010).

Other *pen and paper* techniques that can be embedded into conversations include drawing visual scales that represent time lines, feelings, hopes, etc., and creating lifestyle grids (Jeffers, 1987; see Pound, Parr, Lindsay, & Woolfe, 2000). During the process of using these techniques, opportunities arise to bring to the fore those resources that the person might have forgotten they have that can be thickened during therapy. Discussing issues, steps, and actions using some form of imagery is particularly helpful, as it makes the process more accessible, resulting in fuller engagement. For example, drawing a simple line, pathway, or even a staircase can add clarity and help to support the person in thinking about and working towards her desired goal (Figure 6.1).

Other resources

For many, traditional questioning can shut down what we might need to hear. This is particularly the case for people with communication disability, as they are placed in a situation whereby not only might the story be difficult to tell, but they no longer have easy access to language in order to articulate it. Arts-based methods can help to open up and reveal what the person wants to tell and what we need to hear. They have greater immediacy than language, have stronger emotional appeal, and have the potential to cross the cultural divide. They can help to surface the meaning people attach to brain injury, as well as give insight into the ambiguity of living in the context of disability.

Greetings cards can provide a useful entry point to find out and to gain an understanding of a person's perspective that might otherwise

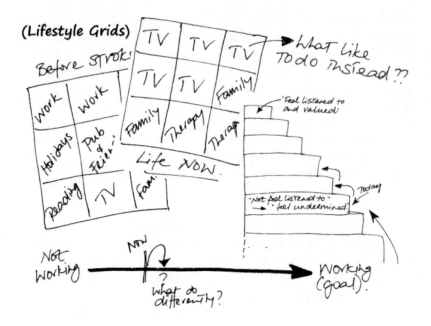

Figure 6.1.   Examples of use of pen and paper.

remain hidden. For example, I have a "deck" of approximately fifty greetings cards collected over the years that I use as a means to support a person to talk about the experience and meanings of living in the context of communication disability. Some people select a card as a concrete representation, while others chose cards that are metaphorical. In this way, a person's narrative can be given "voice" through imagery (Barrow, 2008). I remember a woman, about ten years following the onset of aphasia, selecting a card of Van Gogh's field of sunflowers for how her life was now, saying that things were "ordinary" even though she "couldn't speak". Later, she selected a postcard depicting a lonely figure in blue mist standing in the distance under a tree for how she saw the future. For me, this card has a lonely, eerie feel, and I remember being somewhat surprised at her choice given our previous discussion about her life being "ordinary". On exploring why she selected this particular card, a story emerged of her fear of the future without her mother, to whom she was very close. This then led to conversations about preparing for such a time. The use of greetings cards can also reveal the ambiguous nature of living in the context of disability. Previously, I reported on a woman, "Anne", who selected two cards to represent the ambiguity of living with aphasia: Picasso's *Weeping Woman*, which depicts a woman's face in fragments, crying, and Van Gogh's field of sunflowers (Barrow, 2008). Again the use of imagery provided a way in to understanding the experience of living in the context of brain injury that was not readily articulated and that might otherwise have remained hidden.

Both photo-elicitation and photovoice can be useful techniques to generate discussion and share experiences of individuals' life-worlds. Photo-elicitation is the term used to describe the discussion generated around photographs a person has taken. It increases understanding of the person's experience and the meaning attached to it. Photovoice, on the other hand, refers to the discussion about photos within a group, resulting in the sharing of multiple perspectives. Photovoice can be particularly useful in opening doors to alternative narratives of disability. Lorenz (2010) carried out a study with people with brain injury using both photo-elicitation and photovoice, and found that it provided her with a different understanding of individuals' experience of living in the context of brain injury that she would not otherwise have gained. She gave participants throw-away cameras and asked them to take photographs of whatever they felt reflected their life with brain injury. These photos then guided conversations about their experience. She found that both photo-elicitation and photovoice helped to "put a biographical disruption such as brain injury into perspective in a lived life" (Lorenz, 2010, p. 148). Requesting the person to generate their own photos allows the person to hold the power through both the creation and the sharing of images.

Wilson and Long's (2009) book of *Blob Trees* is based on their original Blob Tree (sometimes referred to as the "tree of life"), published in 1988. The Blob Tree is not gender, race, or age specific. It depicts "blob people" in different poses on a tree; for example, one sits alone at the end of a branch, another stands proudly at the top of the tree, a couple sit arm in arm on another branch, another hangs on to the tree trunk, and so on. The tree can be used to stimulate discussion about a wide variety of things relevant in life. For example, it can be used to gain insight into how a person views things at different points in time by asking them to locate themselves on the tree to reflect those times. I remember a woman with aphasia selecting two figures on the tree to reflect her current life. One was of a figure clutching on to the trunk of the tree, while the other was of a couple sitting arm in arm on one of the branches. In this way the Blob Tree revealed something that went against the problem-saturated story that characterised our meetings up until that time. This "unique outcome" was then explored and thickened in therapy. The Blob Tree can provide a springboard and a point of reference for in-depth conversations related to living with brain injury and as a means to support the goal-setting process and tracking change over time.

The Communication Disability Profile (Swinburn with Byng, 2006) was developed to enable people to express their experience and views of living in the context of aphasia. It consists of a number of picture resources that are designed to explore activities, participation, external influences, and emotions. Integral to its design is the use of diverse depictions sensitive to age, gender, and racial background. This, together with the pictographic resources developed by the Aphasia Institute in Canada (Kagan & Shumway, 2003), is extremely useful to have to hand to support conversations around engaging with life in the context of communication disability (see Appendix 2).

Using stones as a dynamic visual method to explore friendship, Pound (2010) asks people with aphasia to select from an array of stones of different sizes, shapes, and colours to represent people whom they consider friends and to place them in relation to themselves and others. The use of stones in this way can open up discussions about an individual's family and social network as well as how he or she views themselves within such networks in the past, now, and into the future. A photograph can then be taken of the "collage of stones" so that change can be tracked and discussed.

Using these simple techniques and tools provides a means for the person's voice to be heard and acknowledged, so that issues and concerns regarding living in the context of communication disability can be addressed. In addition, they allow one to explore what Thomas (2007) refers to as "impairment effects" (i.e., those restrictions that cannot be environmentally or socially manipulated), "barriers-to-doing" (i.e., environmental and social obstacles that affect *what* we can *do*), and "barriers-to-being" (i.e., hurtful and hostile behaviour of others that affect *who* we can *be* and how we feel about ourselves now and in the future). In this way, the challenges of living in the context of impairment and disability can be externalised and broken up into manageable pieces and addressed.

As with *techniques*, we fit the *tools* we use to support the telling of the story to the specific needs and preferred communication style of the individual concerned. The resources outlined above are not an exhaustive list and inevitably some will work better with some individuals than with others. It is a question of trial and error.

In line with the principles of narrative therapy, being creative and using a variety of techniques and tools provides an entry point to finding out about the sometimes latent resources of the individual that can be thickened and capitalised upon in moving towards a preferred future. During the process, alternative stories of disability might be illuminated, opening the door to other ways of thinking about living in the context of brain injury. Such alternative narratives can nurture feelings of self-esteem and self-worth, as well as the development of a robust "new" identity incorporating communication disability that commands respect (e.g., Barrow, 2008; Nelson, 2001; Pound, Parr, Lindsay, & Woolf, 2000). Many people with communication disability have told of finding new meaning in life as a result of brain injury (e.g., Bolte Taylor, 2008; Khosa, 2003).

Sharing perspectives

Participating in groups provides a valuable context for people to surface a range of stories of living with communication disability. A group context, either formal or a less structured peer-led drop-in format (see Pound, 2011), creates an opportunity for people to share different perspectives of living in the context of brain injury (Lorenz, 2010) and communication disability (Pound, 2011). For example, participating in a group might help individuals to move from the endless "battle" to win the "war" over stroke (Boylstein, Rittman, & Hinojosa, 2007). Particularly for those people where "restitution" is not forthcoming, groups can create a space for other metaphors of brain injury recovery to emerge, thereby enabling the person to feel less isolated and to move forward. In this way, group discussions open the door to alternative constructions of disability that allow people to "think differently about being different" (Swain & French, 2008).

Documentation

As discussed, the use of pen and paper, together with a variety of visual methods, can play an important part in making therapy services more accessible for people with communication disability. Therefore, what documents we develop and how we create them take on even greater significance.

White and Epston (1990) refer to traditional documents in clinical practice as "rituals of exclusion". They suggest that alternative documents need to be developed with the person to transform them into "rituals of inclusion". There are a number of ways we can respond to this call: for example, co-constructing the note together for the health-care record (Mann, 2002), the writing up and/or sharing of a report of the meeting (Pound, Parr, Lindsay, & Woolf, 2000), and developing a handout of their experience and advice for others (Barrow, 2011). The actual process of creating such documents provides opportunities for conversations about their experience that might otherwise remain unspoken. For example, I remember working with a woman with aphasia and it was not until she decided to develop a handout for her family and friends to tell them about aphasia and what it meant for her that some of the significant challenges of bringing up rebellious teenagers in the context of communication disability emerged in any depth. While previous conversations had touched on some of the issues of managing her teenage children, it was the conversations around the development of the handout that acted as a springboard to identify and explore how she could rekindle her many innate resources to manage the delicate and challenging parent–teenager conversations that arose.

When writing documents, we need to take into account the person's ability to read. Many people with aphasia find reading difficult. Therefore, paying particular attention to making documents accessible for the intended audience becomes even more important. See Appendix 1 for tips to make documents more accessible and Appendix 2 for a list of useful resources.

Getting there

For people to reap the benefits of a narrative approach to practice, we need to ensure that they arrive with the energy and frame of mind to engage in the process. Wendy, a woman with aphasia, comments, "The doctor hadn't sent a map. I didn't know. Someone said down there, right, left. I didn't have an inkling. I was thoroughly fed up. By the time I eventually got there I was going slow" (Wendy, quoted in

Parr, Wimborne, Hewitt, & Pound, 2008). The potential barriers that a person may face in accessing and navigating their way through the service need to be acknowledged. Figure 6.2 provides a "map" of just some of the things we need to consider in this regard. This is based on the work undertaken by Parr and colleagues (2008) in the development of the Communication Access Toolkit. This conceptualises communication access within three overlapping domains—interactions, documents, and environments, which they refer to as the "Communication Access Triangle". Considering access in this way helps us to think about, and get a handle on, the many obstacles that people with communication disability might face in accessing services. Minimising potential barriers before the person arrives helps to ensure that they have the energy to be able to tell their story and so gain maximum benefit from the service. (See Appendix 1 for tips on making services accessible.)

I have outlined only some ideas on how to make a narrative approach to practice accessible for people with communication disability as a consequence of brain injury. I have focused on visual and arts-based methods as they can help to reveal what we need to hear, they allow for surprises to come to the fore and they can un-stick routine ways of practice. In particular they are valuable in engaging the person as an active participant in guiding the therapy process. It

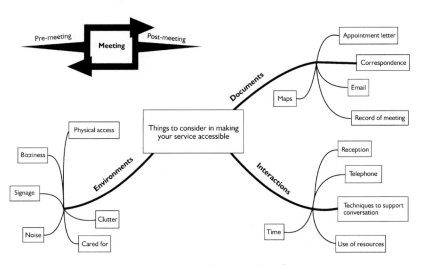

Figure 6.2.   Making your service accessible. Based on the *Connect Communication Access Triangle* (Parr, Wimborne, Hewitt, & Pound, 2008).

can be daunting first meeting someone with communication disability and it can take a while to identify the techniques and tools that are most effective for your work together. The person best placed to advise on this is the person with the communication disability, either through asking them directly or by observing and exploring what works well and what doesn't.

Conclusion

The premise of a narrative approach to practice is that the person's story is heard: "To give the gift of listening is to appreciate receiving the gift of a story" (Frank, 1998, p. 200). It is this that is the foundation of co-constructed therapy that meets the individual's specific issues and priorities in moving towards a preferred future. In so doing, it fulfils what "service users" identify as important in person-centred support, which is supporting choice and control, having the opportunity to set their own goals, to be listened to, and to have a relationship of trust and openness (Glynn et al., 2008). People with communication disability have a right to equal access to services. Sometimes, the very nature of their impairment denies them this right, albeit unintentionally. This needs to be addressed through appropriately supporting communication, so that the person's story is genuinely heard, thereby allowing him or her to engage fully in the therapy process. By using just a few simple techniques and tools, we can make communication access a reality in a narrative approach to practice. In so doing we all benefit, particularly those with communication disability.

Reflective box I

Reflecting on your own narratives of brain injury and communication disability

- If you had a "deck" of greetings cards, postcards, photographs, and other images, which one would you choose to represent communication disability? Why that particular image?
- What goes through your mind when a person with communication disability is referred to you?
- What are your thoughts and expectations of their ability to participate and engage in therapy and in achieving their goals?
- What are your thoughts about *your* ability to work with that person?

Reflective box 2

Think of a person with communication disability with whom you have worked.

- What did you do to support communication so that the person could tell their story? What worked well? In hindsight, what could you have done differently?
- What helped you to record their story and piece it together over time? Is there anything else that would have helped?
- Thinking about the assessments and resources that you use, how accessible are they for people with communication disability? How could you make them more accessible?

Appendix 1: Enabling telling and listening to stories: tips to make communication accessible

Interactions

"Sometimes people talk too quickly . . . words are spinning in my head. Time—give me time. That's very important." (Person with aphasia)

- Adapt talk by using a relaxed natural pace, clear jargon-free use of language, signalling topic change.
- Support talk by writing key words, drawing, using everyday resources (e.g., maps, calendar), specific resources (e.g., diagrams, photos).
- Tune in to the person's cues by being alert to their verbal and non-verbal signals.
- Acknowledge if you do not understand and recap.
- Verify that you have interpreted correctly.

Documents

"Oh, if it's too much . . . I don't bother, I leave it." (Person with aphasia)

- Use clear headings.
- Use bullet points with one idea per bullet.
- Use increased amount of white space between lines of print.
- Keep grammar clear (e.g., avoid passive tense).
- No jargon or acronyms.

- Use lower case as it provides word shape.
- Use a sans serif 12–14 point font (e.g., Arial, Tahoma, Verdana).
- Emphasise key words in bold.
- Sensitive use of appropriate diagrams, pictures, and/or symbols.

Environments

"When I go into somewhere messy . . . I get confusion of what I am thinking and what I want to communicate." (Jasvinder, person with aphasia, quoted in Parr, Wimborne, Hewitt, & Pound, 2008)

- Calm, cared for, and welcoming.
- Clear signage and way-finding.
- Uncluttered.
- Seating and positioning.
- Access to a table for writing.
- Choice and control.

Appendix 2: List of useful resources

Better Conversations: A Guide for Relatives of People with Communication Disability (2005). Connect – the Communication Disability Network. Available from: www.ukconnect.org.

Caring and Coping: A Guide for People with Aphasia, their Family and Friends (2009). Connect – the Communication Disability Network. Available from: www.ukconnect.org

Communication Access: Guidelines and Resources on Communicating with People Who Have Communication Disabilities (2009) Available to download: www.mcss.gov.on.ca.

Making Information Accessible: Guidelines for Producing Accessible Printed and Electronic Information (2010). SAIF – Scottish Accessible Information Forum. Available to download: www.saifscotland.org.uk.

Parr, S. (2004). *The Stroke and Aphasia Handbook*. Connect – the Communication Disability Network. Available from: www.ukconnect.org

Sunderland, M., & Engleheart, P. (1993). *Draw on Your Emotions: Creative Ways to Explore, Express and Understand Important Feelings*. Milton Keynes: Speechmark.

Weiss, B. (2007). *Health Literacy and Patient Safety: Help Patients Understand*. American Medical Association Foundation. Available to download: www.amafoundation.org/go/healthliteracy.

References

Barrow, R. (2008). Listening to the voice of living life with aphasia: Anne's story. *International Journal of Language & Communication Disorders*, 43(S1): 30–46.

Barrow, R. (2011). Shaping practice: the benefits of really attending to the person's story. In: R. Fourie (Ed.), *Therapeutic Processes for Communication Disorders* (pp. 21–34). Hove: Psychology Press.

Bartlett, G., Blais, R., Tamblyn, R., & Clermont, R. (2008). Impact of patient communication problems on the risk of preventable adverse events in acute care settings. *CMAJ*, 178(12): 1555–1562.

Becker, G. (1999). *Disrupted Lives: How People Create Meaning in a Chaotic World*. Berkeley, CA: University of California Press.

Boazman, S. (2003). A time of transition: a matter of confidence and control. In: S. Parr, J. Duchan, & C. Pound (Eds.), *Aphasia Inside Out: Reflections on Communication Disability* (pp. 32–40). Maidenhead: Open University Press.

Bolte Taylor, J. (2008). *My Stroke of Insight: A Brain Scientist's Personal Journey*. London: Hodder & Stoughton.

Boylstein, C., Rittman, M., & Hinojosa, R. (2007). Metaphor shifts in stroke recovery. *Health Communication*, 21(3): 279–287.

Cant, R. (1997). Rehabilitation following a stroke: a participant perspective. *Disability & Rehabilitation*, 19(7): 297–304.

Charon, R. (2004). Narrative medicine. *New England Journal of Medicine*. Feb 26: 862–864.

Charon, R. (2006). *Narrative Medicine: Honoring the Stories of Illness*. New York: Oxford University Press.

Cheng, I. (2010). Transforming practice: reflections on the use of art to develop professional knowledge and reflective practice. *Reflective Practice*, 11(4): 489–498.

Clarke, P. (2003). Towards a greater understanding of the experience of stroke: integrating quantitative and qualitative methods. *Journal of Aging Studies*, 17: 171–187.

Crossley, M. (2000). *Introducing Narrative Psychology: Self, Trauma and the Construction of Meaning*. Buckingham: Open University Press.

Duchan, J. (2011). The social constructions of relationships in healing interactions from ancient times to present. In: R. Fourie (Ed.), *Therapeutic Processes for Communication Disorders* (pp. 153–165). Hove: Psychology Press.

Epstein, R. M. (1999). Mindful practice. *Journal of the American Medical Association*, 282(9): 833–839.

Frank, A. W. (1995). *The Wounded Storyteller: Body, Illness, and Ethics*. Chicago, IL: University of Chicago Press.

Frank, A. W. (1998). Just listening: narrative and deep illness. *Families, Systems & Health*, 16(3): 197–212.

Frank, A. W. (2004). *The Renewal of Generosity: Illness, Medicine, and How to Live*. Chicago, IL: Chicago University Press.

Glynn, M., & Beresford, P., with Bewley, C., Branfield, F., Butt, J., Croft, S., Dattani Pitt, K., Fleming, J., Flynn, R., Patmore, C., Postle, K., & Turner, M. (2008). Person-centred support: what service users and practitioners say. Joseph Rowntree Foundation (www.jrf.org.uk).

Gwyn, R. (2002). *Communicating Health and Illness*. London: Sage.

Hewitt, A., & Byng, S. (2003). From doing to being: from participation to engagement. In: S. Parr, J. Duchan, & C. Pound (Eds.), *Aphasia Inside Out: Reflections on Communication Disability* (pp. 51–64). Maidenhead: Open University Press.

Hilari, K., Northcott, S., Roy, P., Marshall, J., Wiggins, R., Chataway, J., & Ames, D. (2010). Psychological distress after stroke and aphasia: the first six months. *Clinical Rehabilitation*, 24: 181–190.

Hydén, L.-C. (1997). Illness and narrative. *Sociology of Health & Illness*, 19(1): 48–69.

Iwama, M. (2010). Kawa Model. www.kawamodel.com.

Jeffers, S. (1987). *Feel the Fear and Do It Anyway*. London: Arrow.

Kagan, A., & Shumway, E. (2003).*Talking to Your . . . Interactive Resources for People and their Health Practitioners*. Toronto: Aphasia Institute. Available from: www.aphasia.ca.

Khosa, J. (2003). Still life of a chameleon: aphasia and its impact on identity. In: S. Parr, J. Duchan, & C. Pound (Eds.), *Aphasia Inside Out: Reflections on Communication Disability* (pp. 10–20). Maidenhead: Open University Press.

Kleinman, A. (1988). *The Illness Narratives: Suffering, Healing and the Human Condition*. New York: Basic Books.

Lorenz, L. (2010). *Brain Injury Survivors: Narratives of Rehabilitation and Healing*. Boulder, CO: Lynne Rienner.

Mann, S. (2002). Narrative ideas in practice. *Gecko: A Journal of Deconstruction & Narrative Ideas in Therapeutic Practice*, 2: 39–49 (www.dulwichcentre.com.au).

Mattingly, C. (1998). *Healing Dramas and Clinical Plots: The Narrative Structure of Experience*. Cambridge: Cambridge University Press.

Mitchell, K., Skirton, H., & Monrouxe, L. (2011). Amelioration, regeneration, acquiescent and discordant: an exploration of narrative types and metaphor use in people with aphasia. *Disability & Society*, 26(3): 321–335.

Nelson, H. L. (2001). *Damaged Identities, Narrative Repair*. Ithaca, NY: Cornell University Press.

Parr, S., Paterson, K., & Pound, C. (2003). Time please! Temporal barriers in aphasia. In: S. Parr, J. Duchan, & C. Pound (Eds.), *Aphasia Inside Out: Reflections on Communication Disability* (pp. 127–144). Maidenhead: Open University Press.

Parr, S., Wimborne, N., Hewitt, A., & Pound, C. (2008). *The Communication Access Toolkit*. London: Connect Press. Information available at: www.ukconnect.org.

Penman, T., & deMare, T. (2003). Changing places: reflections of therapists and group members of the power and potential of groups. In: S. Parr, J. Duchan, & C. Pound (Eds.), *Aphasia Inside Out: Reflections on Communication Disability* (pp. 91–102). Maidenhead: Open University Press.

Pound, C. (2010). Absent friends: including people with aphasia in friendship research. Social perspectives in acquired communication disorders – Colloquium, London 17–18 June 2010. Poster presentation.

Pound, C. (2011). Reciprocity, resources, and relationships: new discourses in healthcare, personal, and social relationships. *International Journal of Speech–Language Pathology*, 13(3): 197–206.

Pound, C., Parr, S., Lindsay, J., & Woolf, C. (2000). *Beyond Aphasia: Therapies for Living with Communication Disability*. London: Winslow Press.

Shadden, B., Hagstrom, F., & Koski, P. (2008). *Neurogenic Communication Disorders: Life Stories and the Narratives of Self*. San Diego, CA: Plural.

Shakespeare, T. (2006). *Disability Rights and Wrongs*. London: Routledge.

Swain, J., & French, S. (2008). *Disability on Equal Terms*. London: Sage.

Swain, J., Clark, J., Parry, K., French, S., & Reynolds, F. (2004). *Enabling Relationships in Health and Social Care: A Guide for Therapists*. Oxford: Butterworth-Heinemann.

Swinburn, K., with Byng, S. (2006). *The Communication Disability Profile*. London: Connect Publications. Available from: www.ukconnect.org.

Thomas, C. (2007). *Sociologies of Disability and Illness*. New York: Palgrave Macmillan.

United Nations General Assembly (2006). *Conventions on the Rights of Persons with Disabilities*. UN doc A/61/611. www.un.org/esa/socdev/enable/rights/convtexte.htm (accessed 31 August 2013).

Weingarten, K. (2001). *Making Sense of Illness Narratives: Braiding Theory, Practice and the Embodied Life*. www.dulwichcentre.com.au.

White, M., & Epston, D. (1990). *Narrative Means to Therapeutic Ends*. New York, London: W. W. Norton.

Wilson, P., & Long, I. (2009). *The Big Book of Blob Trees*. Milton Keynes: Speechmark.

CHAPTER SEVEN

Helping children create positive stories about a parent's brain injury

Audrey Daisley, Simon Prangnell, and Ruth Seed

Introduction

Acquired brain injury is frequently referred to as a "family affair", with its often devastating effects rippling out to have an impact on not only the injured person, but also those close to them (Lezak, 1988). Substantial research and clinical literature provide excellent guidance for addressing family needs in this context (Kreutzer, Marwitz, Godwin, & Angaro-Lasprilla, 2010), but it has tended to focus on adult relatives with the needs of children in these same families being relatively overlooked (Daisley & Webster, 2008).

In this chapter, we share our experience of working with families affected by brain injuries, with particular focus on the ways in which we have utilised narrative therapy techniques, in the form of narrative therapeutic scrapbooks, to support child relatives. We do this from a number of positions: that of a consultant clinical neuropsychologist (AD) specialised in leading and developing services for families affected by brain injury; as a recently qualified clinical psychologist (SP) with a strong interest in working systemically with families affected by brain injury; and a trainee clinical psychologist (RS) with experience in neuro-behavioural and neuro-rehabilitation settings. Two of us (AD and SP) are also parents, and this has offered us another perspective when considering the needs of distressed young children. Our family support service is located within an National Health Service (NHS) neuro-rehabilitation unit which serves a large number of in and out patients with brain injuries, their families, and carers. The primary focus of our family work is to support the reha- bilitation process and, in doing so, improve both family and individ- ual outcomes. The work we undertake with families is heavily influenced by systemic approaches and, in particular, approaches that draw upon narrative therapy techniques and ideas. However, it is probably important to state that none of us is formally trained in narrative therapy, so it follows that the ideas and approaches to work- ing with children that we offer in this chapter cannot be considered as "pure" in their narrative therapy content as perhaps some of the other work offered throughout this book. However, we are excited by the ideas and possibilities these approaches offer in addressing the needs of this particular group of children.

A child's journey though parental brain injury

You are seven years old and your dad is in hospital. He had an acci- dent last month and everyone has been very worried about him and upset. You do not know how he had the accident, or what really happened but it must be really bad if everyone is crying so much. It is a bit boring going to see him at the hospital but it is funny when he acts a bit strange; he looks like dad but he cannot seem to remember your name and keeps calling you Mark (when your name is really Michael). You think it's funny but mum gets upset if you laugh. Some- times you get upset too, but you do not tell anyone. There are loads of things you want to know though—what really happened to dad? What kind of accident was it? What made it happen? What got hurt— you heard it was his brain. How can you hurt the brain—you can't even see the brain. That can't be true. You hurt your leg once and needed a big plaster on it. Why don't they just put a plaster on dad and then he will be fine. Will this get better? How can dad look just the same but be acting so different—he must be playing a trick on us. When is he going to come home? Will he still be able to watch you play football—there is a match next week and he has already missed two? Is he going to go back to work? . . .

When a parent or close family member sustains a brain injury, children, like their adult counterparts, are abruptly faced with having to manage a whole range of issues, concerns, and challenges. As the example above illustrates, children can be bewildered, confused, and afraid about the impact of this event, have questions about what has happened, about what it will mean for them, and for the rest of the family. They often voice questions and issues that the adult family members have been holding quietly. The dominant themes emerging from the stories that children tell us include: the need to make sense and meaning from what has happened to the parent, the difficulty in understanding the changes and differences they observe between the pre-injury parent and the new, post-injury parent, fears about the future and of grief and loss (of the parent as they were and of family life as it was). Children's accounts also often contain myths and misconceptions about brain injury, especially relating to what they believe to have caused the injury (they frequently blame themselves, and this is typically associated with a range of difficult and conflicting emotions). Crucially, children frequently describe feeling as if their and their family's life stopped when the parent became injured and they express fears about the future and whether life can ever resume some sense of normality again.

Maintenance of a personal narrative is crucial following traumatic and stressful events (Tyerman, 2008), and disruptions in personal narratives are typically associated with greater emotional distress. As such, we were drawn to narrative therapy techniques such as storytelling and metaphor, reauthoring and externalising conversations (White & Epston, 1990) to enable children to create a more coherent, positive, and optimistic account of the parent's brain injury. Narrative techniques were appealing, as alongside children's accounts of loss and fear there was also curiosity and a keenness to tell the story, however difficult. Their accounts were moving and often humorous, and there were stories of hope and possibility that we wished to harness to support children's adjustment to the parent's brain injury.

As such, we found ourselves frequently looking for an alternative, "better fit", and child-friendly way of working with these issues (than the more psycho-educational approaches we had previously been using). Drawing on our interest in narrative therapy, we began to develop therapeutic narrative scrapbooks with children. Douge (2010) notes that this approach "Combines principles of Narrative Therapy with the industry of scrapbooking to provide children with an enjoyable process that enables them to find a new perspective for some of life's difficulties" (p. 684).

This approach to working with children made intuitive sense; storytelling and creative activities appeal to most children, they utilise their existing skills and abilities (which is important at a time when much feels new and unfamiliar to them), and, crucially, the approach places children's own stories and experiences at the heart of the process, positioning them, not the therapists, in the role of expert. Such approaches had been described as being effective in working with children in other contexts similar to our own, for example, therapeutic scrapbooks have been used following bereavement (Kohut, 2011; Maier, 2007), with families in palliative care settings (Allen, Hilgeman, Ege, Shuster, & Burgio, 2008), children with terminal illness (Barber, 2011), and children who have experienced trauma (Lowenstein, 1995), so we were optimistic that they would be applicable to our client group.

Therapeutic narrative scrapbooks after parental brain injury

Getting started: practicalities

Before embarking on the process of developing narrative scrapbooks with children, there are resources and materials that need to be gathered. Some ideas are presented here as suggestions, but this is by no means an exhaustive list of what might be required. It can be helpful to draw these materials together and keep them in one place, such as a resource box or room; this makes it less likely that the resources will "wander" and just makes it easier to carry things between rooms. In practice, we have needed to gather a large range of arts and crafts materials, including items such as paints, coloured pens, glue, glitter, scissors, paper (assorted sizes and colours), pre-made scrapbooks, notebooks, stickers, and so on. Children will be familiar with working with these materials and can be encouraged to contribute their own favourites. It is also helpful to gather together a range of other resources to form a "library" of words, pictures, and images relevant to brain injury and its sequelae, emotions, and family. This can include pictures or words cut from magazines or newspapers, pictures downloaded from the Internet, and photographs. Furthermore, having magazines available for children to search in for key words and pictures that can then be cut out and used for collage style work can be helpful. We have often found that children find it safer and easier initially to express their concerns or emotions using words or images that have been gathered in this way, rather than directly reporting their own ideas. Access to information technology facilities, including a digital camera, the Internet, word processing, presentation and publishing software provides an alternative way of working. It goes without saying that children have different preferences and skills for working in different types of media, thus having a selection available will allow greater flexibility and permit you to be guided by the child's preferences and interest.

In addition to drawing these materials together, some thought needs to be given to the environment in which this work is being carried out. In reality, options may be limited; however, having access to a family room or more child-friendly rooms can be of benefit. Alternatively, taking steps to ensure consultation rooms are somewhat less intimidating can be helpful (e.g., removing/storing equipment), or co-working with colleagues such as occupational therapists, who may have access to craft areas for their own therapeutic work.

The process

Creating narrative scrapbooks provides a means of applying narrative therapy techniques and draws on the creative skill and family expertise of the child, integrating this with what is known about the familial brain injury and subsequent treatment. As outlined earlier, the scrapbook can establish and ensure the consistency and continuity of their personal narrative, both family and injury narratives. The context of a scrapbook is open to the needs and interests of the child; however, a number of suggestions are offered here, based on our experience of developing these books with children. This work can be completed on an individual basis with children, or, alternatively, it can be a joint venture between siblings or other child relatives with adults supporting and adding to the work in between sessions. In this way, as noted above, it provides a chance to unite against the brain injury by collaborating together. The process of scrapbooking comprises several stages (while we want the child to feel empowered to guide the process, we have found it helpful to try to work within a flexible framework so that the key issues are addressed). As such, we have found the Y-shaped model of adjustment to brain injury (Figure 7.1; Gracey, Evans, & Malley, 2009) a useful complementary theoretical framework alongside narrative techniques for guiding the stages and processes of the scrapbooking. The model suggests that, for children, in the context of parental brain injury, distress arises from the threat associated with the discrepancy that they experience/observe between the parent as he or she "ought" to be ("how I think my mum should be", i.e., typically based on the parent as they were before the brain injury), and the person that he or she is currently perceived to be ("how I think my mum is following the brain injury"). Intervention, that is, in this case, the development of a therapeutic scrapbook, focuses on increasing children's understanding of the changes that have occurred in the parent, the family, the child, and relationships since and as a consequence of the injury, with the aim of developing a more coherent account of the injury, the impact of the injury, the skills that the parent might have lost, and the skills and roles that the parent has retained. The aim is for children to reach, via

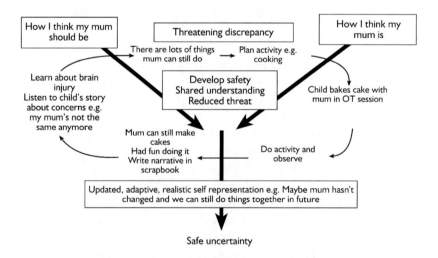

Figure 7.1.   Y-shaped model of adjustment to brain injury
(adapted from Gracey, Evans, & Malley, 2009).

working with us on developing new narratives about the injured relative through scrapbooking, a position of "safe uncertainty" through their achieving a less discrepant (and, hence, less distressing) view of the parent and family situation.

Step 1: Building the family narrative

The first stage of the scrapbooking process invites children to tell us about the story of their family. They and their relatives are often so typically focused on the current problems (namely, the brain injury) that the suggestion to talk about life outside and before the injury can be a relief for many (Douge, 2010). These early externalising conversations help to introduce the notion that the brain injury (the problem) is not what wholly defines the injured parent or the family. We encourage them to use the scrapbook to build the family story, by establishing who is in the family and key family life cycle or other events. In practice, this typically starts by the child developing "profiles" of family members, including pictures, likes, and dislikes (food, music, etc.), details about their work or hobbies, and birthdays. These are sometimes displayed in the scrapbook in the form of a genogram, or family tree. Having done this, pictures and stories from favourite family holidays or other key times can be included; gathering pictures and other reminders can be set as a "homework" task and encourage the family to join together to create the narrative. Family photographs (which tend to portray positive pre-injury events) are talked about in sessions and are used to elicit conversations about their family life, their identity, their experiences and memories. Using photographs to encourage storytelling is a key part of the scrapbooking process, particularly in later stages, as the illness narrative is developed and children are encouraged to take photographs of the "new, changed parent" to elicit alternative conversations.

In practice, we often find families are avoidant or uncomfortable with taking photographs of their injured family member while they are in hospital; similarly, they report taking fewer photographs of themselves as a family during this time, and this might represent an important disruption in the family's documented narrative of themselves and key events. The point in the family timeline at which to start the book is guided by the child. It might be that they wish to start from the day they were born, including baby pictures, moving on to starting nursery and school, and then family holidays. Some children are naturally drawn to dividing their family story into "our family before the brain injury" and "our family after the brain injury", and in these cases children's wishes should guide the process. This initial stage of scrapbooking is usually non-threatening and enjoyable for children (although evoking memories of happier former times can be upsetting); for the therapist, it offers a useful insight into the family before the injury, particularly understanding patterns of relationships and roles—much of which will have been disrupted as a result of the brain injury. It can flag up the issues that a child might grapple with in the next stage of the process when they begin to compile the injury narrative—or when they start to scrapbook the family in its current state.

Step 2: Developing the injury narrative

This stage of storytelling invites children to talk about the often painful account of the parent's injury, its impact on the family and themselves, and the emotions and feelings associated with it. The aim is to encourage expression of feelings and, eventually, through a process of reauthoring and externalising, to help the child achieve a more coherent, accurate, and hopeful account of the events surrounding the family brain injury and subsequent treatment and rehabilitation.

There is a wide range of topics that can be addressed in this section to facilitate conversations; these include factual topics, such as the nature and location of the damage to the relative's brain, the injury's functional impact, and information about rehabilitation and recovery. Discussions of feelings and reactions to brain injury should also be included and issues about the future should be addressed. Children should be encouraged to select areas they would like to talk about and this should guide the content of this section of the scrapbook.

In practice, we have found it important to include detailed information about the cause and location of the injury, the effects of the injury, and how this translates into day-to-day functioning of the injured person, the hospitals at which the family member has been seen, therapy that their relative has been receiving, details about the team working with their relative, and, in some circumstances, details about the places that their relative might be moving to after hospital (for example, if not returning home). The therapist normally has to take a more directive role in this stage, encouraging children to tell the often very painful account of the injury and of the family since its onset.

There are a number of ways of developing the illness narrative and building this story, depending on the age of the child and his or her level of understanding and cognitive development. Initially, the work should feel non-threatening and safe to the child, such as talking about and documenting factual information about the brain injury. For example, work on understanding the cause and location of the injury might involve accessing scans or images of the brain, or drawing pictures from models to help localise the injury. This can then be amalgamated with information about the function of specific parts of the brain, for example, from the Internet or age appropriate textbooks. Clarification of timelines, chronology of events, and possible future timescales can aid the child to hold a more accurate, consistent, and cohesive illness narrative. It is also helpful to identify gaps or discontinuities in the story and provide a chance to "fill in the blanks", provide accurate information, and address misconceptions. For example, Jonny, aged six, had held on to the belief that having had an argument with dad before leaving for school had made his father have the stroke. Further, he believed that being "extra good" now would prevent his father from having another stroke. By learning about the actual causes of stroke and documenting this in his scrapbook, he was able to rewrite this part of the story for himself and be freer of the responsibility he had been carrying.

Similar to developing profiles of family members, children can be encouraged to develop profiles of the team working with their family member. This could include pictures and details about what job each team member performs, based on interviews, Internet research, and information provided by the team. Children might be curious or, indeed, anxious, about the use of equipment (such as hoists) and can again be encouraged to research and record information about what equipment is used for, how it used, possibly including the option of practising using the equipment. Children can also be supported to interview members of the injured relative's therapy team in order to learn more about their relative's rehabilitation. Children often enjoy adopting a different persona or identity for this work: for example, imagining that they are working for a newspaper or a television programme and that they need to interview one of the medical consultants about brain injury. As a homework task, they can draw up a list of possible questions (with the help of an adult relative) they are going to ask the staff members (which can be guided by specific concerns or fears that they might have), and these questions can then be posed to members of the rehabilitation team. For example, questions associated with why a parent needs to perform certain stretching exercises and whether the children can help may be directed towards a physiotherapist.

This does require the support of the therapy team, and, in practice, team members themselves might need some support in participating (such as advance warning of questions, preparing possible answers in advance, clarifying information, help and reassurance in explaining brain injury and their roles in a child-friendly way). Children are also encouraged to work alongside the psychologist to seek weekly progress updates from the therapy team, which are also recorded in the scrapbook. Such "co-research" (Epston, 1999) helps the child obtain alternative information, knowledge, and understanding about the parents that might redress the child's existing beliefs and ideas about them. In addition, hearing other people providing positive stories of the parent's strength, determination, achievement, and skills provides the child with new knowledge. In narrative therapy terms, such re-membering conversations (Myerhoff, 1982) enrich the new emerging narrative of hopefulness that we are trying to foster. The results of this research can then be recorded in the scrapbook.

As the child gathers information and becomes increasingly knowledgeable about brain injury, the illness narrative can continue being expanded and developed using a range of narrative techniques to facilitate the adjustment process. For example, children can be supported to explore unique outcomes or exceptions, such as exploring times when the brain injury "is not present". Daniel, aged nine, had been making a scrapbook with us charting his mother's progress through rehabilitation. The overriding themes arising from his story were of loss and change, where he consistently described his mother as "completely different—not my mum any more—she's all hurt and gone". With the support of rehabilitation staff, Daniel's mother (who had sustained a severe head injury) was able to take him to a local cafe for a snack (this is something that they had always enjoyed doing previously and which Daniel repeatedly said he missed). Photographs of the event were taken and discussed at a later session. Similarly, as rehabilitation progressed, staff and Daniel actively sought and recorded other instances where mum had been able to carry out activities that she had enjoyed previously. Again, these were photographed by Daniel and staff, and recorded in the scrapbook under "things my mum still likes and is good at". This allowed Daniel to experience his mother as more akin to her old self and this presented him with the possibility that his old mother had not "totally gone". Discussions with Daniel about these events focused on mum's retained and regained skills, and these reauthoring conversations further enriched and thickened this alternative narrative that mum was not totally lost. The aim is for children to create a richer and more optimistic narrative about the injured relative, which may instil more hope for the future.

In a similar way, we used the scrapbooking approach to externalise a father's verbally aggressive behaviour (a common post brain injury problem) as part of the brain injury and not as part of father. Luka, aged eight, had witnessed his father engaging in several very upsetting, angry verbal outbursts recently—two of which were directed at Luka himself. Luka said that he felt afraid of dad and wondered why he was "being horrible" all the time to him. We used education and discussion about the types of problems people can have following brain injury and helped Luka see that his dad's outbursts were a symptom of his injury and not the result of any wrong-doing by Luka. In addition, we encouraged Luka to record in the scrapbook times when his father appeared calm, or happy, or interested, in order to thicken this more positive story.

Storytelling and the use of metaphor can be useful narrative techniques to enhance the scrapbooking process (but they also obviously stand alone and can be used in individual work aside from scrapbooking with children to address issues of concern). Storytelling or metaphor can help to establish a coherent narrative, meet the child's information and emotional support needs, and provide a means for increasing their resilience. Stories can be also be used as a method of indirectly assessing children's concerns and fears, which they might not otherwise be able to report verbally. Recently, there has been a rise in the number of story format publications to help children understand and process issues relating to parental brain injury and neurological illness (e.g., *My Mum Makes the Best Cakes* and *My Dad Makes the Best Boats*, by Jo Johnson, 2013a,b). In an early paper, Romano (1976) discussed the importance of mutual storytelling (facilitated by the use of puppets or drawings for younger children) in helping children prepare for parental disability. She provided an example of a child who had been asked to tell a story about a picture she had drawn. Romano states that the child said of the story, "The children are in their backyard; they're bored as their mother is at work and their daddy is sick. They are kind of unhappy" (p. 313). Romano (1976) proposes that allowing children to develop such stories provides them with a vehicle by which they can express, process, and, ultimately, resolve difficult feelings. She states that for children who are too young to develop their own stories, prepared accounts can be helpful. Romano states that the key issue in prepared stories is that there must be a close parallel between the issues facing the characters in the story and those being faced by the children, and yet they must also be sufficiently impersonal to allow the child to be able to process the entire account and achieve an ending—important for instilling hope in children that their own personal story may also reach a satisfactory close.

Case study: Laura

Laura was an eight-year-old girl whose father sustained a hypoxic brain injury following a cardiac arrest. To help understand recent events, Laura was seen by the family support service with her brother and began completing a scrapbook. She was also seen individually for assessment of some specific fears that her mother had identified.

A number of approaches were used to directly elicit her concerns, but she repeatedly told us that she did not have any worries or fears. As such, an indirect externalising approach was taken. Rather than continuing to ask about her concerns, a family of bears was drawn out (with pictures and names) with the therapist and Laura, where the father bear had sustained a brain injury and Laura was asked to write a story about what the other bears in the family were thinking about this event.

Laura's story of the experiences of the young girl bear contained themes of worry, fear, and keeping problems to herself. She told us that the girl bear was worried that the mother bear was upset and was frightened that this would be made worse by the girl bear talking about her worries. The girl bear was worried about upsetting her more, and that if she got more upset her mum might have a brain injury. This immediately gave insight into what appeared to be Laura's concerns.

In this example, creating a family of bears and writing a story about that family provided a means by which Laura's fears could be accessed and discussed safely, and then could be used to guide future working with her. Stories can be written or drawn and presented in books, storyboards, pictures, and collages. Alternatively, they can be audiotaped and later transcribed. The story can be written to provide an account of the events surrounding the injury, the impact of the injury in terms of family relationships or the effect of memory impairment, or can be used as a means of enhancing child's perceived ability to cope.

Anecdotal evidence from our clinical practice suggests that children who have written stories about other children or families who demonstrate mastery or resilience in the face of significant adversity or distress have been observed to have enhanced mastery of their own situation, and their perceived ability to cope has increased. These stories have drawn on the child's interests, using characters from their own favourite stories, and have also involved creating new hero and heroine characters. Similarly, our work often draws on metaphors, including those suggested by us and by children. These metaphors have been an effective and accessible way of describing complicated aspects of brain injury: for example, using stormy unpredictable weather as a metaphor for an injured father's mood swings. This story developed around the ideas of uncertainty and fear of never knowing how the weather will be when the character wakes up, how the weather sometimes changes in the day without warning, and how the central character learnt to carry a magical umbrella to safeguard against the bad weather when it comes. This was balanced with the good feelings when the sun shines. Other stories have drawn on metaphors such as rollercoaster rides to describe the rehabilitation process, symbolising the ups and downs, the thrills but also fear, and the notion that rehabilitation is like a journey.

The ideas presented here represent just a few suggestions for approaches that have been used in our clinical practice. There is a rich variety of alternative techniques and formats that could be used within a narrative framework. These could include writing a newspaper-style report on the brain injury or events surrounding that, and writing a presentation that could be seen by peers or other children affected by familial brain injury. Additionally, the use of emails between children to build up a shared, supportive narrative about their experiences could be explored, as can encouraging ongoing dialogue (via letter-writing between children in similar situations in the old pen-pal style, or emailing, text messaging, and so on). We have also recently started to explore the use of short video clips, containing soundbites from children about key issues in coping with a relative's brain injury made as a resource for other children and for staff training in these issues.

There appears to be a wealth of possibilities for encouraging dialogue with and among children about their experiences, and for them and others to benefit from their stories.

Bringing it all together and ending

In practice, we have found that children enjoy the process of scrapbooking and it provides structure and purpose to their visits to the rehabilitation unit. We feel it fosters positive and active engagement with their relative's rehabilitation, something that children had frequently told us they had felt excluded from. Scrapbooking also offers children the opportunity to be heard, to ask questions and learn more, unlike many forms of intervention. We have found that it allows children of different ages from the same family to come together and work co-operatively. The older children tend to take responsibility for writing and gathering information, with younger children decorating the scrapbooks and adding creative personal touches. Something positive and tangible is developed from the experience, and children typically want to show the scrapbook to others outside the family, such as classmates and teachers. Some children have allowed us to photocopy pages from their books so that other children can see what can be achieved and learn from the wisdom of their experiences. For many children and their families, the scrapbook becomes a reference book for them to consult later; many families report that seeing photographs from the early stages of rehabilitation prompts them to appreciate and acknowledge the progress that their relative has made, fostering a narrative that is more optimistic and hopeful. Above all, the scrapbooking process appears to provide a way of integrating the illness story with the family story, so that there is a place for these in each account.

When is the scrapbook complete?

We encourage families, if they wish, to continue developing the scrapbook once they leave our unit, providing the message that progress will continue and that there will be events to document. This also provides us with the opportunity to discuss with families the likely "up and down" pattern to future recovery (we draw again on metaphors of funfair rides and so on to illustrate this) and try to prepare them for setbacks and disappointments as well as positive events. We maintain contact with families during these early months of being back home so that we can continue to support them. We frequently receive postcards from children telling us about holidays that the family have successfully managed or key events that they have enjoyed. The stories continue . . .

Case example: Hannah's scrapbook

We met Hannah, aged seven, soon after her mother Kathy's admission to our unit. Kathy, in her mid-forties, had suffered a stroke three months previously and had been admitted for neuro-rehabilitation. Hannah was being cared for by her maternal grandparents while Kathy was in hospital, and they reported that they were managing the situation well. There had been no initial concerns about Hannah's adjustment, but recently Kathy had been telling her therapists that Hannah seemed quieter and more withdrawn and Kathy was becoming worried. We agreed to see Hannah within the Family Support Service to talk about this.

We (AD and RS) met with Hannah on a weekly basis, for approximately an hour at a time over a period of three months. The initial session involved us introducing ourselves and what we as psychologists do when we work with children, with an aim of normalising the process for her. Hannah talked very openly with us about a number of concerns (these are outlined in the following sections) and at the end of the session we invited her mother and grandparents to join us to discuss our plan and what the work might involve. Subsequent sessions tended to involve Hannah only, though we updated her family regularly on the work we had been completing. It was agreed that we would help Hannah develop a scrapbook to document what had happened to her mother and what the future might hold, as these two issues were of concern to her from early discussions.

Hannah's family story

Hannah was an only child and had no contact with her father. She lived with her mother, Kathy, and her maternal grandparents provided significant amounts of care and support to the two of them; there were reports from Brian, Hannah's grandfather, that Kathy had always found it difficult to manage Hannah alone. Hannah told us that her grandfather was the "fun one" in the family and that her grandmother "sorts everything". She expressed sadness that Granddad seemed worried all the time now and was no longer fun to be with and that her grandmother could not "sort mum".

We asked Hannah to draw a picture of her family to understand where she placed herself in relation to the key people. She drew herself in the centre of the page, doing a handstand while supported by her grandfather. Around the two of them she drew her mother and grandmother and extended family, all joined by arrows and annotated with their relationships to one another (e.g., "sister of Grandmother"). This suggested to us that Hannah might see herself and her grandfather as being central to the family, with the others surrounding them (but with none given particular importance). The activity in the picture (doing a handstand with her grandfather) highlighted his role as an "active" and "fun" participant in her life. This presented us with an avenue to explore regarding how her mother's role in the family, and in her relationship with Hannah, might have changed from Hannah's perspective. Hannah spoke little of her mother's role, except to say that she had to work frequently.

Hannah attended a prestigious preparatory school and was evidently a bright, creative girl. She had also become closely involved with the family of one of her school friends, who had several young children, and they played an important part in her care while her mother was in hospital. Hannah expressed some confusion about the role this family might play in her future; she had overheard her grandparents expressing concerns that should Kathy not recover fully, they themselves might be too old to be able to manage Hannah's care full time. She believed that she heard them saying that she could live with her friend's family instead; she was both excited and upset about this prospect, but had not shared this with anyone as "there's too much stress around".

The illness narrative

We began by asking Hannah to describe to us what had happened to her mother. The stroke had happened on Hannah's birthday, while her mother was baking her birthday cake. Hannah described how the "pressure had built up in her mum's head because she was cooking really quickly and she was stressed"; this provided us with some insight into the event Hannah attributed to her mother's stroke. It also highlighted a misunderstanding that had the potential for future stress: for example, Hannah having concerns about her mother, or indeed anyone else she knew, cooking or appearing stressed. This was something to return to at a later stage.

Furthermore, Hannah described how she had been the one to phone the ambulance, something that placed her in a central position of responsibility. It was also clear from her description of the event and her mother's subsequent time in hospital that her understanding of the timeline of events was somewhat confused and inaccurate. This raised the issue that Hannah might not be able accurately to judge how long her mother had been in hospital so far, and also how long she was likely to remain there until she returned home.

Bringing the family and illness narrative together in the scrapbook

Hannah's scrapbook began with an introductory page she designed, including a drawing of herself and her mother. She wrote down some questions she had at that point, which included "Will my mum walk again?", "When will my mum be coming home?", and "What does she do in physio?". We were previously curious as to what Hannah had been wondering about, and this technique also helped establish her in the role of "detective", which we had thought she might engage with well. So, thus far, we had established where she positioned herself in the family, and something about the possible relationships she currently had with each family member. We had also heard her story of what had happened from the time of her mother's stroke up until now.

The next step was to begin on the educational avenue of the process. We utilised a children's textbook about the brain with which Hannah engaged well. Hannah also searched for brain images on the Internet and printed and cut these out, making collages in the book that were labelled with what the different parts of the brain did. She also wanted to include some information about "keeping your brain safe", which was an avenue we also explored. We produced a list of different actions the brain controls (walking, drawing, seeing, remembering, etc.), which Hannah grouped together and coloured in. She divided them, with some guidance, into things she thought her mother could still do, might be able to do in the future, and might not be able to do again. This opened up an avenue for discussing how things might be different and how they might stay the same at home for Hannah. We also discussed why her mother's stroke might have occurred to address any misconceptions Hannah might have had. The key in all this was providing age-appropriate information that armed Hannah with a better grasp of what had happened, while not overwhelming her.

We expanded on the idea of Hannah as a "detective" by arranging for her to "interview" her mother's occupational therapist and physiotherapist. This proved a successful approach and gave Hannah a chance to feel more in control of gathering information, rather than hearing it from her grandfather. We also included her mother in a session, so Hannah could ask her what she had achieved and could now do again, and what she still found difficult. The idea behind this was to normalise her mother's current difficulties and to highlight her achievements and her efforts in her brain injury to Hannah. This was all presented in drawings and notes in Hannah's scrapbook.

Difficult discussions

Hannah tended to appear cheerful and positive during sessions, though she gradually became less engaged and more distractible as sessions went on. We decided to address this with curiosity (casually, while we were engaged in a cutting-and-sticking task) and asked if she was less interested in sessions, or maybe was not enjoying them as much as she had first appeared to. Her response to this, however, opened up another avenue—one that had initially been difficult to engage her in conversation about. She said that she did not like discussing her mother as it "makes me sad to think about it". She said that people "all thought she was cheerful but really she was sad inside". A less direct form of questioning, and her having "busy hands" (Douge, 2010) while we discussed it, proved to be a successful approach in terms of opening another avenue of discussion.

The insights that emerged led to a number of activities we included in the scrapbook. One was an "iceberg" drawing, in which Hannah wrote above and below the surface the things about her that people knew and saw on the outside, and the things that were hidden. We also made a little booklet which fitted inside the scrapbook, and which included lists of "Hannah on the outside" ("happy", "bubbly", and "clever") compared to "Hannah on the inside" ("sad", "not clever"). She also talked about having mixed feelings about her mother coming home.

Empowering Hannah

Hannah said she did not talk about how she felt with others and we wondered if perhaps this had been lost in the focus on her mother and her recovery. It might have been particularly true, as her grandfather had taken on the role of primary carer for Hannah, as well as frequently visiting his daughter in the hospital. Having this in mind led on to more practical discussions about what she could do if she was feeling sad, and formed part of the scrapbook that Hannah was happy to show to her mother, which we felt opened up a dialogue between them about how she had been coping. The next part of the scrapbook, therefore, detailed Hannah's thoughts about what she could do if she felt sad. This covered both home and school environments, and we introduced the idea that when our sessions came to an end, she would be able to use these approaches herself.

Hannah's new story

The final part of the scrapbook focused on the things that her mother could still do that Hannah felt were important in their relationship and in her life. It transpired that Hannah and her mother often played a game together where they posted each other notes through a cardboard tube. The notes asked questions about how each other's day had been, how they were feeling, and so on. Hannah took great joy in showing us this game. We discussed how it would still be possible to do with her mother, as her mother's writing was improving over time. She also described how they used to do craft activities together, so we organised a joint session with her mother's occupational therapist, Hannah, and her mother, in which they made Easter cards together as a demonstration of how experiences such as these were still possible. Combined with the discussions with her mother's occupational therapist and physiotherapist about her progress and prognosis, Hannah became armed with accurate information about what was likely to still be possible and what might be more difficult.

Hannah left her sessions with a scrapbook of her drawings, notes, feelings, and ideas about what it might be like in the future when her mother returned home. It was hoped that this would prepare her in some ways for what was ahead. She had a story in the scrapbook of what had happened to her family, and was more knowledgeable and in control of the situation.

Conclusions

Here we have described one approach—scrapbooking—to supporting children who have been affected by brain injury in their family. The techniques embodied in the scrapbooking process have a strong basis in narrative therapy and appear to offer a "good fit" way of addressing children's information and support needs in this context.

The use of scrapbooking as a therapy tool, alongside special stories, creative play, and art, offers a wealth of "playful approaches" (Epston, 1997) to managing very difficult and often traumatic situations for this group of children. Children are helped via the processing and retelling of their stories to achieve realistic hope regarding their injured parent's recovery and their own personal situation. They are helped to express and work towards resolution of difficult feelings, such as anger and guilt (often through storytelling and hearing of how others have overcome similar difficulties). Discussion of the ambiguous nature of the loss of the parent as he or she was is addressed, and the child is helped to find a new, more optimistic way of moving forward while still accepting the difficulties inherent in doing this. Such "double-stories" (Pluznick & Kis-Sines, 2008) acknowledge the difficulties faced by children who have ill parents, as well as the knowledge, skill, and resilience they develop as a result of the experience.

References

Allen, R. S., Hilgeman, M. M., Ege, M. A., Shuster, J. D., & Burgio, L. D. (2008). Legacy activities as interventions approaching end of life. *Journal of palliative Medicine, 11*(7): 1029–1038.

Barber, B. (2011). An autobiographical scrapbook for terminally ill children: a guide to processing death. PsyD Dissertation, Azusa Pacific University. Accessed via: http://proquest.umi.com/pqdlink?Ver=1&Exp=07–07–2017&FMT=7&DID=1955083331&RQT=309&attempt=1.

Daisley, A., & Webster, G. (2008). Familial brain injury: impact and interventions with children. In: A. Tyerman & N. King (Eds.), *Psychological Approaches to Rehabilitation after Traumatic Brain Injury* (pp. 475–508) Oxford: BPS Blackwell.

Douge, J. (2010). Scrapbooking: an application of narrative therapy. *Procedia – Social and Behavioural Sciences, 5*: 648–687.

Epston, D. (1997). *Playful Approaches to Serious Problems: Narrative Therapy with Children and their Families.* London: W. W. Norton.

Johnson, J. (2013a). *My Mum Makes the Best Cakes.* Milton Keynes: Speechmark.

Johnson, J. (2013b). *My Dad Makes the Best Boats.* Milton Keynes: Speechmark.

Kohut, M. (2011). Making art from memories: honouring deceased loved ones through a scrapbooking bereavement group. *Art Therapy Journal of the American Art Therapy Association, 28*(3): 123–131.

Kreutzer, J., Marwitz, J., Godwin, E., & Angaro-Lasprilla, J. (2010). Practical approaches to effective family intervention after brain injury. *Brain Injury, 8*: 113–120.

Lezak, M. D. (1988). Brain damage is a family affair. *Journal of Clinical & Experimental Neuropsychology, 10*(1): 111–123.

Lowenstein, L. B. (1995). The resolution scrapbook as an aid in the treatment of traumatised children. *Child Welfare, 74*(4): 889–904.

Maier, E. H. (2007). Narrative scrapbooking: empathic facilitation of cocreated stories for bereaved and nonspecific adults in supplemental therapeutic support groups. PhD Thesis. Institute of Transpersonal Psychology. Accessed via: http://proquest.umi.com/pqdlink?Ver=1&Exp=07–7–2017&FMT=7&DID=1537003551&RQT=309&attempt=1&cfc=1.

Myerhoff, B. (1982). Life history among the elderly: performance, visibility and re-membering. In: J. Ruby (Ed.), *A Crack in the Mirror. Reflective Perspectives in Anthropology.* Philadelphia, PA: University of Pennsylvania Press.

Pluznick, R., & Kis-Sines, N. (2008). Growing up with parents with mental health difficulties. *International Journal of Narrative Therapy and Community Work, 4*: 5–26.

Romano, M. D. (1976). Preparing children for parental disability. *Social Work in Health Care, 1*(3): 309–315.

Tyerman, A. (2008). Facilitating psychological adjustment. In A. Tyerman & N. King (Eds.), *Psychological Approaches to Rehabilitation after Traumatic Brain Injury*. Oxford: Blackwell.

White, M., & Epston, D. (1990). *Narrative Means to Therapeutic Ends*. London: W. W. Norton.

CHAPTER EIGHT

Using narrative ideas and practices in indirect work with services and professionals

Lincoln Simmonds

Introduction

This chapter discusses how we can use narrative ideas and practices in our "indirect work" of supporting services and other professionals engaged with people seeking help. In this chapter, I have drawn heavily on many of the ideas which have influenced much of narrative therapy practice. I have worked for over ten years within a child and adolescent mental health service context, and more recently have specialised within the field of paediatrics. However, I feel many of the ideas related in this chapter will also be applicable across a range of settings, including working with people with acquired brain injury. Indeed, if we are to move away from narrow perceptions of skills, then seeing the transferable aspects of working in any discipline might be the first step towards enriching our own professional narratives. This, in turn, has the potential to enable new narratives to be co-developed with those who seek our input.

This chapter will particularly consider how we can integrate narrative ideas into our current practices, protocols, and service guidelines. I have covered a number of areas of work with services and professionals, varying from consultation to record keeping. All of the areas discussed focus on how we, as professionals and therapists, can "centre" our conversations with other professionals and our practice primarily upon the preferred accounts (descriptions and explanations) and stories of the people whom we seek to help. In the following pages, I outline why it can be helpful to move away from a purely naturalistic and structuralist approach to working with people.

The more dominant accounts/descriptions/explanations of people's problems in Western society tend to be naturalistic/structuralist in nature. Narrative therapy can provide counterpoints to these often dominant naturalistic/structuralist explanations or views of people's problem experiences. In this chapter, initially, I remind the reader about the nature of naturalistic and structuralist descriptions of people's problems, and why this might (at times) be problematic and restrictive. I then outline a number of the practices, ideas, and strategies from narrative therapy. These ideas can be particularly helpful in opening out alternative accounts, which might be more helpful to the professionals and services we seek to support in their work with people seeking help. I discuss the application of narrative ideas in specific contexts of indirect work. Each area of work is also brought to life through an example of its application with the professionals and services that we are seeking to support in their work.

Hazards and limitations of taking a purely naturalistic/ structuralist descriptions of a person's life and identity

By now, having read this far into this book, you may be quite familiar with the terms naturalistic and structuralist, as descriptions or explanations of people's difficulties. You will also understand that this book certainly does not aim to say that describing problems in such a way is inherently wrong. Rather, it is simply the case that if these naturalistic and structuralist descriptions are always given priority in our thinking about people's difficulties, then we limit possibilities for other, more helpful and useful explanations of people's difficulties and lives. I shall argue this point shortly, but first I give you a brief definition of what I mean by naturalistic and structuralist descriptions:

- *Naturalistic descriptions* are, in this context, descriptions of problems that describe the problems as "truths" about a person's nature, character, or identity: for example, "He is anxious" or "She is depressed".

- *Structuralist descriptions* are, in this context, descriptions about problems that are derived from generalised socially constructed ideas about illness, problems, and the way society feels we should live our lives. Thus, diagnoses, or prominent theories about distress, sadness, or feelings of anxiety (or even ideas about how individuals in Western society should live or be able to achieve things, or overcome difficulties by themselves), fall into these categories of descriptions.

Structuralist/naturalistic understandings of identity can often encourage thinking in therapists that can lead to the judgement of people and their experiences against constructed norms (Walther & Carey, 2009). Walther and Carey further emphasised that these ideas of what is "normal" and what is "abnormal" are further supported through the assessments, measures, and even the inclusion criteria of services that therapists are often encouraged or mandated to use.

Can you think of times when perhaps protocols or guidelines, maybe based on certain assessments/psychometrics, have prohibited your service from working with someone or accessing particular types of help, and you have felt uncomfortable about that?

White (2001) outlined a number of constraints and pitfalls present within viewing people's relationships with difficulties solely from a structuralist/naturalistic perspective. Within his article, he wrote clearly about how there is nothing inherently "wrong" about naturalistic accounts, or inherently right, for that matter, about narrative accounts: rather, we potentially miss out on opportunities to develop more helpful and useful accounts of people's lives if we are constrained to a lens of naturalistic explanations.

White (2001) stated that, often, naturalistic accounts fit more with the individualistic views of life and identity that are often present within Western culture. Thus, he argued that, potentially, such accounts miss out on opportunities for people to be sustained via connection to significant figures in their lives. White (2001) also spoke of how naturalistic accounts of people's lives are indicative of norms that declare how people should live. Thus, he determined that accounts which are grounded in normalising judgements often encourage people to "fall back in line" with various socially constructed norms. I would add, though, that, of course, there are socially constructed norms which every therapist would seek to encourage in terms of those about respecting other's lives and wellbeing. My question to you would be how many of the norms are *simply* expressions of what our society at times states that we *should* be doing? By that, I mean are there socially constructed norms that in no way would impinge on others' rights, welfare, and liberties if we chose to step away from them? For example, as I am writing this, I am wondering what would be the response of others if I were to propose that I step away from paid employment to take up a system of bartering my therapeutic trades to sustain my lifestyle?

> What do you think about these ideas of Western society being dominated by accounts of individualism? Is it the case that we think that individuals should make it on their own, and perhaps within the media we celebrate individual achievement and perhaps talk less about achieving things with others' help and support? I often find that articles about physical health problems talk about individuals "battling the illness" or "overcoming the illness" in terms that talk about them being courageous or strong-willed individuals. However, I also find that such articles tend to neglect, or give less priority to, how people were supported by others in showing more resolve or having more courage in certain situations.

Most therapists, mental health practitioners, and psychiatrists would concede the point that all approaches have their limitations in terms of their explanatory power for people's difficulties, and further acknowledge (when push comes to shove!) that no single approach adequately explains the myriad unique individual presentations of difficulties. Often, though, we find that practitioners tend not to have such discussions with the people they see. I would also argue that we tend not to make examinations on a regular enough basis of the limitations of models/approaches/theories that we privilege. There are questions, however, which we could ask of professionals' theoretical perspectives, or, rather, questions which we could encourage them to ask of themselves:

- Who do you think these ideas most benefit?
- What does this approach say about gender relations?

- What does this approach contribute to understanding other cultures?
- What does this approach contribute to ideas about working individually with people being effective?
- What does this approach say about the effects of ideas, and about how our society affects people and their problems?

For example, if I told you that I suffered from severe anxiety as measured by a standardised robust measure, what would be the treatment you would recommend for me if I gave you five seconds to answer? Would you offer me that same treatment if I then told you that I lived on an estate with significant problems of ongoing violence and harassment of the residents? Would you view my anxiety as problematic, or potentially a protective skill, which I had learnt to keep myself safe?

White (2001) also stated that "naturalistic accounts of life and identity are intimately related to the modern phenomenon of the production of weakness and deficits, and of the disorders and the pathologies" (p. 12). This is both an interesting and challenging argument, as many of us would certainly feel that the more dominant mental health models, which are more strongly tied to naturalistic accounts of experience, do not have the intention of perceiving people as weak or deficient in some manner. However, if we step back to reflect on the models, we might notice that often these theories and explanations are based upon conceptions of naturalistic strengths and resources. If we talk of naturalistic strengths and resources, then we inescapably also talk about the absence of such strengths and resources within people. Hence, by our very postulates, we view people as lacking or deficient in particular strengths and resources. This can often serve the purpose of marginalising those who "fail" to show such strength and resources (e.g., "she is not a confident person"). We can also have the tendency to interpret certain qualities as negative, deficient, or defective.

How do we offer alternatives, alongside or counter, to these structuralist/naturalistic viewpoints? I will say it once again. Our aim is not to denigrate or seek to marginalise structuralist/naturalistic accounts. Instead, the role of the narrative therapist is to offer a range of possibilities and explanations. Think of it as a journey across unfamiliar territory, in which the person we are seeking to help is given a complete map of the territory to experience, as opposed to one set of directions to follow through the wilderness. If a structuralist/naturalistic account of a person's experiences feels most useful and helpful to that person, by *their* decision and judgement, then it is the "right" account. Thankfully, we do have a number of tools in our kit-bag of narrative therapy which can provide alternatives to structuralist/naturalistic accounts and, one hopes, open up further possibilities for describing people's lives, which might lead to more helpful, preferred accounts. An obvious starting point is in identifying unique outcomes (exceptions to the problem): whether they are about the person seeking help stepping into (or intending to step into) preferred accounts of themselves, or perhaps even accounts of professionals identifying times when they have desired, or taken action, to support the person in preferred ways.

One such tool is the use of externalising conversations. Externalising conversations are not a necessary requirement of narrative work, but they can aid the therapist in being able to facilitate the "unpacking" of negative identity conclusions derived from naturalistic accounts (of themselves), which often are born out of socially constructed normative descriptions of people's lives. Externalising conversations provide the space to retell a person's experience from a problematic storyline to one that is more along the lines of them being in *relationships* with problems. This runs contrary to naturalistic views of a problem being due to an inherent weakness or deficit within them, as opposed to the narrative view of the problem being separate to the person.

The reader is probably also aware that often we seek to "personify" or characterise a problem (or unique outcome), and that a simple way of doing this is by putting the word "The" in front of any statements about the problem, or referring to the problem as "It". Jenkins (2011) summed this up nicely by highlighting a structuralist/naturalistic view of resilience in Western society and countering this from a narrative perspective by saying, "resilience . . . cannot be orchestrated, possessed or regarded as a personal duality", and that it is more helpful to think about "not what resilience is but what it can do". Thus, what is a person's relationship with resilience? How can they step more into The Resilience (if they view it as helpful)? How can they renegotiate their relationship with The Resilience? You might be able to see that it is the difference between viewing someone as lacking resilience and seeking to imbue it within them, on the one hand, while, on the other, seeking out examples when someone has used resilience to (in their) view the betterment of their lives. A narrative therapist would then be interested in "thickening" (developing) stories and accounts of using The Resilience in ways that are helpful to the person.

We can also draw on the narrative idea of the absent but implicit: that is, the sense that we can only talk or know about something in relation to something else. We do this by "double listening", which means that we pay attention to what something is not, as well as to what it is. For example, an expression of sadness (what it is) also speaks of someone's hopes for happiness (what it is not). An expression of sadness might also suggest that they have ideas of what happiness is. Walther and Carey (2009) spoke of listening carefully for the "particularities" or differences between events with a preferred story, referred to as a "difference between similarities". By doing this, they encouraged the narrative therapist to seek out further deconstructions of normally assumed categories of descriptions of living.

Often, we can assume that one act of something is the same as the other, if they are given the same label, but, by doing so, we might potentially be making generalised assumptions about the nature of an experience, and, thus, miss out on further descriptions and differentiation. For example, how would different people describe their acts of caring to others? Would they come out with very similar descriptions, or would we find that there are a multitude of descriptions and stories under the heading of caring? Thus, we must also stay alert to the same person having many different accounts and types of a "thing" such as caring, and perhaps ask about the differing categories of the "thing" (e.g., would that act be the same type of caring that you told me about last week, or would you see it as different?). We shall now proceed to talking about how you can apply narrative ideas to different areas of indirect working (working with other professionals and services).

Applications of narrative ideas in specific contexts

Consultation

In this section, I talk about situations in which other professionals/services are seeking to consult with you about a person or persons they are working with. I often find that particular discourses tend to dominate consultation work with other professionals. I have already mentioned that often these more dominant discourses are from naturalistic/structuralist perspectives. In situations in which a professional or service provider have approached a mental health professional for consultation about work with a person, expectations of the mental health professional holding the "expert opinion" can often take the foreground. At other times, there can be discourses that the mental health professional or mental health service needs to work with a person, and perhaps needs convincing in the consultation process to act. The hazards are that such discourses can lead to conclusions that are at times unhelpful to the person, and diminish both their preferred identity narratives as well as those of the professionals working with them. I shall elaborate on these ideas over the next series of paragraphs, and look at ways of being able to counter these expectations (if they seem unhelpful), and developing (preferred) alternative stories/explanations/descriptions to the more dominant (often naturalistic/structuralist) accounts.

It is important to acknowledge that the professionals who come seeking consultation are often in situations that feel "stuck" or overwhelming. I am not suggesting that mental health professionals do not have knowledge, skills, and experience that can be brought to bear in understanding and resolving such difficulties. However, when dominant discourses of "expert opinion" are prevalent, then it guides professionals to think that neither they nor the people at the centre of the work have anything to contribute, other than information-giving in order for the mental health expert to form an opinion, whereas dominant discourses that suggest that the mental health service needs to do something can lead to the diminution of the contribution of the professionals currently working with the person. It can often result in such professionals contributing to discourses in which they see themselves as playing no further role, or consider that they have exhausted their skills and resources to no avail. These discourses can also suggest that the person needs specialist help in order to resolve, or perhaps even contain, their difficulties. These discourses might even suggest that their situation fits with ideas that their problems are beyond "normal" experience, and that specialist help for working with "abnormal" behaviours, thoughts, and feelings is necessary to "fix" the problem.

At times, a mental health professional might have to work very hard indeed to counter such dominant ideas. Using narrative ideas and perspectives can be particularly helpful in countering such claims. A narrative therapist might have to work hard to deconstruct the idea that the mental health professional is the "sole expert" in the room. Deconstructing such ideas can be very helpful starting points, as well as finding ways to create a context in which others' experiences, knowledge, and skills are given more weight in the conversation.

It is important to make explicit efforts to enable colleagues seeking help to remain aware that their experience, knowledge, and skills are valued and can be brought to bear in understanding the difficulties. It is often useful to view colleagues seeking help as experts in being able to help us understand the experiences that the people whom they are helping are having. Often it is important to contextualise, or recontextualise, the consultation space as a "thinking space" in which it is emphasised that everyone participating can bring ideas, thoughts, and stories to share. I seek to extend a clear invitation for people to deconstruct the idea of previous experiences of formal meetings, suggesting instead that people are welcome to share unformed ideas or images as opposed to just "facts". Of course, the main challenge to such an invitation is to keep the discussion firmly centred on what the people whom we are seeking to help would find useful, as opposed to giving priority solely to dominant explanations of people's difficulties.

Of course, the central aim of the consultation is to place the experience of the people we are seeking to help at the centre of the conversation. It is commonplace, though, for consultations to take place without the people we are seeking to help being present. Whether or not we should actually have consultations concerning the people we are seeking to help in their absence is perhaps a matter for discussion outside of the realms of this chapter, as there can obviously be hazards in such discussions taking place. The facilitator of the consultation has to be very active in ensuring that the conversations contribute towards the development of preferred stories of the person we are trying to help. At times, it may be necessary to steer the conversations away from tendencies to theorise, or hypothesise, about the person and their relationships.

The story/account that is most useful and helpful to the person whom we seek to help is the "right one": I shall refer to this as the preferred story or account. The preferred story is one preferred by the actual person, *not* the professionals around the person: the one which the person perceives as the most useful and helpful. It is this story that we seek to thicken within the consultation. There are exceptions to this, though. We are, of course, also accountable for upholding practices that ensure that other people's values, rights, and safety are upheld. Thus, we do not seek to support and thicken stories that run counter to this, even if these are seemingly preferred stories of the people we are seeking to help.

As stated earlier in this chapter, eliciting externalised descriptions can often lead to an increased sense of personal agency, and us bearing witness to richer and thicker descriptions of people's lives (White, 2000, 2004). It is also helpful to seek out exceptions to the dominant problem story, also referred to as unique outcomes. Thus, it is important to ask colleagues seeking help about the person's interests, hobbies, positive relations, hopes, etc.

Referring to what the person would say about the consultation (particularly in their absence) can often bring the focus back to the person's experience, thus realigning professionals to centre the consultation on the person. Such story development often gives scope to identify the person's values, hopes, skills, dreams, and knowledge, which foster a sense of acknowledging the person's agency as a foundation for creating desired change in his or her life. By acknowledging ways in which professionals are already acting that are helpful in supporting the preferred accounts of people whom we are seeking to help, we support the preferred accounts of *their* (the other professionals') professional identities. Of course, all of the above discussions need to be carried out in ways that translate into actions/steps that the professionals seeking help can take to support these preferred accounts. These would be the desired outcomes of such consultations. It would also be important that we feed back the discussion to the person seeking help, if they are not able to be present at the consultation. Narrative therapeutic letters or documents that use externalised statements and highlighted preferred accounts can be particularly helpful in this respect, especially in terms of documents or letters that may have been written by professionals or co-written by the professionals seeking help with guidance from the consultation facilitator, on the explicit agreement that the person is the "editor" of the document/letter, and they can amend/change it and seek clarification, if needs be, on receipt. This would need some consideration in terms of how professionals normally document, record, and formalise consultations through written correspondence, and I present a number of suggestions later.

Example

A team of care workers in an emergency respite provision for young people in crisis came to a consultation. We externalised "loneliness" and "rejection" as affecting a young person in particularly problematic ways: in terms of how they viewed themselves, and how relationships between the young person and staff were in the respite placement. Through using the outsider witness scaffold, the workers were able to make guesses about what the young person valued or hoped for. They gained further insight into that which was being blocked by the loneliness and rejection. They empathised further with this by relating their own experiences of struggling with rejection and loneliness, and then were able to identify ways in which they could make changes in their work with the young person in order to develop alternative preferred stories. These stories were based on newly perceived unique outcomes of connection and acceptance, which ran counter to the loneliness and rejections.

Conducting meetings

Using many of the ideas outlined in this chapter, I have worked to look at ways in which meetings between people we seek to help and professionals can be changed or adapted in order to work more towards developing preferred storylines. It has often been the case that I have used such adapted forums for meetings when the "usual" types of meetings have failed, or the person seeking help has disengaged from the process. My assumptions in doing this have perhaps partly been based on struggling to overturn dominant discourses of how meetings *should* be conducted, usually along prescribed lines, which invariably meet the expectations of the agency in control of the meetings in terms of the way of working, as opposed to making the needs of the person the primary concern. However, I would also add that often this more dominate format for meetings can be helpful and useful to people, so it is usually when it is clear that the norm for meetings is *unhelpful* that I will offer an alternative forum. Finally, it is important also to recognise that some meetings have to be conducted along prescribed lines, particularly in contexts of tribunals or safeguarding issues. This does not mean that other alternative meetings cannot be conducted to supplement, influence, or even address issues that are perhaps marginalised by some of these more dominant structures within the fields of mental health and social care.

It is possible that many professionals view the "norm", or normal format, for meetings as being centred around the persons we are seeking to help. Indeed, various strategies or measures are taken in order to try to prioritise this: for example, use of advocates, allowing comment from the people seeking help, distribution of minutes and reports prior to the meeting, and so forth. However, I wish to outline steps here which I feel provide a firm foundation for having meetings centred on the people we are seeking to help.

First, state to the attendees that you are holding a different type of meeting. It is very important to "lay the context" in terms of setting out how such a meeting may differ from the norm. We would initially aim to have the person whom we are seeking to help set the agenda. Of course, we cannot expect people necessarily to know how to do this. Hence, you should view this as a way of facilitating the people whom we are seeking to help in deciding upon the agenda. I have found the following structure particularly helpful.

1. The person selects whom he or she would find helpful to attend such a meeting: that is, the person selects his or her "team".
2. Participant professionals are invited and are told it is a different type of meeting, meaning that they are given information about the format, what is expected of them, and the likely role of the facilitator.
3. The facilitator is given permission to interrupt if necessary to reguide the conversation in a direction that supports preferred narratives. White (2007) might refer to this as a determination not to "relinquish" the meeting to unhelpful discourses.
4. The person is interviewed in front of the professionals.
5. What is important to the person is highlighted, and preferred directions for the person's life, unique outcomes, etc., are highlighted.

6.   The professionals are then interviewed to seek out their resonant responses, using the outsider witness scaffold. However, the transport question of the scaffold would be centred primarily on how the professionals might now act, with their increased understanding of the person's experiences, to further support the person's preferred narratives or those of other people seeking help.

The meeting is concluded with a summary, which is co-written within the meeting with the person at the centre of the work. The document is then sent out detailing "actions" for supporting the person's preferred stories, or, just as importantly, the preferred stories of other people seeking help who struggle with similar difficulties.

Example of application

I suggested to the various parties involved that an alternative forum for meeting might be more helpful to a young person. This young person had disengaged from the service's formal avenues of help and professionals, but there remained considerable concern about his welfare and future.

I thought carefully with the young person about the type of meeting, or discussions, which would be most helpful to him. Together, we had identified a number of values and hopes for his life, which he hoped to be supported in developing further. We felt the format should be one where I interview him (based on our previous conversations in individual work) about these hopes and values. We felt (the young person and I) that the professionals should be placed in a position of listening, and we would manage how they responded so that it could be in as helpful way as possible. We would also seek to manage what the young person felt would be unhelpful advice: "tellings off" or "lecturing" from professionals. As part of the preparation, we asked for permission for me to steer them away from topics or conversations that the young person was not interested in at that time. I was given the permission to interrupt them if necessary, and to ask them set questions based on the outsider witness scaffold. We also provided some flipchart response sheets for them to respond to the young person's values, again in ways which followed the lines of the outsider witness scaffold. In addition to this, we asked the professionals: "In what ways can you support this hope, or this [item] that the young person feels is very important in his life?" Last, we decided that the meeting would be documented with a narrative letter to the young person, which he could then edit and decide with whom to share it, based upon the interview and the flipchart responses. Actions based upon this would then be decided upon and communicated with the professionals, to help the young person "step into" these emerging preferred storylines.

Record keeping

I would simply ask you to ask yourself if there is room to negotiate with the protocols and dictates of meeting the requirements of your organisation's record-keeping standards. This negotiation would be to see if there is room for the person to be an author of his own notes. Suggested ideas are along a spectrum: of writing notes as you usually do, but allowing the person to see them and have a chance to document his comments alongside the notes. Others have had the remit and freedom to have the person write the notes for himself, but, of course, making it clear that it is the person's document as opposed to the professional's, while others still have co-written notes within sessions with the people they seek to help, but being careful to distinguish who has written what, for obvious medico-legal reasons, but also to give the person a clear sense of ownership of their retellings. It might also provide scope to ask, within the imitations of our organisations, how people would like to keep notes. Often, some people would prefer pictorial forms of note keeping. Some might prefer an audio recording. These ideas also prompt questions of how we make note keeping accessible to those with learning disabilities, or literacy problems. At the very least, I think it would be interesting to debate this with the people you see, and the colleagues we work alongside within our organisations.

Using electronic and virtual contexts

At times I have written to professionals by email or letter in order to seek out specific responses that speak of preferred narratives of people. Of course, professionals will need to adhere to confidentiality guidance and service protocols in using such mediums. First, again, I would establish the context by explaining why such an exercise might be useful, then I would simply write requesting responses by asking questions such as:

- What do you appreciate about X?
- What have you learned about X during your work that has pleasantly surprised you?
- What do you know about what X sees as important?
- What do you know about X's hopes and dreams?
- Can you identify any one who is particularly supportive of X's hopes, dreams, or what he/she values?
- Can you tell a brief story that exemplifies what you appreciate about X?

Peer supervision

How can we devise a peer supervision group or sessions that acknowledge the diversity of experience, theoretical backgrounds, personalities, and life experiences in the service without allowing a particular model or practices to dominate above others? How can we avoid situations in which people holding positions of greater power and responsibility within a service have their voices more highly valued or brought to the fore more than other voices within the supervision group? Thus, how could we avoid other voices or stories being marginalised? Often, these voices are those of people who were somehow viewed as having less "expertise", or less formal mental health experience. Often, outsider witness practices provide an opportunity to construct peer supervision sessions that can run counter to this.

For a number of years, I have been fortunate enough to be part of a peer supervision group which I have found invaluable in terms of helping me in my work and in "staying true" to the values of what I would describe as my preferred professional narrative. It was very hard to narrow a work application down to one example, let alone an example that I could share in this chapter with the permission of the people at the centre of the story. However, looking through notes of the supervision session I had attended, it was very clear to me that the peer supervision sessions facilitated me in bringing my experience of the work as close as I could to the experience of the people I was working with. When I had fixated upon what I felt *should* be happening, the descriptions, explanations, dominant theoretical perspectives, theories, and ideas from my psychology training took centre stage. Unfortunately, at times, this was to the obfuscation of the person's experience. It was at those times that I felt particularly stuck in my work, and the help of the outsider witness scaffold within the peer supervision invariably steered me back to the person's preferred accounts, as opposed to mine and of those of dominant ideas of mental health from a Westernised perspective. I have been encouraged in peer supervision to:

- make space to deconstruct taken for granted ideas;
- empower marginalised people and their voices;
- value the diversity of experience and different knowledges;
- place the people we are seeking to help firmly at the centre of the supervision sessions.

With this in mind, I have previously outlined (Simmonds, 2008) guidance for conducting a narrative peer supervision group, which I shall summarise in the following paragraphs.

It is important to think about the maximum number of people that the facilitator will feel comfortable working with. It might also be important to think about membership of the group: for example, if the approach is unfamiliar to many of the group members then it may be better to seek a commitment from the members of the group over a period of time in order to allow them the scope to familiarise themselves with the approach. The format I find most helpful is simply to identify a worker or workers to bring an issue, dilemma, or material, and then be interviewed about it. Often, we would limit this to one or two pieces of work over a period of an hour and a half. The rest of the group would discuss their responses to the work through being interviewed by the facilitator, using the outsider witness scaffold. The facilitator would then return to the workers to seek their responses to the comments made by the listeners. Then we would finish by talking together about the process of carrying out supervision in this way.

In order to facilitate people who were unfamiliar with such a context/approach, often the facilitator can take the lead in the initial sessions in interviewing the worker and the outside witness group. The facilitator might also find it helpful to give people simple advice and tips to help them adapt their normal supervisory interviewing style to fit more with an outsider witness approach. Suggestions such as:

- slow down the pace of the interview;
- ask fewer questions;
- paraphrase and summarise for more clarification;
- thence aloud, that is, be transparent in thought processes;
- ask the interviewee (person bringing the work problem/ dilemma) what effects the problem issue has on them.

Michael White's workshop notes on the outsider witness group (available at www.dulwichcentre.com.au) can be very helpful in also looking at questions on the outsider witness scaffold, which helps professionals link their experiences to those of the actual people they seek to help—person to person—and, thus, gain further insight into people's preferred accounts.

Conclusion

Over the years, I have noticed how discourses which speak of expertise residing solely in the consultant often prove to be restrictive in terms of producing positive and enduring therapeutic change, unless it is the case that the consultant is willing for her/his service to take on the fuller responsibility for the work, and in a sense "relieve" the colleagues seeking help of the "burden" of the problem-saturated story/situation. Although such dominant stories can be viewed as empowering or freeing the mental health expert, I tend to find that unless this chalice of taking on the burden is accepted, then often the consultant can be viewed as obstructive or withholding of a "cure" or asylum. Of course, all of this pales into insignificance in comparison to the potential harm or minimisation of the person we are seeking to help, in terms of the obscuring and, perhaps, constraint of their preferred stories of living.

I view the ideas which I have talked about in this section of the chapter as "escape ladders", or ways of being able to disrupt the course of conversations which centre solely on the consultant as the expert on other people's lives. I see them as ways of reconnecting with the person's experience, and of refocusing participants in consultations on the person who is seeking help and how to thicken their preferred ways of living and their preferred identity conclusions and narratives.

This chapter does not suggest that the "solutions" to overcoming or dismissing and diminishing problem stories reside solely within the person whom we seek to help. A narrative stance emphasises ideas of connection in terms of how our lives' experiences and stories touch each other, but, crucially, how we can act in ways that are supportive of each other's preferred accounts. This can be particularly evident in services where bio-medicalised neuro experts are looked to for an edict on issues such as social disempowerment. A narrative consultation seeks to engage team members who can work in practical ways to thicken preferred narratives of people. Neither does this chapter argue, as with an often-levelled criticism of narrative therapy, that consultants/therapists show, not use, their power at all. The opposite, in fact, in some ways: narrative therapy consultants taking a narrative therapy stance would seek to remain explicitly aware of the dynamics and relations of power within the consultation (and therapy) and seek to use their power and influence in a transparent manner. Michael White's ideas on therapeutic power and positioning are described clearly by Morgan (2006), who outlined the positions that therapists can hold in therapeutic conversations (and, indeed, consultations). She referred to the position most linked with narrative therapy as being "decentred and influential", this position being one where the worker actively strives to provide a context in which the knowledges and skills of the person at the centre of the conversations are more richly described, and their preferred accounts developed further (thickened).

From such a position, I have been privileged to bear witness to rich story development of the lives of the people we seek to help, and also of those of colleagues seeking help. Often, colleagues seeking help are frustrated and despairing about a problem situation because it is not only affecting the lives of the people they are trying to help, but also obstructing and perhaps disconnecting the professionals from their values about how they work, and what they draw on in terms of how they wish/prefer to carry out their work with people. Often, by working within consultations to reconnect people with their preferred ways of working, inevitably connections and possibilities are found for working in ways that are consistent with the person's preferred accounts.

References

Jenkins, A. (2011). On becoming resilient: overturning common sense – Part 1. *Australian and New Zealand Journal of Family Therapy*, 32(1): 33–42.

Morgan, A. (2006). The position of the therapist in working with children and their families. In: M. White & A. Morgan (Eds.), *Narrative Therapy with Children and Their Families* (pp. 55–84). Adelaide, Australia: Dulwich Centre Publications.

Simmonds, L. (2008). Peer supervision where everyone has a voice. *Clinical Psychology Forum, 191*: 52–53.

Walther, S., & Carey, M. (2009). Narrative therapy, difference and possibility: inviting new becomings. *Context*: 3–8.

White, M. (2000). Re-engaging with history: the absent but implicit. In: *Reflections on Narrative Practice: Essays & Interviews* (pp. 35–58). Adelaide, Australia: Dulwich Centre Publications.

White, M (2001). Narrative practice and the unpacking of identity conclusions. *Gecko, 1*: 28–55.

White, M. (2004). Working with people who are suffering the consequences of multiple trauma: a narrative perspective. *International Journal of Narrative Therapy and Community Work, 1*: 45–76.

White, M. (2007). *Maps of Narrative Practice*. New York: W. W. Norton.

CHAPTER NINE

Outcome evidence

David Todd and Stephen Weatherhead

T his chapter presents a pragmatic approach to the challenge
of gathering outcome evidence, while balancing applying narrative approaches within the predominantly scientific backdrop of brain injury services. In addition to discussing the philosophical and practical discourses, the chapter makes some recommendations, including the increased development of practice-based
research networks, and the collection of multiple forms of outcome
data.

A pragmatic approach to narrative and outcomes

I think it is fair to say that we (DT and SW) come from slightly different starting points in exploring this issue. I (SW) am much more
inclined to position myself within a non-structuralist or social constructionist frame, viewing one's experience as heavily influenced by
the narratives we are able to draw upon at any given time. Whereas I
(DT) feel more comfortable describing myself as a scientist–practitioner; valuing the selective application of scientific methodology and
quantitative research, but recognising the necessity of postmodern

perspectives in seeking to conceptualise the human condition in a complex social world.

The consequence of this is a chapter that takes a pragmatic approach to the issue of gathering outcome evidence which values both narrative and scientific frameworks. One thing we would advocate is that a wider definition of science and evidence is needed (Larner, 2004). We do not want to throw the baby out with the bathwater by adhering rigidly to positivist or non-structuralist frames, so instead we take a pragmatic perspective on both a positivist and non-positivist approach, recognising the value in each. It has been said that different schools of epistemology each metaphorically grab a different part of the elephant and proclaim they have discovered its true nature (Henriques, 2003). We believe that the acceptance of a wider description of research evidence and clinical outcomes will enable us finally to see the elephant. We perhaps pose more questions than answers in this chapter, but we also endeavour to present some ways to shift between the margins of both approaches. The following quote captures our shared perspective, utilising an appropriately neurological analogy: "Science and narrative, the quantitative and qualitative, are not competitors but represent a complementary duality, as intimately connected as the two sides of the cerebral cortex" (Roberts, 2000, p. 440).

It is impossible to incorporate within one chapter the full range of therapies and settings in which the issue of narrative outcome evidence is being discussed. However, please rest assured that their omission is not due to our lack of appreciation of their existence; it is merely a reflection of the wordage at our disposal.

Outcome measurement comes in and out of our consciousness as therapists, depending on a whole range of factors, such as the political and economic climate, professional interest, and dominant discourses in academia, service provision, and commissioning. Underpinning all this are the narratives that we, as individuals, personally hold about evidencing outcomes. The form in which we each individually seek to evidence outcomes is equally susceptible to wider influence; however, most would agree that it is important to capture whether or not an intervention has been useful.

While outcome measurement and form has been a hot topic in neuropsychological services for at least the past five to ten years, it is probably fair to say that brain injury services have been leading the trends in capturing evidence of change since neurological and neuro-psychological study began; it is inherent to the discipline. Think about pioneers such as Wernicke, Luria, and Goldstein, all advocates of evidencing change. The challenge for us in exploring this issue through a narrative lens is the apparent philosophical incongruence between the scientific approach to studying neurological and neuropsychological phenomena, and the non-structuralist perspectives of Foucault, Derrida, Deluze, and others whose arguments are critical of positivist approaches.

Take Beck's *Depression Inventory II* (*BDI-II*: Beck, Steer, & Brown, 1996) as a specific example of this incongruence. The BDI-II is a well-validated questionnaire, with a strong evidence base. It does have flaws, such as its over-emphasis on physiological symptoms, which might muddy the data in health settings. However, it is widely used within brain injury services, and is a more than reasonable assessment of a person's level of depression. It is often used in a pre and post fashion as an outcome measure to evaluate whether an intervention aimed at improving a person's mood has been successful. However, if we look at the specific language used within the *BDI-II*, we can see that it incorporates an internalising form of words.

Pick up any narrative therapy text and you will see that one of the most important aspects of the approach is the externalising concept: "The person is not the problem, the problem is the problem". As a specific example, the *BDI-II* phrase, "I am sad all the time" would sit much more comfortably with a narrative approach if it were written, "The Sadness often encroaches on my life". However, it is not simply a matter of changing a few words. This is much more than semantics, and to rebuff it as such would miss the key premise that narrative approaches are built on the interrelationship of knowledge, language, and power. We cannot simply use different words to explore a problem, or evidence change. We must be certain that we hold the individual, their values, beliefs, descriptions, and sense of self, at the core of our work, in order to resurrect previously subjugated discourses and create a space for a preferred future to emerge.

Brain injury can lead to unique and multi-faceted challenges presented by bio-psychosocial combinations of acquired impairments, activity limitations, and participation barriers, all of which are situated within the personal, social, and cultural context of people's lives. As clinicians working in brain injury services, we routinely work with complexity, and select therapeutic and rehabilitation interventions based on the specific circumstances of each person, incorporating the best available evidence of what is likely to be effective in each case. Roberts (2000) views clinical practice as conducted in the tension between modernism, with its positivistic emphasis on rationality, materialism, and reductionism, and postmodern paradigms. In our experience, the potential disconnect between the "art" of person-centred rehabilitation and the "science" of quantitative research and medical evidence is strikingly apparent when working with people who are experiencing psychological difficulties and existential challenges after neurological injury and acute medical treatment. This tension requires acknowledgement, and demands a "rich description" within outcome measures to assess and understand the effectiveness of brain injury services and interventions.

An exploration of outcome measurement requires situating within the context of "evidence-based practice" (EBP). In recent years, across the Western world, EBP has gained considerable currency with political and professional organisations, and has been the subject of much empirical analysis and philosophical debate (e.g., Sehon & Stanley, 2003). A narrative critique of EBP finds it preferring objective over subjective, the general over the specific, quantitative over qualitative (Roberts, 2000). However, a more critical view of EBP from a social constructionist perspective is as a political movement endorsing a narrow positivism that only values randomised controlled trials (RCTs).

Stepping back from ideology and considering terminology, a narrative reading of how language is used and how the meaning of language can change over time is particularly relevant when considering EBP. Sehon and Stanley (2003) point out that practising any alternative to evidence-based practice implies clinical practice based on something other than evidence. However, what separates EBP from other approaches is the priority it gives to RCTs as the strongly preferred form of evidence. Stripping away the ideological baggage associated with the term, and considering the literal definition of EBP, it is not a question of whether there should be an evidence base or not, but, rather, who controls the definition of evidence and which kind is acceptable to whom (Larner, 2004).

The use of outcome measures enables "the establishment of reference points that can be used to interpret data" (Sperry, Brill, Howard,

& Grissom, 1996, p. 145). This "benchmarking" process of single-case design has a long history in neuropsychological research and addresses some of the practical and ethical limitations of RCTs. For example, the use of repeated outcome measures does not require a control group or alternative therapy conditions, or necessitate any specific inclusion or exclusion criteria for the purposes of developing a homogenous sample.

We seek to advocate the collection and dissemination of multiple forms of outcome evidence, both to assess the effectiveness of an intervention and to guide and improve future therapeutic and rehabilitative interventions by adding to the evidence base. From a narrative position, we seek to outline approaches that can be employed to thicken the description of outcome measures in clinical practice, and, subsequently, improve the quality of the existing evidence base. Consistent with the postmodern distinction between "form" and "content", we will consider approaches to outcome measures that do not merely privilege measuring outcomes themselves, but also acknowledge and value the direct contribution these approaches make to outcomes.

Although we are considering outcome evidence from a narrative perspective, we do not propose that standardised outcome measures for a brain injury population should not be used, but, rather, that they should be employed in conjunction with individualised measures of success, progress, or recovery. As Jacques Derrida, one of the major influences on narrative therapy, makes clear, to deconstruct is not to destroy an institution, but to encourage reflection, promote inclusion, and reduce oppression (e.g., Derrida & Ferraris, 2001). France and Uhlin (2006) argue that different ways of measuring narrative outcomes and rehabilitation or therapy outcomes may complement one another and provide a fuller range of perspectives, reflecting that we live in a "multiverse" of knowledge. Postmodernism holds that no one group has privileged access to the truth, and we are urged to "beware of the tyranny of singular accounts" (Doan, 1998, p. 381).

Seeing the individual in data, and data in the individual

Neuropsychology has always held a strong link between research and practice, which is perhaps one of the reasons why the profession is particularly comfortable with evidencing outcome. However, that evidence has traditionally been in quantitative form. This is perhaps because of the close chronological and philosophical links between the developmental growth periods of the profession, and the enlightenment period (e.g., Descartes and mind–body dualism).

The quantitative leaning is also due to psychometric testing representing an important part of cognitive assessment. Indeed, psychometric testing has been hugely influential in the development of the discipline of neuropsychological practice over the past century. The application of psychometric testing involves quantitative explorations of single cases and is founded on the tradition of exploring the individual in detail, to gain a complete understanding of that individual, when compared to themselves at other time points and to a wider population. However, we must be careful not to walk this path without question, particularly when considering a person's scores as part of a cognitive assessment:

> . . . they [cognitive assessments] do not tell us a great deal about how people with neuropsychological deficits cope in everyday life. Nor do they tell us what brain injured people and their families hope to achieve and what is important to them. (Wilson, Evans, & Gracey, 2009, p. 37)

In order to consider the hopes of the person and his or her family, we must spend some time exploring their narratives. A person's narrative is unique to him, but within that narrative there are aspects that are shared with others who have had similar experiences (e.g., a brain injury). There are also embedded aspects from social discourses (e.g., a brain injury leads to permanent irrevocable change), and, of course, the influence of the listener in relation to the narrative.

For this latter point, consider how passive *vs.* active you are as a clinician during the clinical interview. One of the first things every clinician practising in brain injury services learns is that while the cognitive consequences of a brain injury have some predictability related to functional neuro-anatomy, the same injury can affect two individuals in very different ways. Of course, it is nigh on impossible to exactly replicate the same brain injury in two people: however, the uniqueness is much more complex than that. It is influenced by premorbid life experiences, resilience (psychological and physical), as well as post-injury factors that influence recovery (e.g., social networks). Part of our responsibility, as professionals working within this area, is to gain an insight into those individual contexts and the narratives embedded within them.

Knowledge of the individual nature of brain injury has led prominent research-active clinicians to argue that group studies cannot give us data about an individual's development (Wilson, 2009). Indeed, qualitative, "narrative" evidence is considered a robust adjunct to quantitative assessments. Perhaps the real challenge is not convincing ourselves as clinicians that narratives are a valid form of outcome evidence, but inviting others into that conversation.

You may have noticed the multiple references to Wilson, Gracey, Evans, and Bateman (2009); this is a text that skilfully incorporates "hard" evidence, such as quantitative data, with "soft" evidence, such as patient narratives. We would encourage a similar approach when presenting evidence in any forum, whether it is in discussion with the individual accessing the service, his family, service commissioners, or wider dissemination in journal articles and conference presentations. Towards the end of this chapter, we provide summary examples of how to gather multiple sources of data as outcome evidence. In short, our pragmatic approach is to gather three forms of outcome data.

1. Relevant standardised measures.
2. Idiosyncratic/individualised measures.
3. Brief narrative information gathered at different points before, during, and after the intervention.

Narrative approaches hold the potential to enrich outcome measurement through both epistemological and methodological considerations, and innovations in clinical practice and research: that is, "what" is being measured, and "how" it is being measured.

The process of rehabilitation might be seen as involving a progressive shift in emphasis, with focus on physical problems in the earliest stages, cognitive difficulties in the intermediate stages, and emotional, behavioural, and social problems towards the latter stages (Wood, Alderman, & Williams, 2008). When working in a multi-disciplinary acquired brain injury rehabilitation setting, narrative outcomes can be viewed as methodologies that emphasise most language and higher-order outcomes, rather than focusing on the research of physiological impairments and their treatment. However, from an epistemological perspective, narrative approaches can orientate clinicians to which outcomes are important for each service user, and direct and influence our methodological approach, even with measures of treatment outcome for physical impairments.

Narrative approaches are likely to be of great benefit in informing psychological outcome research with individuals following brain injury; for example, in exploring how narratives change over time after injury, and linking this change with traditional measures of symptoms and functioning. These outcome measures could be considered alongside models of psychological adjustment and recovery after brain injury, which highlight the importance of understanding the service user's experience (e.g., the patient experiential model of recovery (Klonoff, 2010)). Such research would seek to identify the relationship between standardised outcome measures and narrative themes that, in our experience, are particularly salient for individuals following brain injury, including themes of:

- self-efficacy/lack of agency;
- descriptions of improved daily functioning;
- issues of identity and self-definition;
- relationships;
- evaluations of the future.

Research exploring the links between narrative measures and standardised outcome measures has been conducted in non-brain-injury settings. For example, Lysaker, Lancaster, and Lysaker (2003) identified narrative changes that may be associated with improved function in people diagnosed with schizophrenia. In a recent study, Moreira, Beutler, and Goncalves (2008) identified narrative changes associated with improved scores on multiple standardised outcome measures with a group of service users diagnosed with co-morbid depression and substance misuse. In a study comparing narrative change with functional rehabilitation goals, Lysaker and France (1999) found that changes in narrative content (e.g., from "I cannot work" to "I may be able to work") were closely associated with gaining paid employment, a traditional measure of outcome in vocational rehabilitation.

The studies outlined above have been conducted within a positivist framework; however, they support narrative measures as associated with traditional measures of outcome at a group level, and also indicate that narrative measures might be *more* sensitive indicators of change at an individual level. There are examples already in which quantitative and qualitative approaches are being integrated in the form of an outcome measure: for example, the outcome rating scales developed by the Association for Family Therapy, which incorporates Likert scales, open questions, and visual analogue scales, all within one document.

Evidencing the value of therapy and rehabilitation

Renewed interest in narrative approaches comes not just from "top-down" postmodern philosophy, but from a range of sources grounded in "bottom-up" clinical practice, including evolution in therapy and rehabilitation, the service-user movement, and the fact that clinicians, whatever their theoretical orientation and practical commitments, spend their days working with people's stories (Hunter, 1991). The narrative focus on the subjective, qualitative, and specific has led to the call for research on therapy and rehabilitation to be based in real-life clinical practice (Larner, 2004). The challenge is to collate and make available outcome evidence that reflects these complex components of people's lives as explored in clinical practice. Held (1998) argues that the postmodern therapy movement should influence research and contribute process and outcome studies; if not, this is likely to result in a recycling of the "theory to therapy gap" in the form of a "philosophy to therapy" gap.

"Practice-based evidence" (PBE), which is defined as outcome data gathered in routine clinical settings, is a necessary complement to EBP in the research cycle (e.g., Barkham & Mellor-Clark, 2003). PBE addresses the generalisability of results across particular services and settings (effectiveness component), and enables individual differences and variations to be explored (practice component). In order to disseminate this often qualitatively rich outcome data (Pistrang & Barker, 2010), evidence the scope of individual difference, and achieve a degree of robustness, "practice research networks" (PRNs) have been developed. Stratton (2007) notes that much existing clinical practice requires only a small amount of formalisation to generate good research information.

Databases are available that include single-participant study designs with individuals following acquired brain injury (e.g., Psych-BITE). However, the remit of databases developed specifically to investigate impairment treatment efficacy do not necessarily capture PBE demonstrating higher-order outcomes of narrative change. Different PRN structures exist which can be related to their context, including organisational differences of the funding groups behind them, or the clinical settings in which the practice research networks are based (Thomas, Stephenson, & Loewenthal, 2007). It has been argued that there is a need for PRNs to be developed that make available therapy or rehabilitation outcomes that are compatible with social constructionist and constructivist thinking. For example, Stratton, Bland, Janes, and Lask (2010) developed the SCORE, an outcome measure for therapy with relational systems, through a purpose-built PRN.

The co-ordinated collaboration of professionals and services in pooling outcome measures influenced by narrative approaches (for example, through PRNs or clinical databases) represents a valuable resource for demonstrating and advocating the complexity of people's lives following brain injury. We would suggest that narrative measures *and* standardised outcome measures should be simultaneously collected through this process in order to achieve the following: more clearly identify relationships between different facets of experience elicited during rehabilitation or therapy, increase the collection of holistic outcomes, and more accurately reflect the research cycle of evidence-based practice and practice-based evidence.

There has been growing recognition within brain injury services of the need to collate outcome measures that reflect, and explicitly engage, service-user involvement (e.g., Turner-Stokes, Nair, Sedki, Disler, & Wade, 2005). A practical example of this is recording the setting of person-centred rehabilitation goals, and measuring the progress towards achievement of rehabilitation goals (see Chapter Three) (e.g., Cathers, Fryer, Hollingham, Hyde, & Woolridge, 2011). Using person-centred goals as outcomes represents a combination of form and content of research, congruent with narrative approaches. When applied in local contexts, service-user involvement in explicitly setting rehabilitation goals has been found to increase the effectiveness of brain injury rehabilitation (Levack, Taylor, Siegert, & Dean, 2006).

In a study comparing estimates of treatment effects in PBE, in the form of observational studies, and RCTs, Benson and Hartz (2000) conclude that "bottom-up" methodology should be used to exploit clinically rich databases. The advantage of outcome measures from everyday clinical practice is that they represent a form of research evidence that has the potential for large-scale collection, for example, through clinical databases and PRNs. Opportunities for the dissemination of outcome measures from clinical practice is through local learning networks or practice-based research journals (e.g., Dagnan, 2011). Such publications aim to use novel research, including PBE developed from the collection of outcome measures, to share good practice and to help develop practice for others, and to improve the quality of services.

Some questions, some answers, and some more questions

In 2008, I (SW) co-authored an article on the challenge of evidencing outcomes in narrative therapy. In that article we concluded with three questions:

- Should narrative approaches adapt their core philosophy to fit with the current political climate?
- Can outcome measures be idiosyncratic and still retain validity?
- Is there an acceptable compromise or an impending split between clinical psychology practice and narrative therapies? (Weatherhead & Jones, 2008, p. 40)

Since then, I have received many emails from clinicians tussling with those same questions and seeking answers. I have always shied away from giving a structured response, partly because I had not fully formed one, and partly because I did not want to give the impression that there is a "right answer" to these questions. However, we (SW and DT) will now explore these questions, with the caveat that this is simply a snapshot of our shared and current perspective, and not a definitive truth (which, of course, would be the antithesis of the narrative approach).

It has been argued that defining and measuring outcomes in long-term acquired brain injury rehabilitation has proved particularly demanding (e.g., Fleminger & Powell, 1999). Furthermore, it has been recognised that no one methodology does justice to this work. For example, Turner-Stokes (2002) outlined the importance of determining whether outcomes measured will be indicators of neuropsychological or physiological impairment, functional activity, or social participation, according to the taxonomy outlined by the World Health Organization's *International Classification of Functioning, Disability and Health* (*ICF*) (WHO, 2001). In order to respond to the recognition that no single measure is suitable for all purposes, the British Society of Rehabilitative Medicine (BSRM) proposed a "basket of recommended instruments" based on an initial survey (Turner-Stokes & Turner-Stokes, 1997). However, these measures are currently being reviewed and updated because of a number of new developments, including the evolution of new indicators of change, the routine availability of computers in clinical settings supporting the computerisation of information, and the increasing focus on narrative approaches in rehabilitation and the emphasis on person-centred goals (e.g., Skinner & Turner-Stokes, 2006).

Should narrative approaches adapt their core philosophy to fit with the current political climate?

The simple answer to this is no, for to do so would be to compromise the integrity of narrative approaches. However, the reality of brain injury service provision, and many other service contexts, may require a more pragmatic answer. We do not have to adapt the central philosophies of therapy in order to facilitate an approach, but we must allow space for others' philosophies if we are to fully engage in a dialogue about our preferred approach.

Narrative therapy has been described as an evolving set of practices, developed from the philosophic contributions of postmodernism, social constructionism, and constructivism (e.g., Wallis, Burns, & Capdevila, 2011). Indeed, even within the individual, narrative theorists conceptualise each person as containing multiple voices with varying points of view (Hermans, 1999). Probably because of its strong base in a postmodern philosophical orientation, with its fundamental differences from modernist theories of knowledge, there is limited quantitative evidence of efficacy or effectiveness for narrative therapy (e.g., Etchison & Kleist, 2000; Wallis, Burns, & Capdevila,

2011). However, despite the important contribution of relativism in recognising that we are all unique, each of us must also share something in common with humanity in general, including what hurts us and what helps us live better lives (Held, 1998).

There is an ever increasing emphasis in the NHS, and in the independent sector, on "outcome data" and "payment by results". This, combined with a growing shift towards an economic marketplace approach to service provision, means that failing to engage with the dominant discourses will inevitably lead to the marginalisation of approaches that sit outside of the discussions. We may also think of this from a narrative frame by drawing on writings such as those by systemic therapist Tom Anderson, who posits that the best way to facilitate change in a system is to present a narrative similar enough to avoid alienation, but different enough to offer something new. Consequently, if we want to shift the focus from the quantification and monetising of therapy, we must shift the focus from within rather than outside the dominant discourses.

Can outcome measures be idiosyncratic and still retain validity?

We propose that outcome measures consistent with narrative approaches can yield rich, generalisable, and valid practice research. In utilising person-centred measures of change, narrative outcomes hold the potential to increase the "transferability" (as compared with "external validity" from a modernist paradigm) of practice research because they capture the complexity of clinical practice, providing finely grained information and, hence, reducing the inferential distance to identifying specifically what is likely to work with other individuals. Person-centred outcome measures are likely to possess strong "ecological validity", as they are based on the specific real-life context for each individual. In addition, as narrative measures of change provide a "thicker description" of an individual's progress through rehabilitation, this provides greater opportunity for multiple views about the effects of rehabilitation or therapy interventions for that person, thereby arguably reinforcing the "comprehensiveness" of practice research (as compared to "internal validity" in relation to quantitative outcome measures).

Camic, Rhodes, and Yardley (2003) describe the higher-order criterion of research validity as the requirement to be meaningful and useful to at least "some people for some purposes". Therefore, as well as considering the statistical and/or conceptual robustness of the instrument measuring effectiveness of brain injury rehabilitation or intervention, it is necessary that the outcome measured by the instrument is relevant to the service user. Research into how and why therapy works is extremely scarce (e.g., Larner, 2004), let alone what factors contribute to emotional change following the trauma and loss that is often associated with brain injury. The way in which people talk about themselves reveals fundamental relationship patterns which may offer insights into the delivery of therapy and rehabilitation services (Roberts, 2000).

Many different elements of narrative have been cited as important by authors from a range of different contexts; these factors have included coherence, active *vs.* passive agency of the narrator, dialogical flexibility, and narrative continuity *vs.* discontinuity (e.g., France & Uhlin, 2006); however, there is no definitive taxonomy of important narrative elements. In addition, a focus on language might not account for cognitive and communication impairments after brain injury, or accurately capture broader impairment-based rehabilitation outcomes. France and Uhlin (2006) state that narrative assessments of outcome can require significant expenditure of time and effort, and argue that such efforts have not yet proved uniquely valuable information that cannot be obtained by simpler means. The challenge for practitioners working in brain injury services is to identify and utilise individualised narrative outcome or process measures that are both robust and user-friendly.

Valid and reliable instruments (to use the language of positivism) have been used to assess dimensions of narrative (e.g., Lysaker, Lintner, Luedtke, & Buck, 2009). However, herein exists philosophical tension and methodological concerns in reducing complex interaction phenomena by using anchored scales (including Likert scales and semantic-differential scales). None the less, such approaches do provide more space for capturing individual experiences, beyond the "raw score" approach of many standardised tools. Other approaches that can be used idiosyncratically, while retaining a sense of robustness, include goal attainment scales (GAS: Kirusek & Sherman, 1968) and the patient generated index (PGI: Ruta, Garratt, Leng, Russell, & MacDonald, 1994). Measures such as GAS and PGI share the ability to provide quantitative evaluation while giving a more individualised perspective of the person's experience, hopes, and values, and they have been utilised effectively within brain injury services.

Is there an acceptable compromise or an impending split between clinical psychology practice and narrative therapies?

Throughout this book, you will have observed a range of narrative perspectives, from the "purist", highly trained narrative therapy perspective, to those who simply consider narrative to be integral to therapeutic work in brain injury settings. As clinical psychologists, we (DT and SW) are perhaps more comfortably placed in the latter bracket. However, we highly value our colleagues who are particularly skilled in specific therapies, be it narrative therapy, cognitive–behavioural therapy, or any of the many other approaches that are available. Unfortunately, the growing (and already dominant) narrative in guidelines and legislation is inarguably a positivist one. This does have the potential to marginalise the non-positivist therapies, which do not conform to "scientific" forms of appraisal.

We would see it as detrimental to lose these therapies from our teams, to be replaced by highly structured inflexible approaches that do not give space for narrative exploration. There must be a compromise, which stays true to the underpinning philosophy of narrative therapy while engaging with the positivist dialogue. If statutory services, in particular, are to retain access to narrative therapy within the current outcome and evidence-based climate, then we need to be somewhat pragmatic. On a macro level, we can do much to challenge what is considered "evidence", in order to create a shift from the perspective of a "right" approach to outcome measurement, based solely on quantitative measures, to one which is much more process, relational, and/or narratively driven.

There are many options to consider when gathering evidence of post-therapy change, each of which have their own strengths and weaknesses. For example:

- *Standardised measures*: This is a traditional, positivist approach. It speaks the language of people who commission services. However, the approach can be reasonably criticised as reductionist, because it often leads to a person's experience being diluted down to a number calculated before and after an intervention.

- *Process measures*: These can capture what the experience of therapy is like for the individual accessing it. However, they do not necessarily evidence whether a useful change has occurred.
- *Gathering individual narratives*: This is a common tool for evidencing the application of narrative therapy. Unfortunately, it does not make for swift evaluation when considering the usefulness of a service for a large number of people. (Adapted from Weatherhead & Jones, 2011)

This still leaves us with the question of whether the measurement of outcomes, including narrative change, is inconsistent with the values that underpin narrative therapy. Our view would be consistent with Larner (2004), who suggests a "para-modern" approach is needed, combining both modernist and postmodern epistemologies. In this way, narrative explorations and the use of positivistic research are not necessarily incompatible. Indeed, we would subscribe to the view that narrative and standardised approaches to outcome measurement and research can be viewed as necessary and complementary companions (Roberts, 2000).

Some pragmatic offerings

Outcome measures assessing preferred identities following brain injury reflect that we can all be described not only in biological, cognitive, and behavioural terms, but also as ethical, political, and spiritual beings (Larner, 2004). Outcome measures do not need to presume that there is an objective truth that can be measured, but, rather, that there are multiple perspectives. For example, Stratton (2007) points out that "symptom reduction" is not the goal for every service user attending therapy, and it is noted that a significant factor in recovery has been identified as the process of developing a sense of self separate from the diagnosis (Davidson & Strauss, 1992). Outcome measures are needed that contribute to an evidence base helping us to improve our practice, not just convincing service managers and funders.

It is recognised that there are limitations to any one form of outcome evidence working with people following brain injury. Quantitative structured tools risk "factualising" information through the loss of a narrative context, and so creating an illusion of objectivity

(Nash, 1994). Alternatively, developing individualised narrative outcome measures risks creating a compelling narrative over and above the process of seeking objectivity. Roberts (2000) describes this as "accenting the difference between narratisation and novelisation" (p. 439). In addition, basing conclusions on higher-order outcome measures too tenuously linked to the process of setting the outcomes themselves risks resulting in a *post hoc ergo propter hoc* ("after this, therefore because of this") fallacy (Sehon & Stanley, 2003).

Combining quantitative evidence of outcome with qualitative narrative data is an important principle for ensuring the approach to outcome measurement is client directed, rather than model driven. The use of multiple outcome measures enables the assessment of complexity and co-morbidity, while addressing the issue of transportability to real life (Larner, 2004). In considering these complementary perspectives, Richardson (1991) offers the term "crystallisation" as an alternative to "triangulation", as a holistic approach to combining outcome measures allows practice evidence to be examined from various angles. By touching on different aspects of the same phenomena, the different methodological and epistemological approaches yield a more complete story, and enrich our understanding of rehabilitation following brain injury.

Structured outcome measures have been developed outside of narrative therapy contexts, which represent quantitative outcome measures that are semi-structured with scope for individualisation, focus on higher-order outcomes, and can be utilised as process measures (e.g., valued living questionnaire (VLQ); Wilson, Sandoz, Kitchens, & Roberts, 2010). The concept of quantifying personally important values can be applied to values that have been identified using more narrative-friendly methods, including narratives elicited in therapy or rehabilitation sessions. Repeated measures of valued living that reflect preferred identities and skills can then become important assessments and may influence process through predicting change and directing further rehabilitation activities for the individual service user.

Here are some brief examples of how we have approached the gathering of outcome evidence in our own practice; this includes narrative measures, fixed standardised measures, quantified narrative measures, and flexible standardised measures.

Example 1: Individual intervention

Context: Therapy facilitated through private practice, with a young woman struggling with issues relating to trust, anxiety, identity, and pain. Some aspects related to pre-morbid experience, and some to post-brain-injury sequelae.

Intervention: 1:1 integrative psychotherapy, incorporating aspects of narrative therapy, cognitive behavioural therapy, and psychodynamic psychotherapy.

Outcome measures: Detailed narrative gathered, to support a painting of "the pain" produced by the individual accessing therapy (see Appendix 1). European Brain Injury Questionnaire (EBIQ) (Teasdale et al., 1997).

Example 2: Group intervention

Context: Community-based brain injury service.

Intervention: A narrative therapy group for men struggling to adjust to life post-brain injury (Weatherhead & Newby, 2011).

Outcome measures: Open question, asked during 1:1 data collection session, *"Please will you tell me a little bit about your life at the moment."*

The Hospital Anxiety and Depression Scale (HADS: Zigmond & Snaith, 1983)

The Patient Generated Index (PGI) (Ruta, Garratt, Leng, Russell, & MacDonald, 1994)

Example 3: Residential acquired brain injury rehabilitation programme

Context: A young man's progress through a rehabilitation programme founded on a neuro-behavioural model based in a residential community reintegration unit.

Intervention: An interdisciplinary clinical team facilitating a transdisciplinary brain injury rehabilitation programme. Intervention founded on a person-centred goal-setting approach in order to address the barriers to supporting the young man to achieve personally important goals on discharge.

Outcome measures: Person-centred rehabilitation goals, for example, to have a better relationship with my family; to get a job; to get better control of anger—achieved or not yet achieved

Supervision Rating Scale (Boake, 2000); Mayo-Portland (Malec, 2005); HADS (Zigmond & Snaith, 1983); Care and Needs Scale (Tate, 2004)—all administered on admission, discharge, and six months post-discharge.

Individually identified values or domains based on the young man's preferred narrative including, "humour", "spontaneity", "creativity", and "maturity". Progress towards these importantly held outcomes were then quantified and measured.

Conclusions

When considering how to evidence outcomes in practice, we can draw much from Roberts (2000), who stated that relationships between clinicians and service users constantly negotiate intimacy and detachment, subjectivity and objectivity; he argued that each of these is needed, and there are risks in overemphasising, or losing, any of them. In our view, the best approach is to use a combination of different forms of evidence. However, it is a fine balance between capturing data (qualitative or quantitative), and reducing therapy down to a focus on data collection, rather than therapeutic interactions. While we advocate collecting multiple forms of data as outcome evidence, care needs to be taken that the act of collecting outcomes does not impede the therapeutic interaction. Outcome measurement needs to be conducted sensitively and parsimoniously, and in the context of the individual therapeutic milieu.

A potential criticism of using a range of outcome and process measures from a service perspective is one of aggregation; specifically, the difficulty of demonstrating effectiveness of practice on a large scale (e.g., service level) with different components of evidence. However, using a range of measures limits the need for reduction or abstraction of unique outcomes, as all the different facets of experience obtained from the combined measures can be considered collectively (in keeping with Goldstein's holism). This may reflect a shift in the way that outcome data is not only collected and reported, but also interpreted by services and commissioners. Combining multiple heterogeneous outcomes might then become accepted as the norm rather than the exception. Stratton (2007) recommended that clinicians value inclusiveness and coherent integration, arguing that we need to have our practice guided less by ideology and more by carefully gathered and publicly reported indicators of what works; that is, research in its broadest sense.

We would advocate and recommend that practitioners and service providers working with people with brain injuries aim to contribute to the evolution of services through the use of outcome measures by means of initiatives in collection and dissemination.

1.   To facilitate the collection of broad person-centred measures of success, progress, or recovery. This should include the employment of both standardised outcome measures relevant for the individual service user or service setting (as determined by the service context) *and* individualised outcome or process measures as relevant to each individual service user (both structured and/ or narrative forms). Individualised outcome measures would include documenting the setting of person-centred rehabilitation goals, where appropriate, and progress towards these goals.

2.   To endeavour to disseminate such holistic outcome measures as practice-based evidence (constituting important and valid research). Publication of such data can be achieved through a number of available options which provide the potential for wide accessibility, including conducting regular audits of outcome measures, contributing to local practice-based journals, utilising relevant practice research networks (PRNs) or case study databases, or working with academic institutions involved in co-ordinating service-related research projects.

Here are some of the benefits of the wide-scale collection and dissemination of holistic and person-centred outcome measures in brain injury services, reflecting combined epistemological and methodological approaches.

•   It develops an increased understanding of how therapy and rehabilitation work in helping people following brain injury.

- Uses a richer and more detailed outcome dataset (qualitative and quantitative) to predict change and implement anticipatory activities to enhance practice.
- Reflects in practice that there is not a "one-size-fits-all" for outcome measures following brain injury.
- Strengthens a more inclusive and accessible evidence base that does not facilitate and perpetuate a narrowly defined form of evidence.
- Challenges the dominant narrative of assessing services or interventions based purely on the availability of RCTs.
- Changes the culturally defined meaning of the term "evidence-base" to one of holism, where outcomes can be assessed and valued on both an individual level and a group level with different methodologies and epistemologies relevant to each level of interpretation.
- Identifies what aspects of narrative approaches work with people following brain injury, so that these techniques can be improved and promoted, rather than marginalised.

Finally, we do not propose that qualitative or narrative forms of outcome evidence should be an adjunct to quantitative or standardised measures, and neither do we feel that quantitative approaches somehow legitimise individual narratives through more robust assessment. Instead, we suggest that qualitative evidence and quantitative outcome evidence are both valuable and valid. If we are to gain a comprehensive picture of status and change, triangulating multiple forms of data can foster a holistic perspective. This can then, we hope, hold meaning for all potential stakeholders, from the person who has sustained the brain injury and their multiple social systems, to us as service providers, and on to those who commission services.

Acknowledgements

The authors would like to thank Graeme Flaherty-Jones and Hugh Fox for being a key part of discussions and action in this topic.

Appendix 1: Hayley's narrative of pain

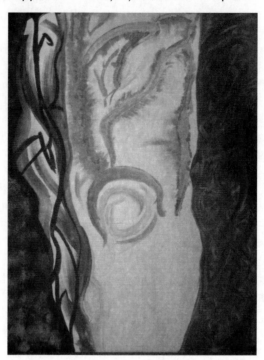

What follows is an excerpt from a recorded conversation with Hayley about her experience of this aspect of therapy. The transcript is included to show how, while it would be possible to capture some of this in a quantitative manner (e.g., through a semantic differential scale with useful/not useful at either end), exploring the full narrative fosters a richer understanding of what it was like for Hayley to partake in this particular aspect of therapy.

Ste: Hayley, we've been working together for quite a while now. Hopefully we've got an understanding now where if I'm talking rubbish you can tell me I'm talking rubbish.

Hayley: Yeah I can

Ste: So I've . . . I'm just wondering whether drawing the picture, doing the painting itself actually made any difference to you. Or whether it's just something you did because I asked you to do it.

Hayley: No at first it was something I did just cos you asked me to do it.

Ste: Aha.

Hayley: But then it became like I was doing it for me. Not for you.

Ste: Right, tell me more about that. Tell me more about what it has done for you. What was it doing for you while you were painting it?

Hayley: I don't know why, but helping to explain your pain, express it through what I do, art. It helps you. It's like you could, people may find it helpful to write things down, like I do, but painting it is another form of doing that.

Ste: Do you remember I said a little while ago when I was asking you to do this, that one of the hopes that I had was that it would move towards changing your relationship with pain?

Hayley: Yes I do remember that now.

Ste: What do you think your relationship with pain is like?

Hayley: I don't think I still have a good relationship with it, but this is dead weird, that I've only just recognised this, but I feel like it's got a bit better after drawing that.

Ste: In what way?

Hayley: Just that I'm able to . . . when I get pain I say to myself, Hayley don't fight with it, sit down, or Hayley you can't do what you were going to plan today, you'll do something else that's not as energise—that's not the right word sorry, you know what I mean.

Ste: Yeah, cos you found pain quite restricting, so pain stopped you going to the shops and things like that for example and—

Hayley: I know but I fought against it

Ste: Yeah, you went and did it anyway and then you—

Hayley: But I still do that sometimes but not as much.

Ste: I wonder whether the process of spending three days painting and sitting with that pain, and trying to get an understanding of it changed your relationship and stopped you feeling so much like you had to fight against it.

Hayley: I'm so glad you told me—well not told me, asked me to paint or draw a picture of my pain. Cos at first I thought how the hell am I gonna do that? But I just sat down and drew where I had the pain. It helped.

References

Barkham, M., & Mellor-Clark, J. (2003). Bridging evidence-based practice and practice-based evidence: developing a rigorous and relevant knowledge for the psychological therapies. *Clinical Psychology & Psychotherapy, 10*: 319–327.

Beck, A. T., Steer, R. A., & Brown, G. K. (1996). *Beck Depression Inventory II*. London: Pearson.

Benson, K., & Hartz, A. J. (2000). A comparison of observational studies and randomized, controlled trials. *New England Journal of Medicine, 342*: 1878–1886.

Boake, C. (2000). *The Supervision Rating Scale*. The Center for Outcome Measurement in Brain Injury. www.tbims.org/combi/srs (accessed 14 March 2012).

Camic, P. M., Rhodes, J. E., & Yardley, L. (2003). *Qualitative Research in Psychology: Expanding Perspectives in Methodology and Design*. Washington, DC: American Psychological Association.

Cathers, R., Fryer, S., Hollingham, K., Hyde, S., & Woolridge, S. (2011). Re-audit of the utility and application of client-centred goal planning in the Cumbria Community Acquired Brain Injury Rehabilitation Team (CCABIRT) service pathway for clients discharged in 2010. *Cumbria Partnership Journal of Research, Practice and Learning, 1*, 35–39.

Dagnan, D. (2011). Editorial. *The Cumbria Partnership Journal of Research, Practice and Learning, 1*: 1.

Davidson, L., & Strauss, J. S. (1992). Sense of self in recovery from severe mental illness. *British Journal of Medical Psychology, 65*: 131–45.

Derrida, J., & Ferraris, M. (2001). *A Taste for the Secret*. Cambridge: Polity Press.

Doan, R. E. (1998). The king is dead: long live the king: narrative therapy and practicing what we preach. *Family Process, 37*: 379–385.

Etchison, M., & Kleist, D. (2000). Review of narrative therapy: research and utility. *Family Journal: Counseling and Therapy for Couples and Families, 8*: 61–66.

Fleminger, S., & Powell, J. (1999). Editorial: Evaluations of outcome in brain injury rehabilitation. *Neuropsychological Rehabilitation, 9*: 225–230.

France, C. M., & Uhlin, B. D. (2006). Narrative as an outcome domain in psychosis. *Psychology and Psychotherapy, 79*: 53–67.

Held, B. S. (1998). The antisystematic impact of postmodern philosophy. *Clinical Psychology: Science and Practice, 5*: 264–273.

Henriques, G. (2003). The tree of knowledge system and the theoretical unification of psychology. *Review of General Psychology, 2*: 150–182.

Hermans, H. (1999). Self-narrative as meaning construction: the dynamics of self investigation. *Journal of Clinical Psychology*, 55: 1193–1211.

Hunter, K. M. (1991). *Doctor's Stories: The Narrative Structure of Medical Knowledge*. Princeton, NJ: Princeton University Press.

Kirusek, T., & Sherman, R. (1968). Goal attainment scaling: a general method of evaluating comprehensive mental health programmes. *Community Mental Health Journal*, 4: 443–453.

Klonoff, P. S. (2010). *Psychotherapy after Brain Injury: Principles and Techniques*. New York: Guilford Press.

Larner, G. (2004). Family therapy and the politics of evidence. *Association for Family Therapy and Systemic Practice*, 26: 17–39.

Levack, W. M. M., Taylor, K., Siegert, R. J., & Dean, S. G. (2006). Is goal planning in rehabilitation effective? A systematic review. *Clinical Rehabilitation*, 20: 739–755.

Lysaker, P. H., & France, C. M. (1999). Psychotherapy as an element in support employment for persons with severe and persistent mental illness. *Psychiatry: Interpersonal and Biological Processes*, 65: 197–206.

Lysaker, P. H., Lancaster, R. S., & Lysaker, J. T. (2003). Narrative transformation as an outcome in the psychotherapy of schizophrenia. *Psychology and Psychotherapy: Theory, Research and Practice*, 76: 285–299.

Lysaker, P. H., Lintner, J. I., Luedtke, B. L., & Buck, K. D. (2009). Quantitative assessment of changes in self experience: an overview of research of the scale to assess narrative development. *Israel Journal of Psychiatry and Related Science*, 46: 111–119.

Malec, J. (2005). *The Mayo–Portland Adaptability Inventory*. The Center for Outcome Measurement in Brain Injury. www.tbims.org/combi/mpai (accessed 14 March 2012).

Moreira, P., Beutler, L. E., & Goncalves, O. F. (2008). Narrative change in psychotherapy: differences between good and bad outcome cases in cognitive, narrative, and prescriptive therapies. *Journal of Clinical Psychology*, 64: 1181–1194.

Nash, C. (1994). *The Use of Storytelling in the Sciences, Philosophy and Literature*. London: Routledge.

Pistrang, N., & Barker, C. (2010). Scientific, practical, and personal decisions in selecting qualitative methods. In: M. Barkham, G. Hardy, & J. Mellor-Clark (Eds.), *Developing and Delivering Practice-Based Evidence: A Guide for the Psychological Therapies: Effectiveness Research in Counselling and the Psychological Therapies* (pp. 65–90). Chichester: Wiley-Blackwell.

Richardson, L. (1991). Postmodern social theory: representational practices. *Sociological Theory, 9*: 173–179.

Roberts, G. A. (2000). Narrative and severe mental illness: what place do stories have in an evidence-based world? *Advances in Psychiatric Treatment, 6*: 432–441.

Ruta, D. A., Garratt, A. M., Leng, M., Russell, I. T., & MacDonald, L. M. (1994). A new approach to the measurement of quality of life: the patient generated index. *Medical Care, 32*(11): 1109–1126.

Sehon, S. R., & Stanley, D. E. (2003). A philosophical analysis of the evidence-based medicine debate. *BMC Health Services Research, 3*, www.biomedcentral.com/1472–6963/3/14

Skinner, A., & Turner-Stokes, L. (2006). The use of standardised outcome measures in rehabilitation centres in the UK. *Clinical Rehabilitation, 20*: 609–615.

Sperry, L., Brill, P., Howard, K. I., & Grissom, G. (1996). *Treatment Outcomes in Psychotherapy and Psychiatric Interventions.* New York: Brunner/Mazel.

Stratton, P. (2007). Enhancing family therapy's relationships with research. *Australian and New Zealand Journal of Family Therapy, 28*: 177–184.

Stratton, P., Bland, J., Janes, E., & Lask, J. (2010). Developing an indicator of family function and a practicable outcome measure for systemic family and couple therapy: the SCORE. *Journal of Family Therapy, 32*: 232–258.

Tate, R. L. (2004). Assessing support needs for people with traumatic brain injury: the care and needs scale (CANS). *Brain Injury, 18*: 445–460.

Teasdale, T. W., Christensen, A. L., Wilmes, K., Deloche, G., Braga, L., Stachowiak, F., Vendrell, J. M., Castro-Caldas, A., Laaksonen, R. K., & Leclercq, M. (1997). Subjective experience in brain-injured patients and their close relatives: a European brain injury questionnaire study. *Brain Injury, 11*: 543–563.

Thomas, R., Stephenson, S., & Loewenthal, D. (2007). *UKCP Report on Practice Research Networks.* London: UKCP.

Turner-Stokes, L. (2002). Standardized outcome assessment in brain injury in brain injury rehabilitation for younger adults. *Disability and Rehabilitation, 24*: 383–389.

Turner-Stokes, L., & Turner-Stokes, T. (1997). The use of standardized outcome measures in rehabilitation centres in the UK. *Clinical Rehabilitation, 11*: 306–313.

Turner-Stokes, L., Nair, A., Sedki, I., Disler, P. B., & Wade, D. T. (2005). Multi-disciplinary rehabilitation for acquired brain injury in adults of working age. Cochrane Database of Systematic Reviews 2005, Issue 3. Art. No.: CD004170. DOI: 10.1002/14651858.CD004170.pub2.

Wallis, J., Burns, J., & Capdevila, R. (2011). What is narrative therapy and what is it not? The usefulness of Q methodology to explore accounts of White and Epston's (1990) Approach to Narrative Therapy. *Clinical Psychology and Psychotherapy, 18*: 486–497.

Weatherhead, S. & Jones, G. (2008). Measuring the narrative: the challenge of evidencing change in narrative therapy. *Clinical Psychology Forum, 188*: 38–43.

Weatherhead, S., & Jones, G. (2011). Dilemmas in evidencing narrative: reflections from workshop conversations. *Institute of Narrative Therapy: Papers & Resources.* Web-based article (www.theinstituteofnarrative therapy.com/Papers%20and%20resources.html).

Weatherhead, S., & Newby, G. (2011). Warehouse of responsibilities: a narrative therapy group for survivors of a brain injury. *Institute of Narrative Therapy: Papers & Resources.* Web-based article (www.the instituteofnarrativetherapy.com/Papers%20and%20resources.html).

Wilson, B. A. (2009). Effectiveness of rehabilitation. In: B. A. Wilson, F. Gracey, J. J. Evans, & A. Bateman (Eds.), *Neuropsychological Rehabilitation: Theory, Models, Therapy, and Outcomes* (pp. 22–37). Cambridge: Cambridge University Press.

Wilson, B. A., Evans, J. J., & Gracey, F. (2009). Goal setting as a way of planning and evaluating neuropsychological rehabilitation. In: B. A. Wilson, F. Gracey, J. J. Evans, & A. Bateman (Eds.), *Neuropsychological Rehabilitation: Theory, Models, Therapy, and Outcomes* (pp. 37–46). Cambridge: Cambridge University Press.

Wilson, K. G., Sandoz, E. K., Kitchens, J., & Roberts, M. E. (2010). The valued living questionnaire: defining and measuring valued action within a behavioral framework. *Psychological Record, 60*: 249–272.

Wood, R. L., Alderman, N., & Williams, C. (2008). Assessment of neuro-behavioural disability: A review of existing measures and recommendations for a comprehensive assessment tool. *Brain Injury, 22*: 905–918.

World Health Organization (2001). *International Classification of Functioning, Disability and Health: ICF.* Geneva: WHO.

Zigmond, A. S., & Snaith, R. P. (1983). The Hospital Anxiety and Depression Scale. *Acta Psychiatrica Scandinavica, 67*: 361–370.

INDEX

Abma, T. A., 59
Abrams, D., xi
absent but implicit, xv, xviii, 55, 71, 78, 85–88, 90–93, 98, 114, 171
Acorn, S., 4, 18
acute disseminated encephalomyelitis (ADEM), 7
Adams, J., 9, 18
Adingono-Smith, M., 59
agency, xiii, xvii, 5, 38, 77, 79, 105, 107, 175, 192, 198
  personal, 8, 58, 79, 85, 90, 92, 98, 174
  sense of, 58, 78–80, 82, 92, 98, 109, 174
Agner, C., 29–30
Al Sayegh, A., xxvi
Aluskas, M., 3, 17
Alderman, N., 191
Allen, R. S., 146
Ames, D., 122
Anderson, T., 197
Angaro-Lasprilla, J., 143

anger, 9, 15, 41, 79, 83, 91, 103, 153, 162, 203
anxiety, xxvi, 14, 54, 103, 151, 167, 169, 202
aphasia, xv, 118, 120–123, 125–126, 128, 130–132, 134, 137–138
  see also: dysphasia
Aphasia Institute in Canada, 132
Aronson, J. K., 4, 6
Atkin, K., xxvii, 2, 4, 8–9
Atkinson, P., 10
Aviles, A., 29–30

Bainbridge, K., 7
Banich, M. T., xxvi
Baptiste, S., 68
Barber, B., 146
Barker, C., 193
Barkham, M., 193
Barrett, L., 56
Barrow, R., 129–131, 133–134
Bartlett, G., 122
Beck, A. T., 187

Becker, G., 119–120, 122
behaviour, xxiv–xxvi, 9, 13, 15–16, 51, 55–56, 60–61, 63–64, 81, 102–103, 107, 110, 120, 132, 144, 153, 172, 191, 200, 202 *see also*: cognitive behavioural therapy
Bell, S., 3, 8
Bellack, A. S., 68
Bennett, B., 17–18
Benson, K., 195
Ben-Yishay, Y., xxvi
Beresford, P., 136
Beutler, L. E., 192
Bewley, C., 136
Bishop, A., 43
Blais, R., 122
Bland, J., 194
Blob Tree, 131–132
Boake, C., 203
Boazman, S., 121, 123
Bolte Taylor, J., 125, 133
Bourdieu, P., 3, 5
Bowen, C., xi, xxvi
Boylstein, C., 133
Braga, L., 202
brain injury (*passim*)
    acquired, xv, xxi–xxvi, 2, 18–19, 51–52, 61–62, 65, 78–80, 86, 98, 102, 115, 118–119, 165, 191, 194–195, 202
    parental, 144–146, 148–150, 153, 162
    rehabilitation, xix, xxiii, xxvi, 51, 53, 55–56, 60, 62, 65, 67, 71–72, 191, 194–195, 198, 202
    survivor, xxv, xxvii, 4, 18, 20
    traumatic, xxvi, 1, 6, 27, 31, 34, 62, 64
Brandstädter, J., 71
Branfield, F., 136
Brewin, C. R., 36, 38
Brill, P., 188–189
British Society of Rehabilitative Medicine (BSRM), 196
Brown, G. K., 187

Bruner, J., 3–6
Buck, K. D., 198
Burck, C., 32, 42
Burgio, L. D., 146
Burns, J., 196–197
Bury, M., xxvii, 8
Butt, J., 136
Byng, S., 122, 132

Calvert, M., 2, 6, 9, 17, 19
Camic, P. M., 197
Canadian occupational performance measure, 67–68
Canam, C., 4, 18
Cano, S., 53
Cant, R., 121
Capdevila, R., 196–197
Carbaugh, D., 8
Care and Needs Scale (CANS), 203
carer(s), xx, 102–104, 107, 109–110, 112, 115, 144, 161
    good, 101, 107
    perfect, 104, 106
Carey, M., 79, 84, 107, 167, 171
Carlson, G., 52
Carroll, L. J., xxvi
Carroll, L. W., 19
Carson, A. J., xxvi
Carter, G., 63
case studies and interviewees
    Anne, 17
    Belinda, 13
    Brenda, 14
    Christian, 62–63
    Claire, 12
    Daniel, 152–153
    Dorothy, 32–34, 37, 40–43, 46
    Ginny, 11, 15
    Hannah, 157–162
    Harold, 15
    Hayley, 206–207
    Jonny, 151
    Judy, 64–65
    Katrina, 82–83, 87–91, 93–98
    Laura, 154–155

Luka, 153
Margaret, 14
Mary, 32–35, 37, 39–41, 45
Nicola, 32–39, 41–43, 45–46
Pauline, 11, 16
Princess, 32–37, 39–40, 42–45, 47–49
Rachel, 12, 15
Sean, 32–35, 37–46
Susan, 13–14
Trish, 103–104, 106–111
Vince, 12, 14
Warren, 30–39, 41–42, 45–46
Wendy, 134–135
Cassidy, J. D., xxvi
Castro-Caldas, A., 202
Cathers, R., 54, 194
Chamberlain, D. J., 2, 19
Charbel, F. T., 29–30
Charon, R., 3, 6, 17, 119–120, 126
Chataway, J., 122
Cheng, J., 129
Christensen, A. L., 202
Chu, E. D., xxvi
Clare, L., 63
Clark, D., 5–6, 17
Clark, J., 120
Clarke, P., 123
Clermont, R., 122
Cloute, K., 4, 36, 40
Coetzer, R., xxvi
cognitive behavioural therapy, 199, 202
cognitive impairment, xxvi, 3, 63
Collicutt McGrath, J., 52
Combs, G., 84
communication access, 135–137
    toolkit, 135
    triangle, 135
communication disability, 117–118, 121–127, 129–130, 132–137
Conrad, N., 68
constructivist epistemology, xv, xviii
Context and Discourse Map, 101, 111, 114
Cook, J. A., 68

Copeland, M. E., 60
Coronado, V. G., xxvi
coulds of living, 104, 110, 111–113
cranioplasty, 28–33, 36, 38–43, 46
craniotomy, 28, 39–40
Croft, S., 136
Crossley, M. L., 32, 44, 46, 121
Crow, L., 9

Dagnan, D., 195
Daisley, A., 143
Dattani Pitt, K., 136
Davidson, L., 200
Dean, S. G., 67, 70, 194
decentred position, xv, 106, 108
Deegan, P., 70
Deloche, G., 202
Deluze, G., 187
deMare, T., 125
Denzin, N. K., 10
Department of Constitutional Affairs, 52
Department of Health, 52, 57
depression, xxvi, 11, 14, 54, 82–83, 167, 187, 192
Derrida, J., 78, 85, 95, 187, 189
Descartes, R., 190
Desjardins, M., 20
discourse(s), xvi, xxiii, 18, 20, 55, 70, 101–115, 172, 176, 181, 185, 187, 190
    dominant, xvi–xviii, 18, 30, 102, 105–106, 108–109, 113, 172, 175, 186, 197
    narrative, 55
    normative, 101, 105–106, 108
    shoulds of, 101, 104, 110–113
Disler, P. B., 194
Doan, R. E., 189
Doering, B. K., 68
Doran, G. T., 58
double listening, xvi, 86, 92, 171
Douge, J., 146, 149, 160
Duchan, J., 119
Dujovny, M., 29–30

Duncan, J., 63
dysarthria, xvi, 122
dysfunction, 31, 81, 84, 91–92
dysphasia, xv, 122 *see also*: aphasia

Easton, A., xxvii, 2, 4, 8–9, 10, 20
Edmondson, R., xxv
Ege, M. A., 146
Ekstedt, H. F., 29
encephalitis, xvi, 10–14, 16–19
    lethargica, 9, 18
    related narratives, 10, 12, 18
Encephalitis Society, 2, 10, 21
Epstein, R. M., 125
Epston, D., 102, 120, 134, 145, 152,
    162
Etchison, M., 196
European Brain Injury Questionnaire
    (EBIQ), 202
Evans, J. J., 52–54, 60, 71, 148, 190–191
evidence-based practice (EBP), 188,
    193–194
executive function, xv–xvi, 52
Exner, C., 68
externalising conversations, xvi, 112,
    145, 149, 170

Feeney, T., 64, 66
Feinberg, T. E., 18
Fenton, W., 68
Fernandez, P., 29–30
Ferraris, M., 189
Fisher, A., 108
Fleming, J., 136
Fleminger, S., 196
Flynn, R., 136
Fodstad, H., 29
Foster, M., 52
Foucault, M., 102–104, 106, 187
Fraas, M. R., 2, 6, 9, 17, 19
France, C. M., 189, 192, 198
Franits, L. E., 59
Frank, A. W., 6–8, 20, 117, 119–121,
    124–125, 136
Freedman, J., 84

Freeman, J. A., 53, 58, 69
French, S., 120, 133
Freud, S., 81
frustration, 45, 79, 91, 93, 103–104,
    109, 126, 182
Fryer, S., 54, 194

Garratt, A. M., 198, 202
Gavriria, M., 29
Gelech, J. M., 20
Gergen, K. J., 32, 65
Gergen, M. M., 32
Gerhardt, U., 3
Gingell, S., xii
Glynn, M., 136
goal attainment scales (GAS), 198
goal management training (GMT),
    63
goal setting, xx, 51–55, 58–62, 65–67,
    69–72, 123, 128–129, 132, 202
    see also: intervention
Godwin, E., 143
Goldstein, K., 72, 187, 203
Goncalves, O. F., 192
Gracey, F., 52–53, 71, 148, 190–191
Grant, F. C., 29–30
Green, M. F., 68
Grissom, G., 188–189
Gwyn, R., 120, 126

Hagstrom, F., 119, 123
Hammersley, M., 10
Harré, R., xii
Harrington, A., 5, 18
Harrison, B., 3, 5, 20
Hart, T., 53–54, 60, 71
Hartz, A. J., 195
Harvey, P. D., 68
Haslam, A., 6
Haslam, C., 6
Hayes, S. C., 65
Heaton, R. K., 68
Held, B. S., 193, 197
Hellawell, S. J., 36, 38
Henriques, G., 186

Her Majesty's Stationary Office
(HMSO), 52
Hermans, H., 196
Hewitt, A., 122–123, 127, 135, 138
Hilari, K., 122
Hilgeman, M. M., 146
Hinojosa, R., 133
Hippocrates, 119
Hogan, B. A., 9, 19
Holliday, R., 53
Hollingham, K., 54, 194
Holm, L., xxvi
Hong, J., 63
Hospital Anxiety and Depression
Scale (HADS), 202–203
Hovey, R., 5
Howard, K. I., 188–189
Hunter, K. M., 193
Hydén, L.-C., 3, 6–7, 18, 121
Hyde, S., 54, 194

identity, xvii–xviii, xxii–xxiv, 2–3, 6,
31, 37–38, 40, 43, 65–66, 68–69,
80, 82, 84, 95, 102, 105, 107, 114,
119, 123, 133, 149, 166–167,
169–170, 192, 202 see also:
metaphorical identity mapping
map(s), 65–66
preferred, 113, 172, 182
sense of, 32, 65–66, 80, 83, 123
identity-orientated goal training
(IOGT), 66–67
Inabuchi, T., 29
independence, 37–38, 40, 43, 59, 65,
90, 120
intervention(s), xxvii, 19, 27–28, 46,
55–56, 58, 60, 62–64, 67, 82, 148,
156, 186–189, 191, 198–199, 205,
235
goal-setting, 64
group, 202
individual, 202
narrative, 21
neurosurgical, 28–29
physical, 67

rehabilitation, 63, 188–189, 197
surgical, 27
therapeutic, 1, 18, 32, 188–189, 197
interviewees see: case studies
Iverson, G. L., 37
Iwama, M., 129

Janes, E., 194
Jeffers, S., 129
Jenkins, A., 170
Jenkins, R., 5
Jetten, J., 6
Jillings, C., 4, 18
Joachim, G., 4, 18
Johansen, R. K., 1, 8, 17
Johnson, J., 153
Jones, C. A., 4, 6
Jones, G., 195, 200
Josselson, R., 42

Kagan, A., 132
Kangas, M., xxvi, 64
Karniol, R., 55
Kat, L., 59
Kayes, N., 53, 65–67, 70
Kemp, M., 6–7
Kendall, E., 2
Khosa, J., 122–123, 133
Kielhofner, G., 56, 68
Kirusek, T., 198
Kis-Sines, N., 162
Kitchens, J., 68, 201
Kleinman, A., 119, 121
Kleist, D., 196
Klonoff, P. S., 54, 68, 72, 192
Kneebone, I. I., xxv
Knibbe, J., 59
Kohut, M., 146
Koski, P., 119, 123
Kovareky, D., 59
Kraus, F., xxvi
Kraus, J., xxvi
Kreiswirth, M., 3
Kreutzer, J., 143
Kuipers, P., 52

Laaksonen, R. K., 202
Lancaster, R. S., 192
Lange, R. T., 37
Larner, G., 186, 188, 193, 198, 200–201
Lask, J., 194
Latham, G., 53
Laughren, T., 68
Law, M., 68
Lawrence, R. J., 61
Lawton, J., 2–4
Leclercq, M., 202
Leng, M., 198, 202
Leon, A. C., 68
Levack, W. M. M., 54, 58, 67, 69–70, 194
Levine, B., xxv, 63
Lezak, M. D., 143
Lieblich, A., 32, 42
life
    altering/changing, 12, 119–120
    family, 145, 149
    good, 96–98
    real, 197, 201
    reduced, 83, 90–91, 94, 96
    story, 64–65
    style, 65, 129, 168
Lilisquist, B., 29
Lillrank, A., 6, 8–9
Lincoln, N. B., xxv
Lincoln, Y. S., 10
Lindsay, J., 129, 133–134
Linge, F. R., 6
Link, B. G., 43
Lintner, J. I., 198
Locke, E., 53
Loewenthal, D., 194
Long, I., 131
Lorenz, L. S., 3–4, 17, 20, 127, 131, 133
Love, J. A., 29
Lowenstein, L. B., 146
Luedtke, B. L., 198
Luria, A. R., 6, 187
Lysaker, J. T., 192
Lysaker, P. H., 192, 198

MacDonald, L. M., 198, 202
Maier, E. H., 146
Malec, J., 203
Malley, D., 71, 148
Mallinson, T., 68
Mann, S., 134
Markus, H., 54
Marshall, J., 122
Marwitz, J., 143
Mattingly, C., 8, 117, 120, 126
May, T., 107
Mayo, D. J., 68
Mayo-Portland, 203
McAdams, D. P., 42
McCaffrey, R. J., xxv
McColl, M. A., 68
McDonald, S., xxvi, 64
McKinlay, A., 43
McLellan, T., 43
McPherson, K. M., 53, 65–67, 70
meaning
    privileged, xvii, 85
    subjugated, xviii, 85
Medved, M. I., 3, 6
Meeter, M., xii
Mellor-Clark, J., 193
memory, xii, xv, xxiv, 34–36, 39, 44, 52, 62, 92, 149–150, 155
    autobiographical, 35
    loss, 39, 83
metaphorical identity mapping (MIM), 66
Mindt, T., 18
Mitchell, A., 4, 36, 40
Mitchell, K., 121
modernism, xvi, 81, 188, 196–197, 200
    see also: postmodernism
Monrouxe, L., 121
Moreira, P., 192
Morgan, A., 79, 182
Moy, J., 52
Muenchberger, H., 2
Mullan, F., 18
Murray, M., 3, 6, 43
Murre, J. M. J., xii

Myerhoff, B., 152
Myles, S. M., 65

Nair, A., 194
narrative (*passim*) *see also*:
    encephalitis, self
  analysis, 24, 27, 32
  approach(es), xi, xix, xxi–xxii,
      xxiv–xxv, xxvii, 19, 21, 51–52,
      54–58, 63–66, 68, 72, 77–81, 83,
      98, 118–120, 123–124, 127,
      134–136, 185, 187, 191–197,
      205
  perspective(s), xxv, 85, 117, 170,
      189, 199
  practice, xi–xii, xvii, xxiii, 51, 84,
      101, 105, 110–111, 117–119,
      123, 125
  professional, 29, 165, 179
  scrapbook, 146–147
  therapy, xii, xx, xxii–xxiv, 32,
      51, 61, 64–67, 78–79,
      101–102, 108, 115, 118, 133,
      143–145, 147, 152, 162,
      165–166, 169–171, 173–174,
      182, 187, 189, 195–196,
      199–202
Nash, C., 201
National Health Service (NHS), 144,
    197
naturalistic
  accounts, 167, 169–170, 172
  approach, 166
  descriptions, xvi, 166–167
  perspective, 167, 172
  strengths, 169
  view(point), 166, 169–170
Neal, R., 2
Neistadt, M. E., 67
Nelson, H. L., 120, 133
neuro- (*passim*) *see also*: intervention,
    rehabilitation
  biology, xii
  disability, 1, 4–5, 9
  illness, 1, 3, 5, 7, 9, 153

psychology, xii, xxiii, xxv, xxvii,
    29, 55, 57, 62, 63, 143, 186–187,
    189–190, 196
  science, xi–xii, xxi, 31
  surgery, 27–29
Newby, G., 202
Noble, I., 7
Nochi, M., 2, 19, 35, 38, 42, 45, 70
non-structuralist *see also*: structuralist
  frame, 185–186
  ideas, 105
  orientations, xxii
  perspectives, xvii, 187
  philosophy, xxiv, xxvi, 56, 106
Norcross, N. C., 29–30
Northcott, S., 122
Nurius, P., 54

objective/objectivity, xv–xvi, 35, 69,
    72, 188, 200–201, 203
O'Brien, M., 5–6, 17
Opher, S., 7, 17
Opzoomer, A., 68
outsider witness, xvii, 175, 177,
    179–181

Palmer, S., xi, xxvi
palsy, xvii, 39–40, 44
Pape, S., 9
Parker, I., xii
Parr, S., 123, 125, 127, 129, 133–135,
    138
Parry, K., 120
Paterson, B., 4, 18
Paterson, K., 125
patient generated index (PGI), 198,
    202
Patmore, C., 136
Patrick, D. L., 68
Patterson, T. L., 68
Paul, J., 5
peer supervision, 179–180
Pellett, E., 66–67, 70
Penman, T., 125
Pennebaker, J. W., 19

Phelan, J. C., 43
Pinhasi-Vittorio, L., 6, 17–18
Pistrang, N., 193
Plato, 119
Playford, E. D., 53, 58, 69
Pluznick, R., 162
Polatajko, H., 68
Pollock, N., 68
positivism, xi, xvi–xvii, 56, 186–188,
    192, 198–200
Postle, K., 136
Postmes, T., 6
postmodernism, xvi–xvii, xxiii–xxiv,
    xxvi, 185, 188–189, 193, 196, 200
    see also: modernism
Potter, S., xxvi
Pound, C., 123, 125, 127, 129,
    132–135, 138
Powell, J., 196
practice-based evidence (PBE),
    193–195, 204
practice research networks (PRNs),
    193–195, 204
Prigatano, G. P., xxi, xxvii, 17–18, 69,
    71
Puente, A. E., xxv

Ragan, S. L., 18
randomised controlled trials (RCTs),
    188–189, 195, 205
rehabilitation (passim) see also:
    brain injury, intervention
    clinician(s), 56, 58, 63, 69
    environment, 53, 67
    goal(s), 56–58, 60, 62–64, 66, 69–71,
        192, 194, 203–204
    journey, 58–59
    neuro-, xi, xiii, xxiii, xxv, xxvii, 144,
        157
    process, 51, 54–55, 62–63, 66, 69–70,
        144, 155
    professional(s), 58–59, 61, 67, 69
    programme(s), xxv, 51, 202
    service(s), 51, 54, 58–60, 62, 67, 70,
        198

team(s), xxii, 55, 61–62, 65–66,
    70–71, 152
relativism, xvii, 197
re-membering, 66
    conversations, xvii, 152
Rengachary, S. S., 28–29
resilience, 31, 81, 153, 155, 162,
    170–171, 190
Reynolds, F., 120
Rhodes, J. E., 197
Richardson, L., 201
Rief, W., 68
Rier, D. A., 3
Riessman, C. K., 3–4, 32
right hemisphere language
    impairment, xvii, 122
Rittman, M., 133
Roberts, G. A., 186, 188, 198, 200–201,
    203
Roberts, M. E., 68, 201
Robertson, I. H., 63
Robinson, M., 6, 19–20
Romano, M. D., 153–154
Rose, A., 37, 68
Ross, M., 55
Rothermund, K., 71
Rous, R., 56
Roy, P., 122
Russell, I. T., 198, 202
Russell, S., 79, 84
Ruta, D. A., 198, 202
Ryland, H., xxvi

Sanan, A., 28–29
Sandford, D., xxvi
Sandoz, E. K., 68, 201
scaffolding, xviii, xxi, 88, 93–95,
    105, 107, 111, 175, 177,
    180–181
Schacter, D. L., 69
Schipper, K., 59
Scott-Findlay, S., 4
scrapbook, 146–154, 156–157,
    159–162 see also:
    narrative

Sedki, I., 194
Segal, D., 2, 4–5, 20
Sehon, S. R., 188, 201
self, xxiv, 2–3, 5, 32, 37–39, 41–42, 54,
    60, 65, 69–71, 77, 80–84, 87–89,
    92, 96–97, 105
  -actualisation, 72
  -aware(ness), 69, 71
  criticism, 110
  -definition, 192
  -determination, 54
  -efficacy, 54, 60, 67, 71, 192
  -esteem, 71, 81–82, 121, 133
  image, 6, 69, 81
  loss of / lost, 20, 32, 34, 38, 70,
      78–80
  metaphors of, 80–81
  -monitoring, 64
  narrative, 35, 55, 59, 63–65, 68–71,
      120
  new, 42, 47
  old, 32, 37, 41–42, 47, 153
  pre-injury, 70
  presentation, 32
  sense of, xxiv, 5, 30, 34, 66–67,
      77–78, 80, 82–83, 96, 98, 102,
      123, 187, 200
  story of, xv, 77, 79, 84–85, 89–91,
      93, 98
  sufficient, 43, 90
  -understanding, 52
  -worth, 55, 133
Shadden, B., 119, 123
Shakespeare, T., 121
Shaw, A., 59
Sherman, R., 198
Shoulds to Coulds Map see:
    Context and Discourse Map
Shumway, E., 132
Shuster, J. D., 146
Siegert, R. J., 52–53, 56, 58, 67, 69–70,
    194
Simmonds, L., 180
Skinner, A., 196
Skirton, H., 121

Skultans, V., 4, 6
SMART (specific, measurable,
    achievable, realistic / relevant,
    timed), 57–58, 63, 66, 70
Smith, B., 6
Smith, C., 3
Snaith, R. P., 202–203
social constructionism, xv, xviii, 56,
    65, 185, 188, 194, 196
Solms, M., 69
Sopena, S., 56
Sparkes, A., 6
Sperry, L., 188–189
Squire, F., 3
Stachowiak, F., 202
Stanley, D. E., 188, 201
Stapley, S., 4, 8–9
Steer, R. A., 187
Stephenson, S., 194
story (*passim*) see also: *life, self*
  development, 90–91, 98, 155, 174,
      182
  preferred, xvii, 66–67, 77, 79, 84–85,
      88, 95–96, 171, 173–175,
      177–178, 181
  problem-saturated, xvii, 132,
      181
  -telling, 117, 123, 145–146, 149–150,
      153–154, 162
  trauma, 84–85
Stover, E., 68
Stratton, P., 193–194, 200, 204
Strauss, J. S., 200
Strosahl, K., 65
structuralist *see also*:
    non-structuralist
  accounts, 169–170, 172
  approach, 166
  descriptions, 166–167
  ideas, 105
  perspectives, xviii, 167, 172
  post-, xi–xii
  understandings, 105, 107, 167
  viewpoints, 169–170
Stuss, D. T., xxv, 63

subjectivity, 18, 65–66, 68–69, 122, 188, 193, 203
Supervision Rating Scale, 203
Suzuki, N., 29
Suzuki, S., 29
Swain, J., 120, 133
Swinburn, K., 132
syndrome of the trephined (ST), 30

Tamblyn, R., 122
Tate, R. L., 203
Taylor, K., 194
Taylor, W. J., 52–53, 56
Teasdale, T. W., 202
Teske, J. A., 3–4
thicken, xviii, 55, 64, 70, 128–129, 132–133, 153, 171, 174, 182, 189
Thomas, C., 132
Thomas, R., 194
Thorne, S., 4, 18
Threats, T. T., 57
trauma/traumatic (*passim*) *see also*: brain injury
  emotional, 92, 98
  experience, 10, 27, 46, 86, 91–92, 146
Turkstra, L. S., 4, 6
Turnbull, O. H., 69
Turner, M., 136
Turner-Stokes, L., 194, 196
Turner-Stokes, T., 196
Tuval-Mashiach, R., 32
Tyerman, A., 145

Uhlin, B. D., 189, 198
unique outcomes, xviii, xxii, 67, 84, 129, 132, 152, 170, 174–176, 203
United Nations General Assembly, 123

valued living questionaire (VLQ), 68, 201
Van Der Kolk, B. A., 35
Vendrell, J. M., 202
violation, 78, 86–87
violence, 78, 82, 91, 169
Vygotsky, L. S., xxi, 71, 88

Wade, D. T., 194
Wallis, J., 196–197
Walther, S., 107, 111, 167, 171
Weatherall, M., 53, 65–67
Weatherhead, S. J., 195, 200, 202
Webster, G., 143
Weingarten, K., 121
Wellness Recovery Action Plan (WRAP), 60
Wernicke, C., 187
White, M., 61, 66, 79, 84–86, 88, 91–93, 96–97, 99, 102, 104–105, 108, 120, 134, 145, 167, 169, 174, 176
Whitehead, L. C., 3, 6
WHO Collaborating Centre Task Force on Mild Traumatic Brain Injury, xxvi
Wiggins, R., 122
Williams, C., 191
Williams, W. H., xxvi
Wills, E., 7, 17
Wilmes, K., 202
Wilson, B. A., 52–53, 56, 63, 190–191
Wilson, K. G., 65, 68, 201
Wilson, P., 131
Wimborne, N., 123, 127, 135, 138
Wittenberg-Lyles, E., 18
Wood, R. L., 191
Woolf, C., 129, 133–134
Woolridge, S., 54, 194
World Health Organization, 56–57, 61, 63–64, 196

Worrall, L., 57
Wykes, T., 68

Yardley, L., 197
Yates, P., 4, 36, 40
Yeates, G. N., xi, xxvi

Ylvisaker, M., 64, 66–67, 70

Zigmond, A. S., 202–203
Zilber, T., 32
zone of proximal development, xviii, xxii, 71

The Encephalitis Society

Support, Awareness & Research for Inflammation of the Brain

We provide **support** to people affected and their families

We provide evidence-based **information** and are backed by a Professional Panel of clinical experts

We raise **awareness** and provide training to health, social care and education professionals

We promote and collaborate on **research**

www.encephalitis.info

We are the only resource of our kind in the World.